# THE TANTRIC WAY

श्रीकृष्णमूर्तिलक्षणम्

समचक्राद्वारदेशे कृष्णवर्णसुशोभना ।

साकृष्णमूर्तिविज्ञेया पूजितासौख्यदायिनी ॥

श्रीकृष्णमूर्तिः

AJIT MOOKERJEE • MADHU KHANNA

# THE TANTRIC WAY

## ART SCIENCE RITUAL

*148 illustrations,*
*18 in color, and*
*80 line drawings*

Thames & Hudson

*Frontispiece: Manuscript leaf illustrating cosmic form of Kṛishṇa with appropriate symbols. Rajasthan, c. 19th century. Ink and color on paper.*



Published in the United States of America in 1989 by Thames & Hudson Inc., 500 Fifth Avenue, New York, New York 10110

thamesandhudsonusa.com

Reprinted 2003

Library of Congress Catalog Card Number 88-51353
ISBN 0-500-27088-0

Printed and bound in Slovenia by Mladinska Knjiga

*Contents*

To
Dr Manfred Wurr
*on the tantric path*

ACKNOWLEDGMENTS

Archaeological Survey of India, New Delhi 10, 37 (right), 77 (right), 79, 80, 85, 128, 165, 173, 181, 188, 194, 195
Achim Bedrich collection, Munich 101, 102, 114, 191
Bharat Kala Bhavan, Banaras collection 42, 52, 58, 160
Kalyan S. Coll, Barcelona 47
Michael Cooper, London 139
S. C. Duggal, New Delhi 88
Robert Fraser collection, London 138, 157
H. Harrer, Kitzbühel 31
Dr H. Hünger 178
Government of India Tourist Office, London 145
Kasmin Gallery, London 63
Max Maxwell, London 83, 84, 137
Ajit Mookerjee collection, New Delhi *frontispiece*, 8, 12, 16, 17, 19, 20, 22, 25, 28, 33, 35, 36, 37, 40, 44, 45, 50, 53, 54, 56, 57, 65, 66, 69, 70, 72, 73, 74, 76, 77 (left), 89, 90, 91, 92, 93, 96, 99, 104, 106, 107, 113, 115, 116, 121, 124, 130, 134, 142, 143, 147, 148, 149, 150, 151, 162, 164, 169, 171, 176, 182, 186, 189, 192, 193; photographs 46, 87
Priya Mookerjee 158, 159
National Museum collection, New Delhi 131
Hans-Ulrich Rieker collection, Hamburg 11
Thomas Gallery collection, Munich 34, 38
Victoria and Albert Museum, London 78
J.-C. Ciancimino, London 67
S. L. Vohra, New Delhi 117
Hans Wichers collection, Hamburg 48, 49, 81, 167
Jan Wichers collection, Hamburg 29, 71, 82, 103, 108, 118, 135, 140, 152, 172, 175
Meggy Wichers collection, Hamburg 129
Dr Manfred Wurr collection, Hamburg 184, 187

# *Preface*

In this space age, when so many are striving towards an understanding of the man-universe relationship, the study of tantric doctrine and its practical application is especially significant. Great enthusiasm has, in recent years, developed for tantra, its timeliness and universal appeal. In order to meet this growing interest and desire for further knowledge of tantra, this book gives the reader a glimpse of the phenomenon that is tantra and its related manifestations in art, science and ritual. Pre-eminently an exposition of a practical method, *The Tantric Way* outlines an expanded concept of man, for a creative awareness of one's psychic sourçes through a comprehensive system of thought and experiential techniques. It should not, therefore, be considered a doctrine but the beginning of a new outlook. If our readers are stimulated to further exploration of tantra and to its assimilation as a whole, which always begins by working on one's own self, the purpose of this book will be fulfilled.

We owe a debt of gratitude to Dr Manfred Wurr, for providing facilities for research and assistance with grants, direction and support, without which this work could never have been written; to Mr Michael Paula and Wissenschaftlicher Verlag Altmann G.m.b.H., Hamburg for co-operation and encouragement; to Mr Hans-Ulrich Rieker, who read through the manuscript; and finally to Dr Sanjukta Gupta, for many helpful suggestions on Sanskrit mantras.

A. M.

M. K.

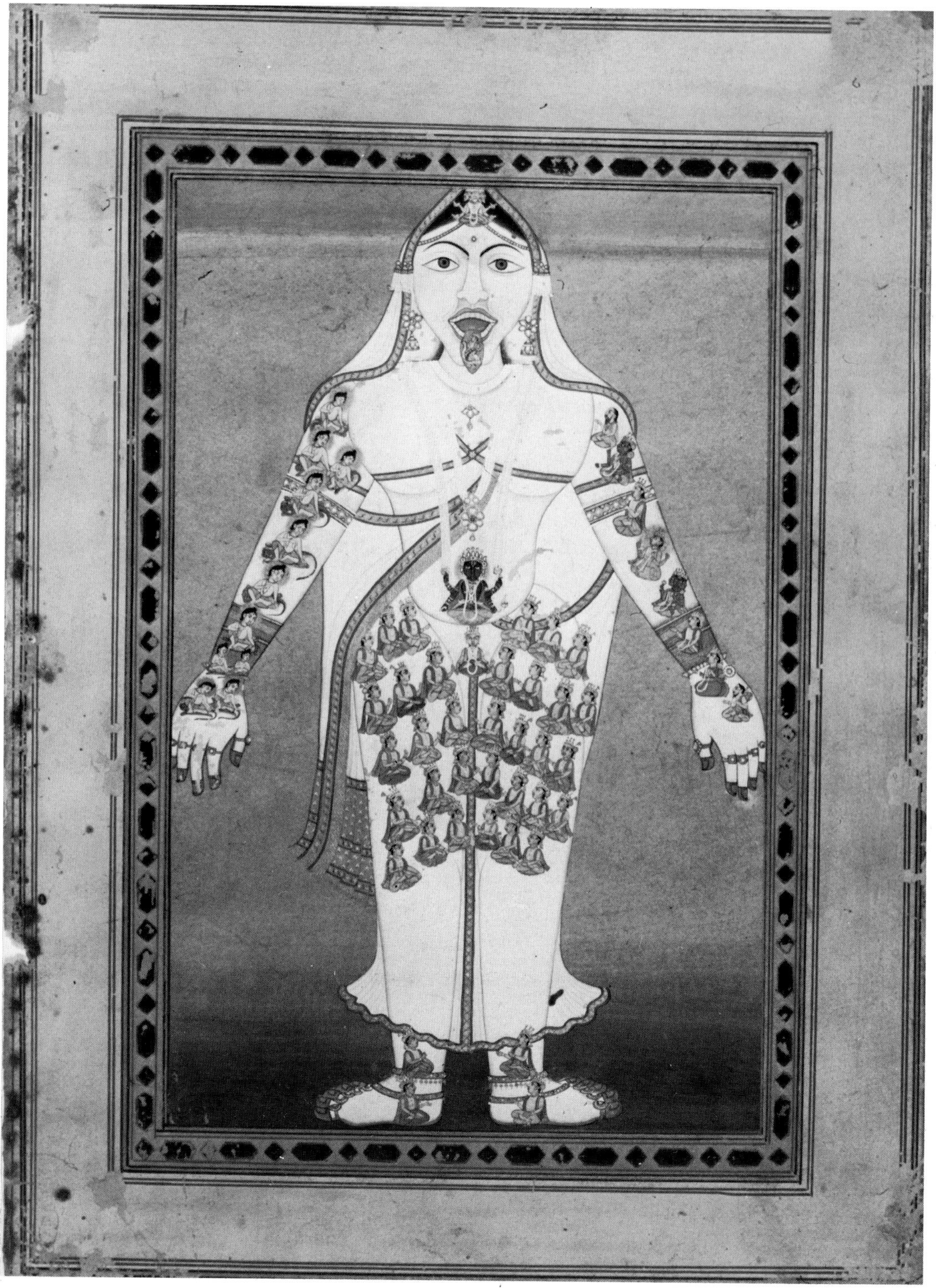

# *Introduction*

Tantra is a creative mystery which impels us to transmute our actions more and more into inner awareness: not by ceasing to act but by transforming our acts into creative evolution. Tantra provides a synthesis between spirit and matter to enable man to achieve his fullest spiritual and material potential. Renunciation, detachment and asceticism – by which one may free oneself from the bondage of existence and thereby recall one's original identity with the source of the universe – are not the way of tantra. Indeed, tantra is the opposite: not a withdrawal from life, but the fullest possible acceptance of our desires, feelings and situations as human beings.

Tantra has healed the dichotomy that exists between the physical world and its inner reality, for the spiritual, to a tantrika, is not in conflict with the organic but rather its fulfilment. His aim is not the discovery of the unknown but the realization of the known, for 'What is here, is elsewhere. What is not here, is nowhere' (*Visvasāra Tantra*); the result is an experience which is even more real than the experience of the objective world.

Tantra is a Sanskrit word derived from the root *tan-*, to expand. From this point of view the tantra means knowledge of a systematic and scientific experimental method which offers the possibility of expanding man's consciousness and faculties, a process through which the individual's inherent spiritual powers can be realized. In a looser sense the term tantra is used as a label for any form of 'expanded' literature that is remotely, if at all, associated with the doctrines of tantra. In such cases, the word is used almost as a 'suffix' (like the Sanskrit term 'śāstra') to indicate a systematic treatise. Care, therefore, should be taken to differentiate between original scriptures and pseudo-tantras; tantras like *Rakshasi Tantra* and many other similar texts, for instance, are not part of the authoritative doctrine. Because of its interchangeable connotations, the term tantra has been subject to a great deal of misinterpretation and is sometimes wrongly associated with spurious practices, vulgarizing it to the level of a fad.

*Vāk-devī. The goddess represents the subtle element of sound by which the universe of 'name' and 'form' comes into existence. Rajasthan, c. 17th century. Gouache on paper.*

*Āsana. This type of terracotta figurine represents the earliest example of āsana. Harappa, Punjab,* c. *3000* BC. *Terracotta.*

It is difficult to determine the exact time when the word tantra came to be used; nor is it possible to determine when tantric principles and practices were first introduced. Tantric ritual-symbols are found in the Harappan Culture (Indus Valley Civilization, *c.* 3000 BC) in the form of yogic postures, and in the Mother and the fertility Cult. Tantra's broad base is undoubtedly of Indo-Aryan origin and part of the totality of the ancient Indian tradition. There is a close affinity between the Tantras and the Vedas (*c.* 2000 BC) and, indeed, some tantric rites are based on Vedic practices. In its subsequent development, tantra shows the influence of the Upanishads, the Epics and the Puranas, until its full development in the early medieval period.

The tantras are mostly anonymous; their authorship is ascribed to divine source. Numerous and profusely varied, they have such names as *Āgama, Nigama, Yāmala.* Generally, they are cast in the form of instructional dialogue. The type of tantra in which Śiva addresses his consort Pārvatī, for example, is known as *Āgama,* revelation, whereas *Nigama* indicates texts in which the dialogue is addressed by Pārvatī to Śiva. The *Āgama* has four parts: the first deals with knowledge or metaphysical questions, and here it closely resembles the Upanishads; yoga forms the second part; the third part deals with ritual practices and the fourth deals with man's social and personal conduct and temperament. The original tantras may be grouped into three sections (according to each one's patron deity): the Śaiva *Āgamas* (Śiva), the Vaishṇava *Āgamas* (Vishṇu) (or *Pañcharātra*), and the Śākta *Āgamas* (Śakti), besides the later Buddhist *Āgamas* composed in Tibet.

There are early references to tantrism in Hindu, Buddhist and Jain literatures, although tantric practices are older than the texts. References to the tantras generally and to their particular rites are found in many Purāṇas, and even tantric works like *Liṅga, Kālika* and *Devī* were formed as distinctive Purāṇas. The earliest codified tantric texts date from the beginning of the Christian era, if not earlier, and some have been assembled as recently as the eighteenth and nineteenth centuries. Tantra literature took a long period to develop and no particular age can be assigned definitely. The antiquity of each work has to be determined in relation to available evidence. Thus, for example, several tantric texts have been found written in Sanskrit Gupta characters, which establishes their date as AD 400–600; in addition there exist manuscripts of Śaiva *Āgamas* from South India from the sixth century. Buddhist Tantras are also very old and may also be traced back to the beginning of the Christian era. Between the seventh and eleventh centuries a

*Seal illustrating a yogi in meditation with a trident symbol at his back, signifying transcendence of the seven phenomenal planes of existence. Provenance and date unknown. Steatite.*

number of tantric texts were assembled and have come down to us from various sources, notably from Kashmir Śaiva works of the ninth and tenth centuries and the Tamil Śaiva poets of the same period, as well as from Buddhist and Vaishṇava sources. The Kulāchāra sect of tantism is said to have been introduced by the tantric Nātha saints. Even Śaṅkara (8th century AD) mentions the existence of 64 Tantras in his *Ānandalahari*, a part of the *Saundaryalahari*. The exact number of tantric texts is difficult to ascertain, though it is generally held to be 108. In addition there is a

*Worship of the trident, emblem of Śiva. Rajasthan, 18th century. Gouache on paper.*

great number of commentaries and digests which have originated in various parts of the country, and testify to the wide popularity of the tantras and their rituals. Tantric influence, however, is not limited to India alone, and there is evidence that the precepts of tantrism travelled to various parts of the world, especially Nepal, Tibet, China, Japan and parts of South-East Asia; its influence has also been evident in Mediterranean cultures such as those of Egypt and Crete.

Tantrikas are broadly divided into various sects according to the deities they worship and their rituals. The principal sects are Śaivas (worshippers of Śiva), Vaishṇavas (worshippers of Vishnu), and

Śāktas (worshippers of Śakti, or female energy). These major groups are divided into various sub-sects. The most important centres where tantric worship is still prevalent are Assam, Bengal, Orissa, Maharashtra, Kashmir, the foothills of the north-western Himalayas, Rajasthan and parts of South India.

According to popular legend, tantric sacred places (*pīṭhasthānas*), came into existence when Śiva carried away the dead body of his consort Satī, or Pārvatī, which had been dismembered by Vishṇu into fifty-one parts that fell on different places all over the country. These became tantric pilgrim centres. Many of these places are strongholds of tantric tradition: the Kāmākshyā temple of Kāmrūpa in Assam, for example, is believed to be the place where Satī's yoni (female organ) fell and is regarded as a living centre of her immeasurable power. The worship of Śakti is very popular among tantrikas so that tantra is regarded as belonging essentially to the Śākta group and perhaps for this reason, tantra has come popularly to be understood, generally though mistakably, as Śakti-worship.

Pre-eminently a practical way of realization, tantra has adopted diverse methods to suit the needs of different followers according to their condition and abilities. Although they have a common goal, each individual has the freedom to follow the path of tantra in his own way. Such freedom does not mean a mere negation of bondage but a positive realization which brings pure joy so that universal knowledge becomes, as it were, self-knowledge. Accordingly, the tantras have evolved a framework of theory and practice, both spiritual and physical, for achieving the ends and values of life.

One question often asked – whether tantra is a religion or a form of mysticism – is best answered in the words of Woodroffe: 'The tantra, in fine, is from its very nature an encyclopaedic science. It is practical, and has no concern with wordy warfare. It lights the torch and shows the way, step by step, until the sojourner comes to the end of his journey.'[1] Although it appears to be a mystic way based on metaphysical concept, yet, in the last analysis, tantra practice sheds its mysticism and becomes a verifiable experience to the one who seeks; in so far as it is based upon human experience in the very act of living as a source of the amplification of consciousness, the tantric method is a scientific approach. In its strictest sense tantra is neither religion nor mysticism but an empirical-experiential method which has been absorbed as a cultural pattern valid for everyone and not limited to any exclusive group or sect.

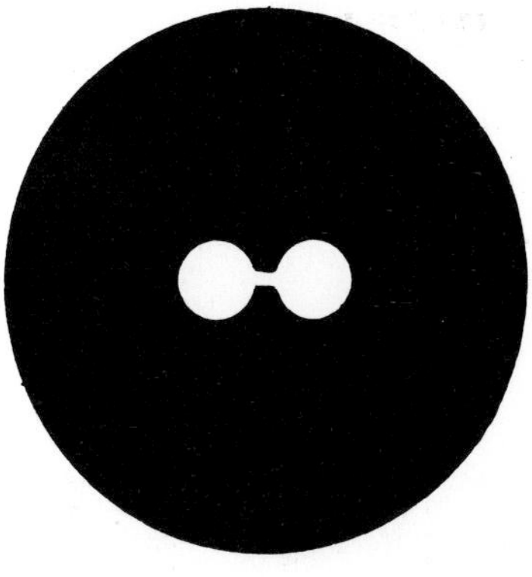

*Sālagrām, a cosmic spheroid.*

Though derived from the essential tenets of Indian philosophy the fundamental conceptions of tantra are not much concerned with abstract speculations but indicate and explain practical ways and means to the goal. Tantra evolved out of the same seeds in which the traditional system germinated and therefore grew up in the mainstream of Indian thought, yet in the course of time it received its nourishment from its own sources, which were not only radically different from the parent doctrine but often heretical and directly opposed to it. In this way tantra developed largely outside the establishment, and in the course of a dialectical process acquired its own outlook. The tantric approach to life is anti-ascetic, anti-speculative and entirely without conventional perfectionist clichés.

The fact that tantra paid more attention to the 'experimental' dimension of life does not imply that its wide ranging psycho-experimental techniques existed in a vacuum. It has highly elaborate systems of atomic theory, space-time relationship, astronomical observations, cosmology, palmistry, astrology, chemistry, alchemy, and the like. Human experience owes to tantra the discovery and location of the psychic centres in the human body and its various yogic disciplines, which are supported by visual and abstract symbols. Tantras are unique in the sense that they posit an element of realism in nature and life in their diverse manifestations. No phenomenal manifestation is antithetical to self-realization. However ephemeral life may be, everything that exists has its own positive dimension. Hence, instead of drawing away from manifested nature and its obstacles, the tantrika confronts them in a face-to-face relationship. Perfect experience results in the experience of the whole, i.e., consciousness as being and consciousness as the power to become.

Because of general ignorance regarding their real meaning, tantric rituals such as sexo-yogic practices which ought not to be confused with yogic postures, virgin worship, etc., have been misunderstood and distorted. Some tantric philosophical and ritualistic patterns were traditionally the possession of a few initiates who formed a close circle and who guarded the system with great care, permitting access to none but qualified aspirants. As a result, pseudo-orientalists recoiled with a puritanical shudder from this 'mysterious cult' and ridiculed it; this attitude was shared by their Indian counterparts in the nineteenth century. At the beginning of this present century the pioneering works of Sir John Woodroffe and other scholars cleared away the misconceptions which obscured its profound teachings.

The basic tenets of tantra can be explained and understood in either ascending or descending order. From its summit, one can start at the cosmic plane, at tantra's precepts concerning the ultimate reality and come down to its notion of creation and the constituents of the objective world, and finally arrive at its understanding of the human body and its properties, and the psychic processes which interlink man and the universe. Conversely we may start from the tangible self and ascend in stages through man–world–cosmos, culminating in the nature of the ultimate reality. These are, in fact, the various grades of tantric thought around which its diverse rituals and art forms are interwoven. Tantrikas have developed a systematic method whereby 'cosmic cross-points' are created in the relative plane, at which the individual encounters the universal noumena. These cosmic cross-points can be achieved either by working on one's self through the human body (Kuṇḍalinī-yoga), through performance of rites and rituals, or visually through such forms and figures as yantras, maṇḍalas and deities (which comprise the mainstream of tantric art), or verbally by the repetition of seed syllables (mantras). Hence tantra's diverse methods which invoke the involvement of all senses, at different levels – physical, mental or psychic – in concert or singly. All these practices nevertheless are directed towards self-enlightenment and a realization of the vision of unity.

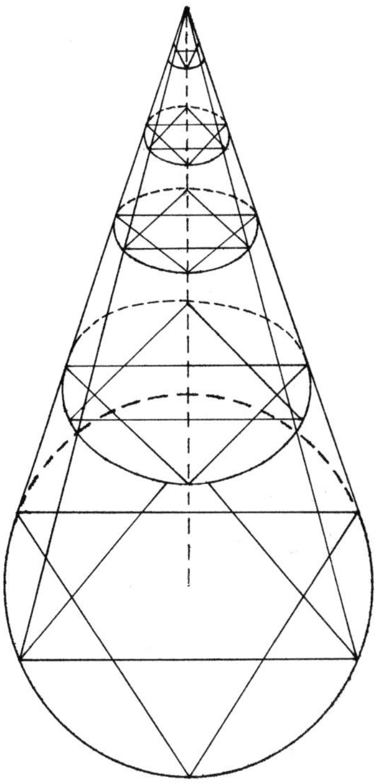

*Diagram of the six chakras, psychic centres in the human body.*

Central to tantra's teachings is the concept that Reality is unity, an undivisible whole. It is called Śiva-Śakti, Cosmic Consciousness. Śiva and its creative power, Śakti, are eternally conjoined; the one cannot be differentiated from the other, and Cosmic Consciousness is endowed with the essential potential of self-evolution and self-involution. It is only in the relative plane that Śiva-Śakti are looked upon as separate entities. The individual has the potential to realize and equate himself with Cosmic Consciousness: to intuit this reality is the purpose of tantra. The individual is not isolated but integrated in the entire cosmic scheme, and so the process of realization is self-fulfilling. It cannot be attained by methods of negation of escape. To achieve awareness of the individual/Cosmic Consciousness equation requires a close symbiosis of the individual and the Beyond – the experience of totality of being and becoming.

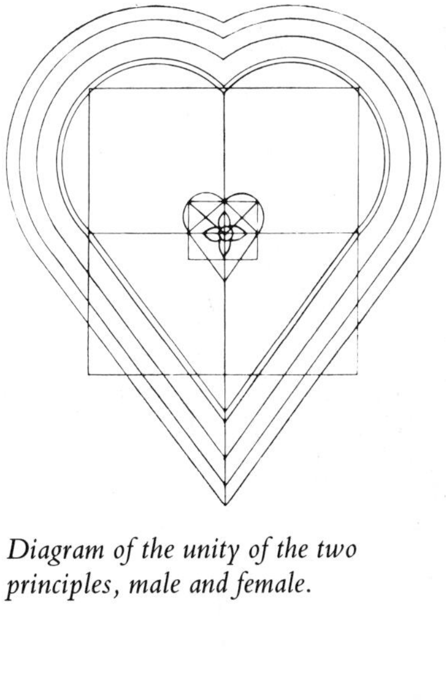

*Diagram of the unity of the two principles, male and female.*

All manifestation, according to tantra, is based upon a fundamental dualism, a male principle known as Purusha (Cosmic Consciousness) and a female principle known as Prakriti (Cosmic Force of Nature). Purusha is identified as Cosmic Consciousness, whose nature is static and which is the transcendental plane where there is but one undifferentiated unity, Śiva, Prakṛiti, Nature, is synonymous with Śakti (female energy); the kinetic energy quantum of the cosmos is the prime mover of creation, out of which the world is born and into which the world is dissolved. Purusha and Prakṛiti are the cosmicized versions of the earthly, phenomenal male and female. Though distinct in their qualities, they are inseparable since they are essentially two aspects of one principle. In reality, the whole world, the entire manifold of experience, is Śiva-Śakti, Purusha and Prakṛiti, Male and Female. Tantra's aim is to realize this integrated wholeness of polarities through active contemplation: achieving this integration of polarity means becoming Śiva-Śakti, united as one. At the experience of unity, ecstatic joy (ānanda), ineffable in human terms, is felt. Both the Hindu and Buddhist tantras accept this dualism, although there is the fundamental difference between them that the latter consider the male principle a kinetic aspect (Upāya) and the Female static (Prajñā). Both schools stress the principle of duality in non-duality and hold that the ultimate goal is the perfect state of union of the two.

Tantrism is a system of 'the rediscovery of the mystery of woman'. Apart from certain historical factors which may have influenced tantra to adopt practices associated with female worship, the chief reason for giving high status to woman and elevating her to the level of a cosmic force is that the female principle is considered to be essentially the kinetic aspect of consciousness. In tantric rituals every woman is seen as a counterpart of the feminine principle and becomes a reincarnation of cosmic energy, symbolizing the ultimate essence of reality. Tantra holds the concept of a composite female principle which, though running parallel to male, transcends it. According to this concept, Śakti is endowed with all aspects of life, creative to dissolutive, sensual to sublime, benign to horrific. Śakti's universal power is the prime mover and mother-womb of the recurring cycles of the universe, and as such reflects the procreative powers of eternal substance. She also symbolizes total life-affirmation and is a source of all polarities, differentiation and distinction of elements. The tantrikas also identify the power of Śakti with the Absolute or One, since she projects the divine bi-unity of male and female principles. In the process of self-actualization, the highest goal identified with the arousal of the Kuṇḍalinī is recognized as a microcosmic version of the feminine power of Śakti.

*Yogini in meditative posture. South India, c. 17th century. Wood.*

The objective world, with its infinite diversity, evolves out of

*Śakti seated in union with Śiva. Śakti, the kinetic energy, the prime mover of all creation, and Śiva, inert as a corpse, represent the positive–negative dualism whose interpenetration gives rise to all creation. Orissa,* c. *18th century. Brass.*

the union of opposites, the male and female principles. There is a complementary force similar to a positive and negative charge continuously attracting the two. Hence, every conjunction of opposites produces bliss and ends in primordial spontaneity. In that balanced and integrated state, Prakṛiti or Nature, composed of three forces or guṇas in Sanskrit called sattva, rajas, and tamas, is in a state of perfect equilibrium. Sattva (essence) is the ascending or centripetal tendency, a cohesive force directed towards unity and liberation. Rajas (energy) is the revolving tendency, which gives impetus to all creative force. Tamas (mass) is the descending or contrifugal tendency, the force which causes decomposition and annihilation. In their unmanifested state, these guṇas are not individually distinguishable because they balance each other perfectly. The *Devībhāgavata* describes this state thus:

Before creation this world was devoid of sun, moon, and stars, and without day and night. There was no energy and no distinction of directions. The Brahmāṇḍa [the universe] was then destitute of sound, touch, and the like, etc., devoid of other forces, and full of darkness. Then but that one eternal Brahman [Cosmic Consciousness] of whom the Srutis speak, and the Prakṛiti [Cosmic Force] who is existence, consciousness, and bliss, alone existed.

When this balance is disturbed there is a loss of equilibrium. This is the process of evolution and the world is recreated anew, the cycle continuing ceaselessly. Thus, in other terms, tamas is inertia, the magnetic force, and rajas is the kinetic force, while sattva is the balancing force between the two opposites. When these forces are in balance, there is no motion, no manifestation, no flux, only perpetual stillness. When this balance is agitated, all the forces begin to combine and recombine, evolution takes place and the universe is slowly projected in the 'form of waves' till there comes a period when everything has a tendency to revert to the primal state of equilibrium.

This phenomenon can be explained by a parallel from modern physics, as described by Lincoln Barnett in *The Universe and Dr Einstein*:

> The universe is thus progressing toward an ultimate 'heat death' or as it is technically defined, a condition of 'maximum entropy'. When the universe reaches this state some billions of years from now all the processes of nature will cease. All space will be at the same temperature. No energy can be used because all of it will be uniformly distributed through the cosmos. There will be no light, no life, no warmth – nothing but perpetual and irrevocable stagnation. Time itself will come to an end. For entropy points the direction of time. Entropy is the measure of randomness. When all system and order in the universe have vanished, when randomness is at its maximum, an entropy cannot be increased, when there no longer is any sequence of cause and effect – in short, when the universe has run down – there will be no direction to time, there will be no time. And there is no way of avoiding this destiny.[2]

Tantra absorbed and elaborated upon the sum total of traditional scientific knowledge in mathematics, astronomy, iatrochemistry, alchemy. The invention of the decimal, of numeration, including the discovery of zero in ancient India, is one of the greatest contributions to human knowledge. Some other discoveries include the heliocentric system of astronomy, the concept of lunar mansions, or nakṣhatras; the precision of equinoxes and the determination of their rate; the establishment of the luni-solar year; the construction of an astronomical calendar on a scientific basis; the rotation of the earth on its axis; the knowledge of geometrical principles and a contribution to algebraic symbols; the spherical shapes of the moon, sun, earth and other planets; the mean distances of the planets based on the theory of equilinear motion with an elaborate account of various types of motion such as rectilinear and curvilinear (vibratory and rotary), momentum and impressed motion; the assumption of inter-planetary attraction in order to explain equilibrium. Tantra's

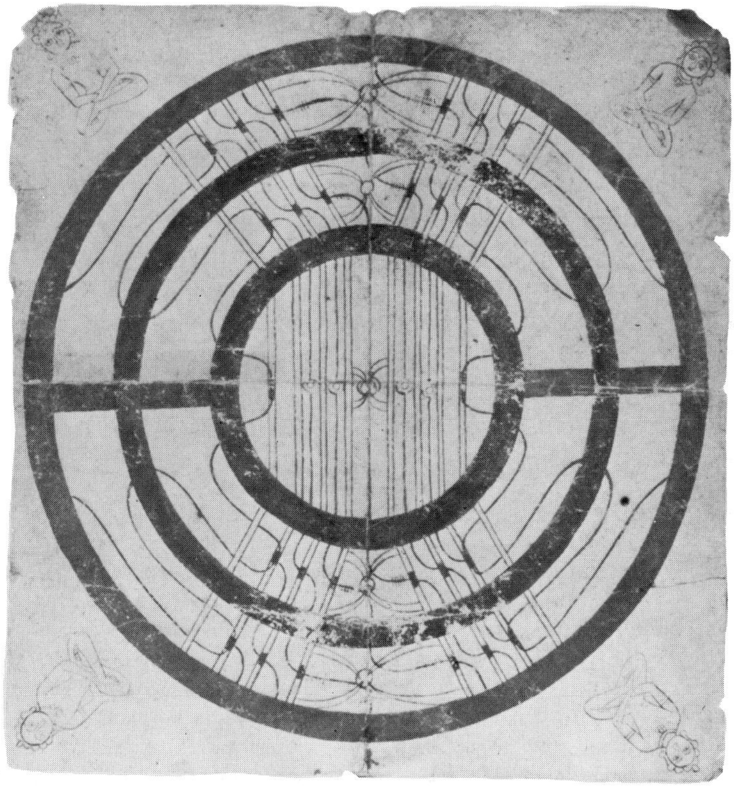

*Diagram of Jambu-dvīpa, the island continent. In Puranic and Tantric cosmology the Jambu-dvīpa is the cardinal centre in relation to the universe. The symbolic Mount Meru in Jambu-dvīpa is the* axis mundi *surrounded by a number of concentric energy zones. Rajasthan, c. 18th century. Ink on paper.*

notions concerning time and space, the nature of light and heat, gravity and magnetic attraction, the wave-theory of sound, are strikingly similar to the concepts of modern science. It must, however, be borne in mind that these scientific generalizations were based on intuitive insight, yogic visions and practices, and intense observation of natural phenomena, conditioned by an ontological viewpoint, and were not determined by experiments carried out in accordance with modern methods. These discoveries have a direct bearing on tantric thought, its precepts and practices: for example, astronomical observations, for tantrikas, have a utilitarian value in so far as they are used to determine auspicious times for rites and rituals and also are indicators to man's destiny in relation to the varying positions of the planets.

During the sixth or seventh century AD Indian alchemy (Rasāyaṇa), esoteric in essence, reached its highest development among the tantrikas. Mercuric and sulphur preparations and chemical substances, but principally mercury, were assumed to possess life-prolonging properties. Even today some tantric yogis take mercury as a substitute to food to preserve the vital elixir of

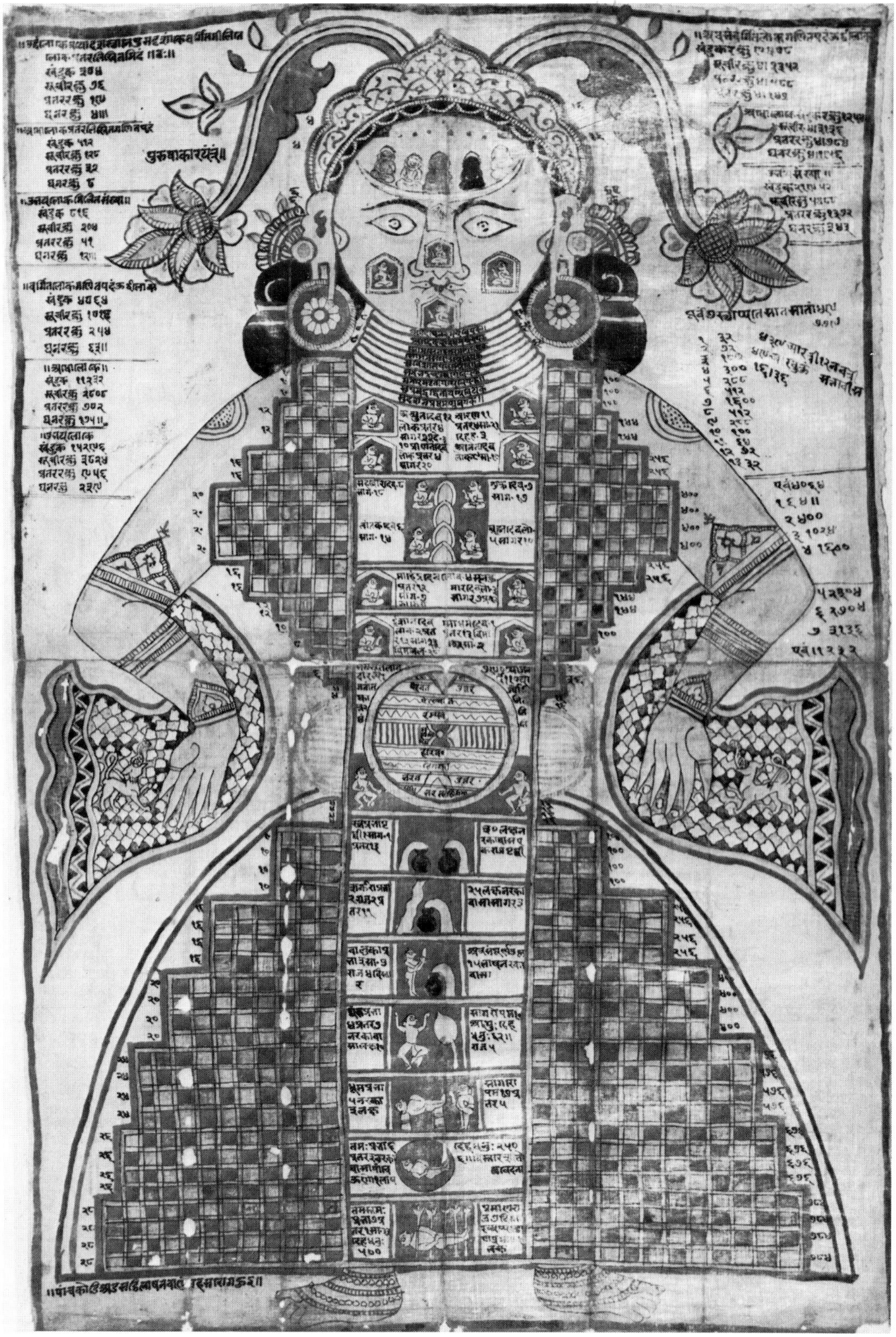

life, for it is believed that only when the body is perfectly attuned and strengthened can it experience and sustain the full intensity of the cosmic state.

The forces governing the cosmos on the macro-level govern the individual in the micro-level. According to tantra, the individual being and universal being are one. All that exists in the universe must also exist in the individual body. One of our major limitations in discovering the essential unity between the microcosm and the macrocosm is that we are accustomed to analyse the world into its separate parts, with the result that we lose sight of these parts' inter-relationship and their underlying unity. The way to fulfilment is through recognition of the wholeness linking man and the universe. In recognizing this unity, on the other hand, this norm extends our ego-boundaries and liberates us from a limited attitude towards the external world. As this feeling develops, the external and internal are no longer polarized: they do not exclude one another nor are they actually separate, but are integrated into a cohesive whole. Thus, the tantrikas see the universe as though it were within ourselves, and ourselves as though we were within the universe. It is, however, difficult to visualize the extent of our latent potentialities because we are usually aware of a very small fragment of our being. The outer self is only a small projection of the larger inner self. A vast reservoir of latent force is waiting to be discovered. The human body, with its psychological and biological functions, is a vehicle through which the dormant psychic energy, Kuṇḍalinī Śakti, can be awakened to finally unite with the Cosmic Consciousness that is Śiva.

The Kuṇḍalinī Śakti, the coiled and dormant cosmic power, is at the same time the supreme force in the human body. According to tantra, this coiled-up energy remains unmanifest within us and is said to be a latent reservoir of psychic power. The Kuṇḍalinī Śakti ('coiled-up energy') is the central pivot upon which our psychophysical apparatus is based. A transformation and reorientation of this dormant energy is only possible through what is called the arousing of the Kuṇḍalinī through the psychic centres in the human body, by activizing its ascent it transcends our limitations. When the Kuṇḍalinī sleeps, man is aware of his immediate earthly circumstances only. When she awakes to a higher spiritual plane, the individual is not limited to his own perception but instead participates in the source of light. Thus in her ascent, the Kuṇḍalinī absorbs within herself all the kinetic energy with which the different psychic centres are charged. By awakening the Kuṇḍalinī's dormant force, otherwise

*Purushakāra Yantra. Painting illustrating the drama of the universe in the body of cosmic man. Rajasthan,* c. *18th century. Gouache on cloth.*

*Cosmic energy symbolized as the serpent power. South India, 18th century. Wood.*

absorbed in the unconscious and purely bodily functions, and directing it to the higher centres, the energy thus released is transformed and sublimated until its perfect unfolding and conscious realization is achieved.

Kuṇḍalinī's rising, in the language of modern science, means the activation of the vast dormant areas of the brain. The neurological capacities of the human being are incalculable: according to recent findings each individual possesses around 10 billion brain cells; a single brain cell may be in relationship to 25,000 others; the number of possible associations is astronomical, therefore, being a quantity larger than the number of atoms in the universe. At each second, the brain receives approximately 100 billion sensations and it is estimated that it fires off around 5,000 signals per second. In contrast to the vast reservoir of our potentialities, we are aware of only one millionth of our own cortical signalling. And so vast areas of the brain, which the neurologists call 'silent areas', remain 'wasted assets', untapped and unutilized. Once these areas are completely active, we have begun to communicate with our own higher consciousness. The opening of this centre to its fullest capacity enables the Kuṇḍalinī to ascend to the highest psychic centre, Sahasrāra, the place of the Cosmic Consciousness, symbolized by a thousand petalled lotus located just above the head. In the process of Kuṇḍalinī-yoga, it is said, even the pattern of the electrical impulses in the brain is altered. Through tantric disciplines, the ascending Kuṇḍalinī vitalizes the psychic centres in the human body, technically called chakras, until it finally reaches the Sahasrāra where a mystic union takes place. The aspirant thus realizes, in a transcendental experience, his union with Śiva-Śakti.

The Kuṇḍalinī Śakti can be aroused through various meditative techniques and processes including the practice of yogic Prāṇ-āyāma, the control of the vital cosmic life-force. Rhythmical breathing makes all the molecules of the body move in the same direction in order to gain control of the mind. If the air in our lungs at any moment contains 10,000,000,000,000,000,000,000, atoms, we can imagine what current is generated by the movement of all the molecules in the system, bringing the restless mind into single-pointedness. In this state the vibrations of the body become perfectly rhythmical and the nerve current is changed into a motion similar to electricity, generating a power so tremendous that the Kuṇḍalinī is aroused.

The attainment of supernatural powers, known as the Siddhis, is considered to be the indirect result of this practice. There are considered to be eight great Siddhis among which the following are best known: Aṇimā, the power of becoming infinitely small so that one can see things of the minutest size, even the inner structure of the atom; Mahimā, the power to become immensely large so that one can perceive enormously vast things, the functioning of the solar system and that of the universe; Laghimā, or weightlessness, 'the power to control the earth's attraction on the body by developing in each cell the opposite [centripetal] tendency'. Others are the power of leaving the body and entering into it at will, mastery over the elements, and supernormal hearing so that one can hear 'the grass as it grows'.

The ascent of Kuṇḍalinī is accompanied by an experience of a mystical light of various colours. The colours of the division of Prāṇa do not correspond on what we ordinarily associate with the solar spectrum but are the arrangement of colours on a supernormal plane. There is a similarity here to Goethe's analysis: 'Colours have a mystical significance. For every diagram that shows the many colours is suggestive of primeval conditions which belong equally to man's perceptions as to Nature.'[3]

In recent years physiological scientists have been concerned to find out whether restriction of awareness to an unchanging stimulus results in a 'turning-off' of consciousness of the external world, as it occurs in, say, the practice of meditation. Their experiments have shown that when a subject is exposed to a continuous visual input or an unchanging stimulus called a 'ganzfeld' (a patternless visual field) or a 'stabilized image', the subject loses complete contact with the external world. This phenomenon is, further, attributed to the structure of the central nervous system. The results of the tiny electrical potentials recorded on the electroencephalograph (EEG) have shown the appearance of the alpha rhythm in the brain. Similarly, recent studies of yoga also reveal that meditation is a 'high alpha state'. Likewise, during the practice of Kuṇḍalinī-yoga when attention is focused in a state of one-pointedness by means of various meditative techniques (repetition of mantra, concentration on yantra, rhythmic breathing, etc.), the adept loses contact with the external world. In consequence, experts conclude that meditation is neither 'esoteric nor mysterious' but is a 'practical technique which uses an experiential knowledge of the structure of the nervous system' and hence is very much within the scope of practical applied psychology.[4]

Tantra teaches that the Kuṇḍalinī Śakti can also be unravelled by the practice of āsanas, the sexo-yogic disciplines: 'One must rise by that by which one falls.' Those very aspects of human nature which bind us can be stepping-stones to liberation. In this discipline, sexual impulses become a pathway for opening the realities of the cosmos, pointing towards the oneness of the finite and the infinite. The ritual of tantra āsanas has developed into a formidable series of psycho-physical practices to promote the type of discipline conducive to meditation. In the act of āsana, a man and a woman unite, and its fulfilment lies in the realization of one's potential with the experience of joy. During sexual union the adepts

*Tantric āsana, or sexo-yogic posture. Orissa, c. 18th century. Gouache on paper.*

withdraw their minds from their environment. The mind aspires to be free. The retention of sexual energy increases inner pressure, thus transmitting the sex force into a potency so powerful that the psychic current is liberated.

Tantra āsana demonstrates the way by which sexual energy can be harnessed for spiritual fulfilment. It teaches us to explore our senses rather than to subdue them. The *Guhyasamāja Tantra* categorically affirms; 'No one succeeds in attaining perfection by employing difficult and vexing operations; but perfection can be gained by satisfying all one's desires.' The tantras are unique in the sense of being a synthesis of the opposing dimensions, bhoga (enjoyment) and yoga (liberation). Our hedonistic urges based on the pleasure principle can be transformed for a spiritual experience. To involve oneself in gross pleasure, therefore, can itself be regarded as an act of spirituality, provided it is indulged in with a right intention and motivation and after adequate initiation. Thus sexo-yogic practices become a yoga, or a means for a spiritual edification, a vehicle, though conventional wisdom regards sex as profane and an obstacle to any form of spiritual progress.

Sex is regarded as a physical basis of creation and evolution. It is the cosmic union of opposites, of the male and female principles, and its importance merits fulfilment on the biological plane, Tantra, however, makes a distinction between momentary pleasure and the joy of union. This joy of union is equated with supreme bliss (ānanda), obliterating differences between male and female in a state of complete union. In this state all impulse and function become Śiva-Śakti. This ecstasy is experienced as the Kuṇḍalinī rises and unfolds itself.

A very dynamic role is played by the female aspirant in the practice of tantra āsana. She is looked upon as an intermediary between the transcendent and the imminent, and is regarded as an embodiment of Śakti, the active principle. Potentially, she embraces within her all the positive attributes with which Śakti is endowed. She 'is', in flesh and blood, the goddess. Thus in the tantra ritual, woman as the reflection of the female principle, becomes the object of worship. She is symbolically transformed into a goddess through rituals as in 'Kumārī-pūjā' (virgin worship) or 'Śakti-upāsanā' (female worship). In the ritual the female adept is an essential archetypal and iconographic image, and is not an ordinary woman.

The extent to which tantra can integrate this archetype into its discipline is shown in the life of Chaṇḍidās, a high priest rebel-poet of 15th-century Bengal, and his love for the washer-maid, Rāmi.

The washer-maid represents the primordial Female, a personification of its totality. Faced with opposition, Chaṇḍidās approached his temple deity, the goddess Bāshuli, who said to him: 'You must love this woman, [as] no god can offer you what this woman is able to.'[5] The songs of Chaṇḍidās, echoed so often by Bengal's Sahaja sect, an offshoot of tantrism, proclaim the worship of love:

*One who pervades*
*The great Universe*
*is seen by none*
*unless a man knows*
*the unfolding*
*of love.*[6]

To a Sahajiyā (literally, the unconditioned 'spontaneous man') the washer-maid, a domni or outcaste woman, is considered to be the ideal partner for ritualistic worship. Not conditioned by any social and ethical taboos, she enjoys freedom and detachment. Tantra's broad-based attitude includes the identity between 'the noblest and most precious' and the 'basest and most common'. The more common the woman is, the more she is exalted. In old Bengali documents there are instances of disputes between the adherents of parakiyā (āsana with another man's wife) and its opponents, the champions of conjugal love (svakiyā). The latter were the losers, which shows the extent of the influence of the parakiyā ideal. The psychological aspect of parakiyā love was greatly influenced by the philosophy of eternal love projected in the life of Rādhā, another's wife, the hlādinī-śakti or power of bliss, which is the very essence of Kṛishṇa. Their inseparable union is a divine 'sport' or 'līlā'. This is emphasized in the Sahaja ritual, in which a woman participates as if she possessed the nature of Rādhā and a man that of Kṛishṇa. Thus, tantric doctrines cut across all class stratifications and social barriers, indeed, some of its sub-sects, like the Bauls, go so far as considering that intense awareness of one another can remain constant only when the lovers are not bound to one another by the social contract of marriage.

Tantric rites and rituals are complex and elaborate disciplines involving a series of practices. Adept are called sādhaka (male) or sādhikā (female), and the discipline they follow is known as sādhanā. It is imperative that the adept should be initiated by a qualified guru or spiritual teacher; there is wide variation in the mode of instruction. In the primary stages, the adept is given an ordinary initiation by means of an elaborate ritual, though a more

*A group of tantrika ascetics. Rajasthan, c. 18th century. Bronze.*

advanced aspirant's initiation is higher and imparted through a disciple imbued with deep spiritual experience.

Three kinds of spiritual aspirants have been distinguished in the tantras according to their mental dispositions or stages of spiritual consciousness: Paśu, Vira, and Divya. When one is still in bondage (paśu) and subject to the common round of conventions, he is led along the tantric way by devices suitable to his competency. One who is more capable of psycho-spiritual experience of a stronger ethical nature (vira) and had the inner strength to 'play with fire', as tantra says, is at the middle of the extremes. A man of divya disposition is the most developed. His meditative mood is spontaneous in him and he is always ready to imbibe spiritual experiences, always in ecstasy enjoying the 'inner woman' and 'wine'. In this state the 'inner woman' is the Kuṇḍalinī Śakti in the body of the worshipper and 'wine' the intoxicating knowledge derived from yoga, which renders the worshipper senseless, 'like a drunkard'.

There are several kinds of tantric practices for the awakening of the Kuṇḍalinī Śakti; among them and most important are Dakshiṇāchāra or Dakshiṇa Mārga, the right-hand path; Vāmāchāra or Vāma Mārga, the left-hand path, in which woman (vāmā) is included; and Kulāchāra, which is a synthesis of the other two. In addition, there are also the mixed practices, such as the Vedic, Śaiva and Vaishṇava. The followers of the left-hand path practise the Pañcha-Makāra rites (five M's), whose name refers to the five ingredients beginning with the letter M: Madya, wine; Māṁsa, meat; Matsya, fish; Mudrā, parched cereal; and Maithuna, sexual union. The symbolic content of these ingredients varies for different classes of aspirants. According to tantra, those who are unable to cut the three knots of 'shame, hate and fear' are not worthy of being initiated into this path. The fundamental principle of the left-hand path is that spiritual progress cannot be achieved by falsely shunning our desires and passions but by sublimating those very aspects which make one fall, as a means of liberation.

During rituals, different rites are performed among which, nyāsa, the 'ritual projection' of divinities and elements into various parts of the body by the adept, is extremely important. While practising nyāsa, often done with mudrās or finger gestures, the adept takes the attitude that mantra-sounds or forces are working to stimulate the nerve currents for the proper distribution of energies through his whole body. He thus projects the power of the divinities and at the same time touches the different parts of his body in order to symbolically awaken the vital forces lying dormant.

Tantrikas also perform other group-rituals known as Chakra-pūjā or Circle-worship, of which Bhairavī-chakra is the most important. In this ritual, the female guru, is worshipped, and the practice of the rite is confined to only the highly advanced initiates who are generally admitted to the inner circle, which encourages a group-mind where each initiate shares a 'psychic blueprint'.

These group rituals are an attempt to tie together experiential and cognitive awareness through in-group practices which have not only spiritual but therapeutic value for the adepts. Sharing is essential to understand one's self deeply. These rituals are a

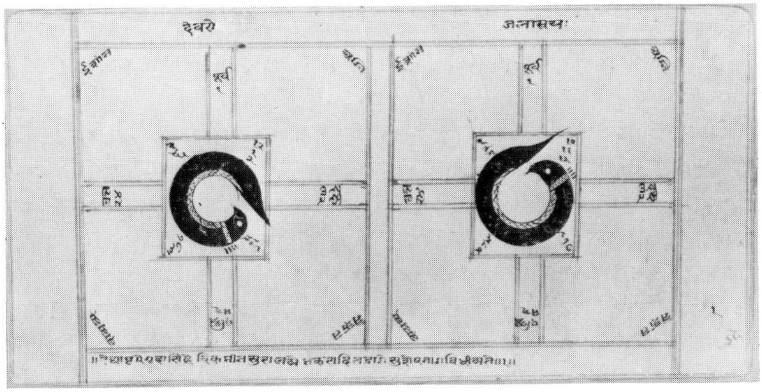

*Kuṇḍalinī in its kinetic aspect. Rajasthan, c. 19th century. Gouache on paper.*

'microlab', where one can participate in wide-ranging experiences which develop one's own potential in a group setting and make the aspirant aware of integrated wholeness through interpersonal contact. The application of many and diverse ritual practices such as gestures (mudrās) and touching the various parts of the body (nyāsa) not only have symbolic significance but a psychological basis as well: they are 'empathy building' methods which deepen concentration and expand the awareness of the aspirants.

The use of such things as incense, flowers, sandalwood paste, honey, etc., and eating and drinking together, foster sensory awakening and experience through the senses. Likewise the frequent outbursts of the 'joy chorus' are deep moments of group interaction binding each adept into a common genre. Periodic observance of these rituals acts as reinforcement and contributes to the complete cycle of spiritual development as well as adding harmony to life.

During the performance of special rituals tantric aspirants sometimes resort to the use of drugs, drinks and chemicals: drinking bhāṅg, a drink made of hemp leaves; or smoking gāñjā, an intoxicant; or smearing the naked body with specially prepared ashes. These are used not for mystical illumination but to counteract the influence of adverse conditions such as extreme cold or heat, hunger and thirst, especially when a prolonged ritual is performed under the sky at midnight in solitary places or at a high altitude.

In today's psychedelic rituals, many people have recourse to conscious-expanding experiences by means of drugs, to feel the 'isness of things'. According to the findings of a Harvard Psilocybin Project, the persons who took drugs reported that 'One moment of clock time in an LSD session can be an eternity of ecstasy. . . . These reports, interestingly enough, are quite similar to the accounts given by the adepts of Kuṇḍalinī Yoga and certain forms of Tantrism.'[7] The resemblance of the LSD experience to that of the yogi is only a close approximation to its real nature. There are essential differences between the two. A 'chemical pilgrimage' is a short-lived experience initiated and prolonged by artificial means and exists isolated from life. On the other hand, a yogi's experience is the outcome of a discipline, set within a certain psychological and spiritual framework. His outer life is controlled by his inner, so that even while withdrawing from the outer world he is not alienated from life, since he is firmly established within himself. Every movement, thought and action is performed for the attainment of a prescribed goal. He awakens his inner forces

*A practising tantrika in the Himalayas.*

but at the same time maintains perfect lucidity and self-control, the resulting experience of which is neither hallucinogenic nor artificial. His experience is an everlasting one, whereas a 'chemical pilgrimage' is principally indulged in spasmodically for momentary thrills invariably bringing depression and in many cases ending with drug addiction.

In tantric rituals, particularly in the twilight (sandhyā) rituals performed at the conjunction of day and night or at midnight, a secret language known as Saṅdhyā-bhāshā or Saṅdhā-bhāshā is used by which a state of consciousness is expressed in ambiguous terms with erotic meanings. The symbolic contents of these terms are not intelligible to non-initiates, thus, for example: 'inserting his organ into the mother's womb', 'pressing his sister's breasts', 'placing his foot upon the guru's head', 'he will be reborn no more'. In saṅdhā terminology, the 'organ' is the contemplating mind; the 'mother's womb' is the Mūlādhāra chakra, or base centre; the 'sister's breasts' are the heart centre (Anāhata chakra), and the 'guru's head' is the brain centre (Sahasrāra). These code terms, if translated, mean, to quote Agehananda, 'He practises mental penetration through the successive centres, and when he reaches the uppermost centre, he will not be [re-] born. According to some scholars, Saṅdhyā-bhāshā means 'twilight' or 'secret' language, though others call it Saṅdhā-bhāshā, or 'intentional' language, in which many passages of tantric texts are composed. Whatever its meaning, it has an equivocal significance, partly to conceal the real meaning of the terminology from non-initiates but also, as Eliade says, 'Chiefly to project the yogin into the "paradoxical situation" indispensable to his training.'[8] The process of destroying and reinventing terminology, and even a guru's abusive language, recall present-day 'agression rituals' practised in group psychotherapy as a form of linguistic catharsis, using offensive language as a means to avert psychotic behaviour and to live constructively with the collective psyche. In tantrism, however, abusive language has a double meaning, 'concrete' and 'symbolic', mainly to transubstantiate that experience into awareness.

Tantric rites and rituals can be performed either on the mental plane or by the use of mantras or sacred words, diagrams, deities, ritual ingredients. These accessories are not considered and used according to their function in daily life but have deep spiritual significances. Mantras are indispensible to tantric discipline. Literally translated, the word mantra means 'that which when reflected upon gives liberation'. A mantra cannot be enlivened

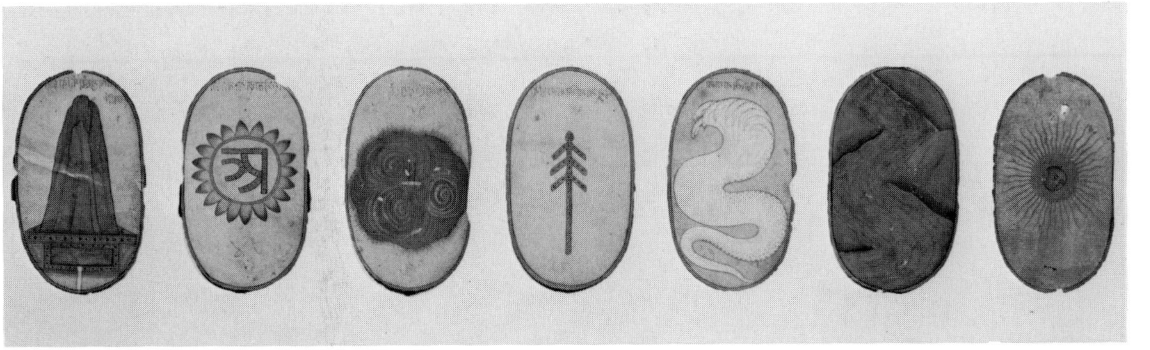

*A set of seven paintings illustrating various phases of cosmic evolution and involution. Rajasthan, 18th century. Gouache on paper.*

until it is repeated and creates a wave pattern (japa), accompanied by a clear grasp of its meaning and a proper articulation of its letters. Each letter of the mantra is charged with energy and creates vibrations in the inner consciousness. Sound vibrations are said to be the manifestation of the Śakti and consequently are sound equivalents of the deities. Mantras may seem meaningless and unintelligible to the non-initiate, but to the adept who has received right instruction from a guru, they are seeds of spiritual power.

The Primal Sound as the monosyllabic mantra Oṃ is the basis of cosmic evolution. All the elemental sound-forms of mantras emanate from this eternal sound. Sound and form are interdependent, and every form is a vibration of a certain density; conversely, every sound has a visual equivalent. Sound is the reflex of form and form is the product of sound. All that is animate and inanimate are vibrations of a particular frequency. All the mantras have their colour forms, and when a mantra is pronounced properly its visual correlates begin to manifest. The dynamic power-pattern rooted in sound by which it is revealed is called a yantra.

A yantra, which means 'aid' or 'tool', is generally drawn on paper or engraved on metal, either to aid meditation or as a tangible image of the deity. Just as a mantra is a sound equivalent, the yantra is a diagrammatic equivalent of the deity and consists of linear and spatial geometrical permutations of the deity. The primal abstract shapes, such as the point, line, circle, triangle, square, are harmonized in composition to provide a formal equilibrium which is both static and dynamic. A common feature of the yantra is that it possesses an element of centrality around which the whole figure is built up. The centre as point of origin and balance evokes the idea of emanation and radiation. Enveloped in vertical and horizontal extensions it conveys a sense of formal mathematical order and regularity.

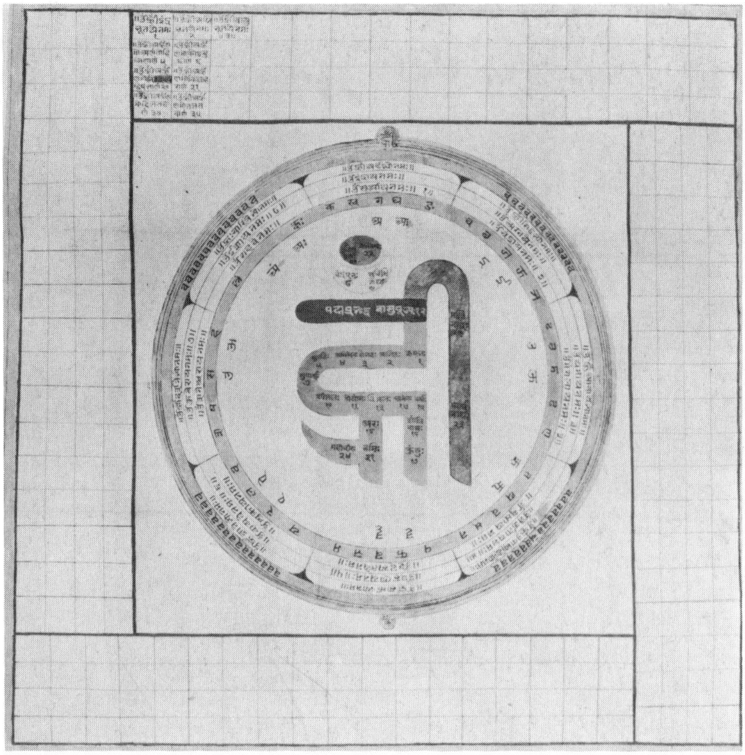

*Oṃ, the cosmic sound, is a combination of three syllables – a, u, m – that represent three phases of the cosmic cycle – creation, preservation and dissolution – condensed into a single sound unit. Rajasthan, c. 18th century. Gouache on paper.*

Thus, yantra represents an energy pattern whose force increases in proportion to the abstraction and precision of the diagram. Through these power-diagrams creation and control of ideas are said to be possible. The principle behind this tenet is that just as each form is the visible product of any energy pattern rooted in sound, so, reciprocally, each visible form carries with it its own implicit power-diagram. Hence the yantra ought not to be considered a schematic sketch of tantric astronomical and astrological maps and computations, but a linear image revealed to the adept. All the elemental geometrical figures of which a yantra is constructed and other forms of meditative diagrams or psycho-cosmic energy charts have symbolic values. They can be composed into a complex structure to represent forces and qualities of the cosmos in elemental forms. For the tantrika, therefore, these diagrams are potent in that they are not only conscious entities, but, symbolically, consciousness itself.

As in the yantra one looks for an affinity between the centre which represents the focal area of psychic power and the core of one's own consciousness, so also in the maṇḍala a similar identity is sought and expressed. The maṇḍala, the word means circle, is an archetypal image signifying wholeness and totality. It represents

*Shyāmā (Kālī) Yantra. Rajasthan, 18th century. Gouache on paper.*

the cosmos or the potent core of psychic energy, and is a perennial balance of force whose beginning is in its end, whose end is in its beginning. Within its perimeter a complexity of visual metaphors – square, triangle, labyrinthine patterns – represent the absolute and the paradoxical elements of totality. Usually painted on cloth oı paper, the maṇḍala is widely used in tantric worship and forms an essential part of the ritual. The adept is initiated to visualize the primal essence of the maṇḍala in its external form and then to internalize it through contemplation into a psychic force. Thus the circle as a symbol of wholeness functions as a 'paradigm of involution and evolution'.

Like the maṇḍalas and yantras, the egg-shaped Brahmāṇḍa, the globe-shaped Sālagrāma, and the Śiva-liṅga, mostly in stone and used for ritual, manifest a realization of the wholeness. In the Brahmāṇḍa, 'Brahma-Aṇḍa', the totality is represented in the form of an egg. The Brahman (the Absolute) is symbolized as a curve which surrounds the universe and forms the egg (Aṇḍa), the Cosmic Egg (Brahmāṇḍa). Śiva-liṅga is a term commonly applied to the phallus, though according to the *Skanda Purāṇa,* the liṅga means the all-pervading space in which the whole universe is in the process of formation and dissolution. Liṅga stands in the yoni – the

*Brahmāṇḍa, cosmic spheroid, a symbol of all-pervasive reality. Banaras, contemporary traditional form. Stone.*

*Liṅgam with the serpent power, Kuṇḍalinī, ascending to its apex. Banaras, contemporary. Stone.*

womb of Prakṛiti, symbol of the female principle or the kinetic aspect giving rise to all vibration and movement. In a state beyond manifestation or a state of repose or balance, the yoni is represented by the circle, the central point being the root of the liṅga. In differentiated creation, however, or a state of activity it becomes distinct, and the circle is transformed into a triangle – the yoni, the source of manifestation. Thus the point, Bindu, in the circle is an acceptance of all: it neither posits nor negates but incorporates all into its endless form. These are essential figurations in the symbolism of tantra, whether expressed in abstract form or anthropomorphically, as when the Liṅga-yoni is revealed in the form of Ardhanārīśvara, possessing male and female attributes, conjoined together, signifying psychic totality.

Through successive stages of the transformation of matter and its reduction to its absolute essence, the tantric artist's first concern is to bring out the hidden universality of basic forms. He does not attempt to absorb something external but releases what he has experienced inwardly. Concerned with the realities of life, tantra art is firmly rooted in spiritual values. This form of com-

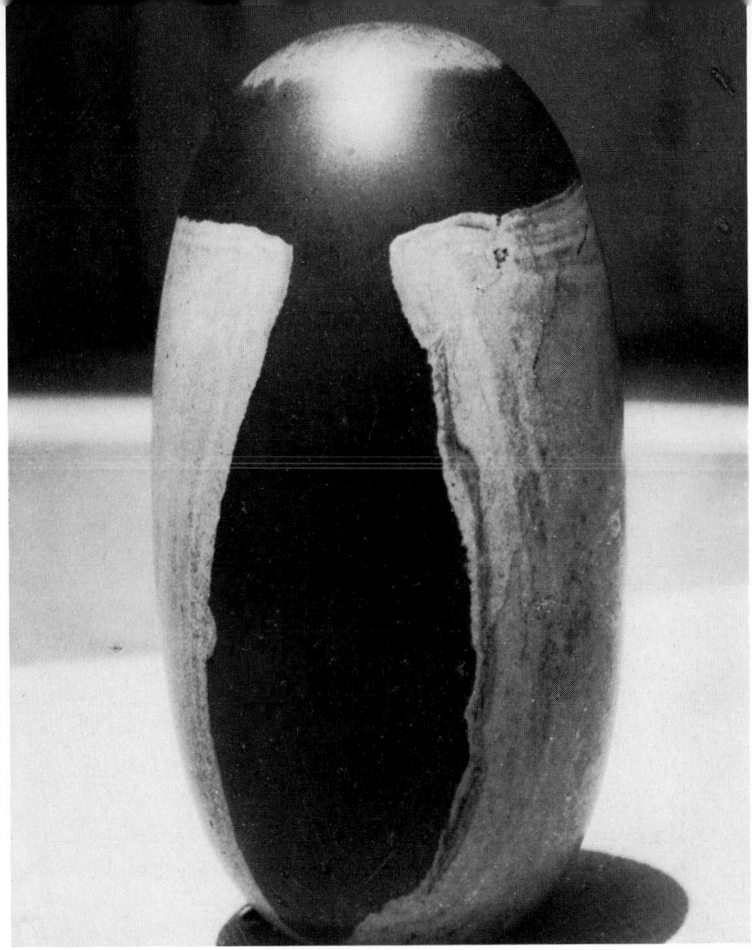

munication becomes a way of life and creates concepts and forms whereby deepest intuitions are crystallized and conveyed to others, thus giving universality to the personal expression of art.

In tantric imagery, the power-patterns and configurations are built up from primal abstract forms to complexity. This form of imagery is intuitively apprehended and is based on irreversible cosmic principles. There are no variables, but a continuum of spatial experiences whose 'essence' precedes its existence: the whole meaning is already present before the form is executed. These art forms retain their intrinsic character and serve to create visual reactions both psychological and spiritual.

Tantra art, like most other forms of Indian art, is anonymous, coming down to us from very ancient times. Some of the art objects are dated and their provenance is known; others, like Brahmāṇḍas, Sālagrāmas, Śiva-liṅgas, are expressions of ageless types which have survived due to their extensive use in worship and ritual. However, the traditional task of codifying the philosophical and scientific norms of tantra is fast disappearing and can be found only in isolated areas.

*Ardhanārīśvara. The natural markings on the egg-shaped sculptural form illustrate the divine biunity of male and female principles in a single unit. Banaras, contemporary expression of traditional form. Stone.*

*Ardhanārīśvara. This hermaphroditic image of Śiva and Pārvatī as half male and half female illustrates the dual principles in harmonious unity. Brij Nagar Museum, Rajasthan, c. 12th century. Stone.*

*Hari-Hara. Painting illustrating Vishṇu (Hari) on the left fused with Śiva (Hara) on the right. The androgynous deity, widely worshipped in South India as Aiyaṇar, symbolizes the creative power of preservation and dissolution of the eternal cycle of the universe. Kangra, c. 18th century. Gouache on paper.*

Combining as it does art, science and ritual, tantra shows the way to self-enlightenment. The way to the goal is within, in every atom of our being. We learn it by living it. Both external and internal practices are necessary.

Today's artist employs abstract forms of representation to express the complexities of life and nature, an approach which in tantra art dates back several centuries. Many of the tantric forms, their colour combinations, patterns and structures, bear striking resemblance to the works of contemporary artist.The essential difference between the two, however, is that the tantric artists expose in their art mysteries of the universe and the laws which govern them. Tantra art has a deeper significance when compared with barren abstraction, which has arisen principally from a search for the unconventional. Tantra art owes its origin to a deep spiritual faith and vision. Philip Rawson observes:

> The essence of these works is that they are all meant to provide a focus for meditation. Their diagrams are meant to open doors in the mind that reflects them, and so open for it a new and higher level of consciousness. It is not surprising that the current Pop-LSD cult, led by Dr Timothy Leary, should have latched on to one or two of these visual images – though I am sure few of the devotees realize how far this art goes. They may well discover from this book[9] that it could offer them far more than a simple breaking-down of conceptual cages. It could give them something on which to build a permanent intuition, as inner vision that does not need repeated 'trips'.[10]

Equally significant are tantra's views on the expanded concept of man which reflects his relationship to the vast-scale cosmos within which a single individual has the possibility of extending his awareness into the outer reaches of space. It conceives of the human body as the physical substratum to highest awareness, and the raw material for further transformation, where even conjugal love and sex are considered a means to supreme joy and spiritual edification; its unconventional and spontaneous approach to life, with its psycho-experimental content, offers a complete reorientation of our outlook on the world at large.

Similarly important are tantra's concepts of the polarity principle determining the relationship between man and woman, a creative interaction in which the conflict between outward and inward, of head and heart, can be resolved. In the tantric method, the female force is all-important, since it offers the key to a creative life in the act of living it. The preponderance of masculinity, with its aggressiveness and relative lack of feminine qualities, has created an imbalance in today's society. To experience the basic sensation of being 'I' in its totality is to equilibrate the two opposites, masculinity and feminity. In tantric terms it means a synthesis, a development of feminity within each one of us. The higher our spiritual evolution, the more feminine-affirmative will be our level of consciousness, in relation to the masculine-negative.

Thus tantra opens up a new vista in its ideological and spiritual concepts, and its spectrum of experiential techniques provides a possible psychotherapeutic alternative in the quest of a love and joy that unite.

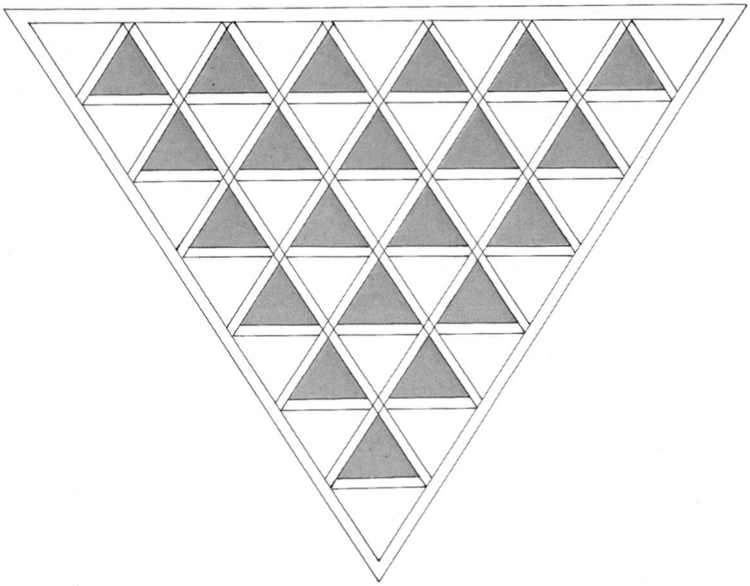

*Janan yantra.*

# *ART*

The art which has evolved out of tantrism reveals an abundant variety of forms, varied inflections of tone and colours, graphic patterns, powerful symbols with personal and universal significance. It is specially intended to convey a knowledge evoking a higher level of perception, and taps dormant sources of our awareness. This form of expression is not pursued like detached speculation to achieve aesthetic delight, but has a deeper meaning. Apart from aesthetic value, its real significance lies in its content, the meaning it conveys, the philosophy of life it unravels, the world-view it represents. In this sense tantra art is visual metaphysics.

## *Unity*

The foundations of tantra art are based on the spiritual values which surround Indian art in general. Though it projects visual imagery in its own special manner, tantra art shares a common heritage.. According to age-old tradition, the beautiful and the spiritual form an inseparable whole. Beauty is a symbol of the divine. A striking enunciation of this principle can be found in *Samyutta Nikaya* (V.2): Ananda, the beloved disciple of the Buddha said to the Master, 'Half of the holy life, O Lord, is friendship with the beautiful, association with the beautiful, communion with the beautiful.' 'It is not so, Ananda, it is not so,' said the Master; 'It is not half of the holy life; it is the whole of the holy life.' If beauty reflects divinity, conversely and by implication reality must be made visible in terms no less than the highest ideals of beauty conceived by man whatever the nature of the semblance – by means of a symbol, a pattern, or an anthropomorphic form. Admittedly, this approach aspires to a transcendent vision, arising principally from untutored vision of 'closed-eye perception'. An act of creation becomes, as it were, a contemplative process, an orchestral symphony in which both the seer and the seen become

*Oṃ, the Primal Sound as the monosyllabic mantra, is the basis of cosmic evolution. On the left the tantric Trinity, Brahmā, Vishṇu and Śiva, with the Śakti on the right. Manuscript page, Rajasthan, 18th century. Gouache on paper.*

*Rāma and Sītā, conceived as Vishṇu and Lakṣmi in the Suriya or sun-disc maṇḍala. Rajasthan, c. 18th century. Gouache on paper.*

one. What follows from this hypothesis is that what merely influences the senses and titilates the eye is no longer creative. To reduce art, as Coomaraswamy pointed out, and speak of it 'exclusively in terms of sensation is to do violence to the inner man'.[11] The scope of art is limited if it does not emancipate us from surface perception.

That emancipation is precisely what tantra art aims at achieving. Through the vocabulary of art, it teaches us to understand the world in a way that our experience of it is enriched and deepened. It frees our mundane reactions so that our dissipated perceptions – a mass of indistinct spatial configurations – are woven into a significant idea and, consequently, we do not lose their psychological impact. Being essentially a product of the thinking eye, equilibrated by reason, tantra art affirms the Kantian dictum, if we apply it to the context of art, that 'form without content is meaningless, content without form is blind'. From this perspective, tantric imagery is not an arbitrary invention derived from the chaos of artistic manipulation because, in the last analysis, behind the symbols are the purest abstractions revealed and visualized during contemplation.

In a quest for unity, the tantric artist identifies with the universal forces and is driven to find a truer reality beyond appearances by which a synthesis can be achieved between the external world and the interior model: a macrocosmic vision which allows the artist to come into familiar contact with the space-time continuum. The world of art and the world of experience, though different in their very nature, are not separate entities. Art is not wholly divorced from experience; a thread of continuity binds one world with the other. The tantric artist is not alienated from nature, but is very much in unison with the order which constitutes it. His art is a projection of an intrinsic consciousness permeating the outer and the inner worlds. In this sense the artist is a link between art and life stretched to a point between life and cosmos.

The art of tantra expresses this unity amidst the diverse physical forces which constitute nature, and the many is thus harmonized into a whole. The appearance of unity is a reality to the artist and is reflected in the images he creates. To break the dimensional limits of a work of art in the quest for a psycho-physical unity with the essential forces of nature is a universal urge, not subject to the limitations of time. The contemporary artist Lucio Fontana comments: 'I do not want to make a painting. I want to open up space, create a new dimension for art, be one with the cosmos as it endlessly expands beyond the confine of the picture.'[12] The continuity which effects cohesion and unity illustrates that synthesis and gives art a universal significance. In the words of Aurobindo, it reveals:

*a fourth dimension of aesthetic sense,*
*where all is in ourselves, ourselves in all.*

Most tantric images tend to stress the analogies between the individual and the cosmos, and the life forces which govern them, and in a way mirror Aurobindo's statement. They are reflections of something taking place in real life and constantly reminding us through the visions of the yogis what our true nature is.

In this form of representation, tantric images have a meditative resilience expressed mostly in abstract signs and symbols. Vision and contemplation serve as a basis for the creation of free abstract structures surpassing schematic intention. A geometrical

*Yoni, the emblem of Śakti, the creative genetrix of the Universe. South India, early 19th century, coco-de-mer.*

configuration such as a triangle representing Prakṛiti or female energy, for example, is neither a reproduced image nor a confused blur of distortion but a primal root-form representing the governing principle of life in abstract imagery as a sign. In these types of representation which are abstract as opposed to imitative, universal as against individualistic, cognitive as opposed to emotional, the tantric artist's vision of reality is deeply conditioned by tradition and inheritance, subjugating his purely personal subjective expression to a generic one. Tantric art embraces and reflects the continuity of tradition: once a particular image was revealed and accepted, it continued to retain its significance through the centuries. Thus tantric forms have acquired a timeless quality and a common denominator. They function as signs which pre-exist and are conditioned by pre-established codes similar to mathematical formulae. They are, therefore, not subject to constant metamorphosis.

## *Symbolism and Imagery*

Tantric forms are represented in a purely allegorical manner where representation of one order of ideas is achieved by an image used as a symbol. The forms have acquired meanings through usage and cultural conditioning. Many tantric symbols appear to be absorbed subliminally and produced spontaneously and unconsciously in contemplative vision or creative psychic manifestations; conversely, they have a communicative aspect and elicit ideas with strong metaphysical undertones. Their real significance lies in their function as psychic associations in the conscious mind.

Symbols seldom appear directly, and their inner meaning ever eludes the eye; however enigmatic they may appear, they are only the means of knowing reality in images. Hence the wide-ranging symbology of tantric art necessitates some acquaintance with the tantric texts. Most of the symbols are very old and can be traced back to the Vedic period (*c.* 2000 BC). In the Ṛig Veda, the creative principle of life is conceived of as a 'golden embryo' or Hiraṇya-garbha, the womb of energy from which the universe develops. The same symbol is crystallized in the conception of the Śiva-liṅga, or Cosmic Egg, in the tantras. Ageless symbols live incarnate from one period to the other and continue to survive

*Sālagrāma, symbol of Lord Nārāyana or Vishṇu, in his aspect as Sridhara. Banaras, contemporary expression of traditional form. Stone.*

*Brahmāṇḍa, the 'Cosmic Egg', used in ritual as manifesting a realization of wholeness. The entire universe is symbolized in this egg-shaped form. From the Narmada river-bed, Western India. Stone.*

*Śiva-liṅga with yoni-pitha, beneath a banyan tree. The figure of the bull of Śiva, Nandi, stands between an early iconographic image of Śiva, on the left, and his symbol, liṅga with yoni, on the right. Bastar, Madhya Pradesh, c. 13th century. Stone. The brass figure of Nandi is a contemporary tribal artefact.*

through successive generations. In this respect the varied forms of tantra present a living art functioning within the confines of defined traditional limits.

Tantric imagery cannot be understood purely on the level of art criticism, analysing it on the basis of style, form, compositional elements, colour symbolism, and the like. Its concept overrides the percept, for tantra is predominantly a way of knowledge, a way of life with its exclusive concern for enlightenment. Its art, therefore, is intimately related to living rites. Art and ritual in tantra are umbilically dependent. As ritual enfolds the entire multiplicity of life, equally it also creates and multiplies art symbols to suit its specific context. Art and ritual merge into each other and combine their resources in exploring and expressing the meaning of existence, affording an experience to the neophyte which leads him to inner realization. Art, thus, holds out a new dimension to ritual and makes its generic symbols emotionally cogent to the individual.

Most tantric images, if not all, serve as intermediaries between the transcendent and the immanent to a greater or lesser degree, forming indissoluble cosmic links through which reality is made visible and eventually apprehended. Of necessity, they follow a specific semantic code, though there may be a variation in technique and medium. This can, perhaps, be demonstrated by a parallel. The Mevlevi Dervishes, by their whirling movements, induce ecstatic states to dispose the psyche to return to its centre. Here, dance ceases to be an exercise of the muscles or mere bodily movement and is instead an interpreting medium which brings the dancer to transforming self-realization. Similarly, in tantric art ritualized symbols are freed of their illusory existence and acquire a dynamic potency. They function as a psychic matrix which ultimately aids the initiate to illuminate himself. In this interaction, therefore, the relationship of art to ritual becomes clearer: these forms become vehicles of self-enlightenment. Having arisen from ritual they are absorbed back into ritual: ritual becomes the *sine qua non* of art. By combining with ritual, art assumes a social function, and it is precisely this aspect which supports the continuity of tradition. If ritual vanishes from the scene because of changes in the structural pattern of society, art forms will also atrophy and in the last analysis will become merely 'history'.

Art's intimate relationship to ritual is not limited to transcendentally ideal forms but extends to include real objects found in the natural environment of the Sādhaka (spiritual aspirant). In this

*River-bed where the egg-shaped Brahmāṇḍas, or elliptical stones known as Bānaliṅgas, are found. Their cosmic spheroid shape, marked with auspicious signs and with a natural polish, result from the action of strong water currents. Those gathered from the bed of the Narmada river in Western India are highly prized and are known as Narmadeśvara. They are the Śaivite counterparts of Vaishṇavite Sālagrāmas.*

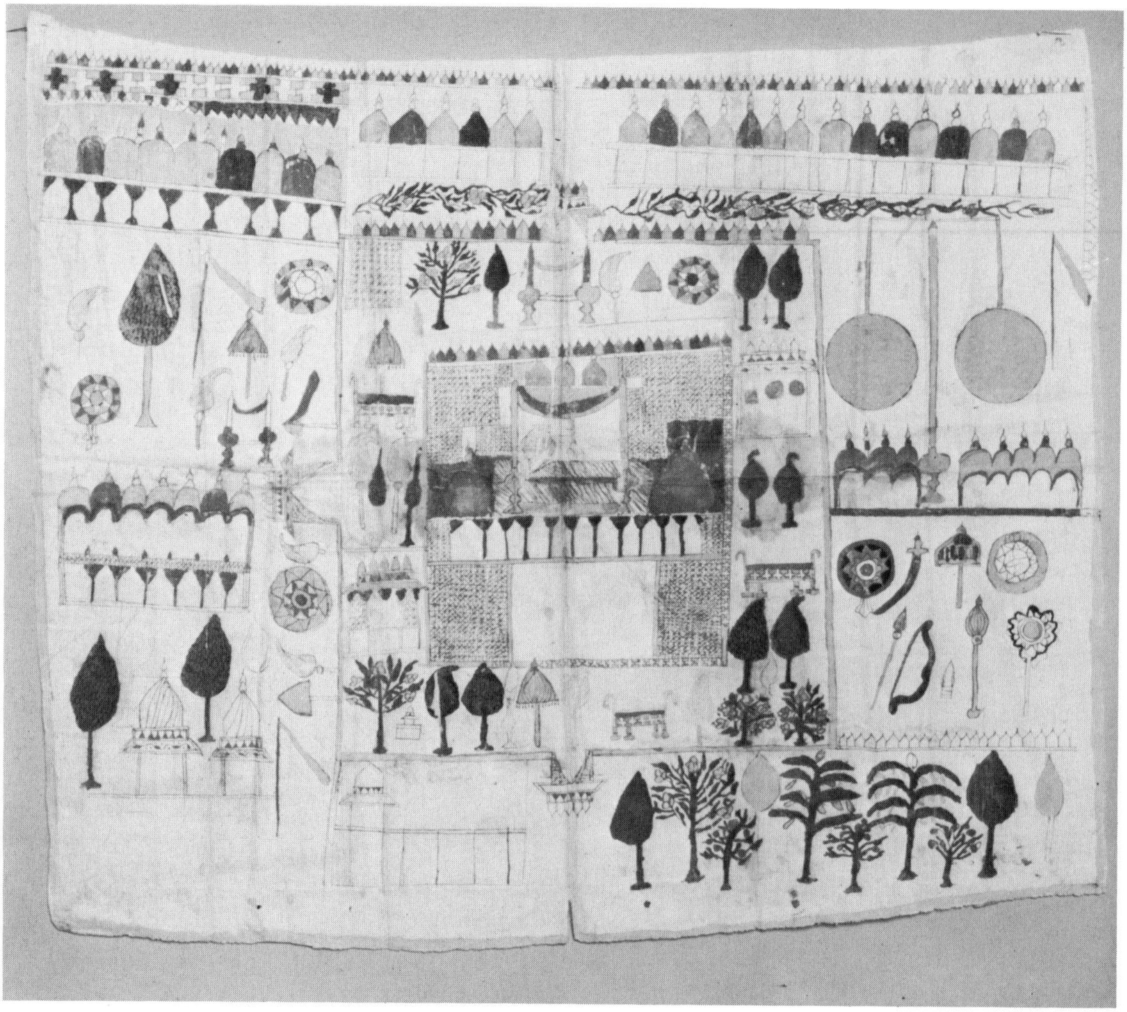

*Auspicious symbols. All the principal divinities are related by association to certain traditional insignia representing the Universal One. Rajasthan, c. 18th century. Ink and gouache on cloth.*

respect as well tantra art illustrates its synthesizing force by striking a balance between beauty and functionality. For a tantrika, art has a clear-cut purpose within its defined limits, and there is little scope for ambiguities, experimentation or individual mannerism.

To understand its pictorial range, tantric imagery can be broadly grouped into (1) psycho-cosmic forms and diagrams such as yantras and maṇḍalas: (2) visual representations of the subtle body or its constituents; (3) astronomical and astrological computations; (4) iconographic images, āsanas and certain accessories used in rituals. The purely formal qualities of tantra's diverse imagery can be distinguished into abstract and representational; as we find in the ovoid form as opposed to its

*The tree of life. The individual soul (the bird at the right), symbolic of worldly attachments, eats the fruits from the tree of life, while the universal soul (the bird on the left) looks on with detachment. Rajasthan, c. 18th century. Gouache on paper.*

figurative representation. The *Śukranitisāra,* a medieval Indian treatise, explains this distinction in terms of the qualities the art form represents and the corresponding emotive response it evokes. These qualities are sāttvika (serene and sublime images), rājasika (dynamism and kinaesthetics) and tāmasika (the terrifying aspects of Prakṛiti), true to the characteristic antinomianism of the tantras.

## *Yantras and Maṇḍalas*

In tantric abstraction, the yantras and maṇḍalas exemplify dynamic relationships concretized in the rhythmic order elaborated out of the multiplicity of primal forms. A yantra is conceived and designed, as Heinrich Zimmer points out:

*Yantra. Rajasthan, c. 17th century. Copper plate.*

As support for meditation and serves as (1) a representation of some personification or aspect of the divine, (2) a model for the worship of a divinity immediately within the heart, after the paraphernalia of outward devotion (idol, perfumes, offerings, audibly uttered formulae) have been discarded by the advanced initiate, (3) a kind of chart or schedule for the gradual evolution of a vision while identifying the Self with its slowly varying contents, that is to say, with the divinity in all its phases of transformation. In this case yantra contains dynamic elements.

We may say, then, that a yantra is an instrument designed to curb the psychic forces by concentrating them on a pattern, and in such a way that this pattern becomes reproduced by the worshipper's visualizing power. It is a machine to stimulate inner visualizations, meditations, and experiences. The given pattern may suggest a static vision of the divinity to be worshipped, the superhuman presence to be realized, or it may develop a series of visualizations growing and unfolding from each other as the links or steps of a process.'[13]

As the yantra is constructed step by step, the sign begins to convey a lived experience.

Yantra is a pure geometric configuration without any iconographic representation. Some yantras are constructed wholly before meditation and are images of the cosmos, while others are built up in stages during the entire process of meditation. The first sort provides an immediate model to the adept for identification, while in the second his concentration progresses gradually, along with the construction of the image, until it is completed.

Yantras are of various kinds, representing deities like Śiva, Vishṇu, Kṛishṇa, Gaṇeśa, and various manifestations of Śakti such as Kālī, Tārā, Bagalā, Chinnamastā; each has its corresponding yantras. In some yantras, the sound equivalents of the deities are symbolically represented by the Sanskrit seed syllables inscribed in the spaces within the pattern: 'Twofold is the aspect of Divinity, one, subtle, represented by the mantra, and the other, gross, represented by an image' (*Yāmala*). The mantric syllable symbolizes the essence of divinity. Other yantras do not represent deities but are emblems of an energy pattern of the cosmos and are worshipped for various purposes, mainly for the attainment of spiritual enlightenment. It must be emphasized, however, that, of whatever type they may be and for whatever purpose they are invoked, yantras are usually represented in pure geometrical abstraction. The predominant elementary forms of which yantras are constituted are the point, line, circle, triangle, square and the lotus symbol; all of these forms are juxtaposed, combined, intersected and repeated in various ways to produce the desired objective.

Thus it is clear that the tantrikas dispensed with conventional ideas of the dynamics of form, and concentrated instead on another aspect. They had recourse to the explanation of primordial forces and vibrations in order to understand the hidden logic behind phenomena, so that in tantric abstraction, form is seen in the context of its origin and genesis, in terms of the basic impulse which has shaped it. In this way, for example, tantra regards vibration as a primary cosmogenic element which gives rise to all structures and movement. If we could penetrate the reality behind appearances, ostensibly static structures could be seen as vibrational patterns, which are often illustrated in series of tantric paintings. As movement increases, form is condensed into a 'whole' which is represented as a mathematical point of zero dimension. When the movement decreases, currents and eddies are set in motion and form becomes more differentiated; the bindu begins to evolve into a primary geometrical shape till the multiple spaces interpenetrate, overlap, collide and generate energy to form the whole pattern. The diagrams of tantra art which reveal expansion and contraction of forces in the ongoing process of creation could aptly be termed forms where energy is represented as immobilized.

*The goddesses Dhūmavati (right) and Chinnamastā (left), with their appropriate yantras below. Dhūmavati, one of the important goddesses of the tantric mahāvidyās, is pale in complexion to symbolize the upper spheres. Chinnamastā, in her creative and destructive aspects, signifies apparent dissolution and return to the elements. The classical imagery of these two icons is transformed into a geometrical energy-pattern, or yantra. Though differing in appearance, the representational and abstract patterns bear a simultaneous likeness in meaning and content. From an illuminated manuscript page. Nepal, c. 1760. Gouache on paperboard.*

To the tantrika these abstract terms reveal a significant order of nature and resemble what to us, in the twentieth century, would seem like the energies of science. Cymatics, a field of research which studies the tangible effects of wave and vibrational processes in material and in nature, has revealed many richly diverse structures: vortices, hexagons, rectangles, overlapping patterns, some of which resemble the primary shapes at the basis of tantric imagery. The effects of cymatic phenomena are demonstrated, for example, in the fact that when lycopodium powder is excited by vibration, a number of circular piles which rotate on their own axes are formed. If the vibrations are intensified the piles migrate towards the centre.

Commenting on this process Dr Hans Jenny, exponent of cymatic research, states:

Whether the heaps unite to make larger ones or whether they break up into a number of smaller piles, they invariably form whole units. Each of them is participative in the whole in regard to both form and process.

This brings us to a particular feature of vibrational effects: they may be said to exemplify the principle of wholeness. They can be regarded as

*The Universe and the terrestrial sphere. The sixty-three layers, in the upper and nether worlds and the central earth zone, merge into boundless space. Rajasthan, c. 1800. Gouache on paper.*

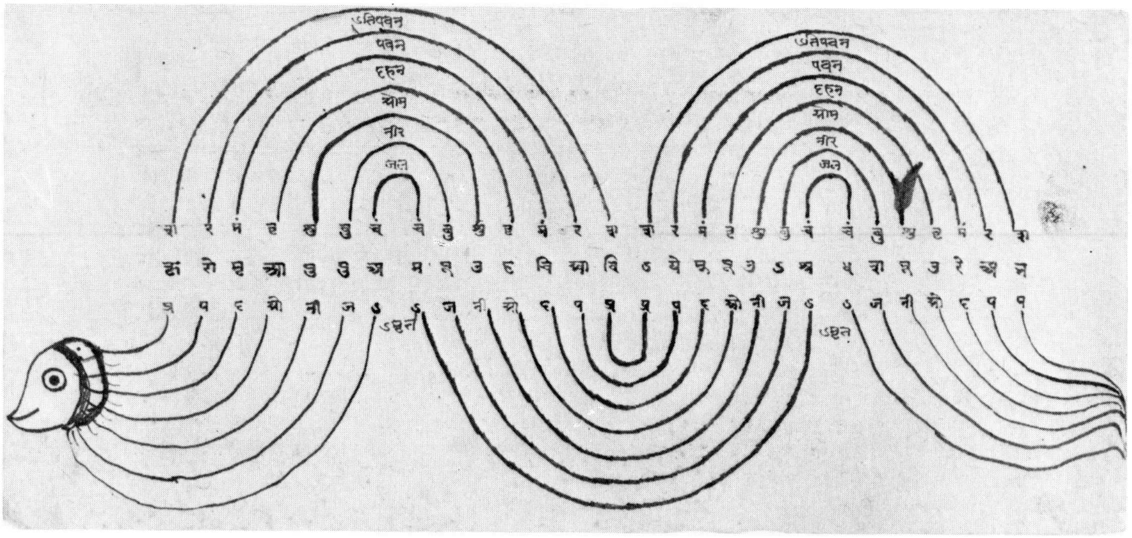

*Diagram illustrating the eternal recurrence of the sevenfold division of the Universe as a cosmic river of time and reality. A manuscript page from Rajasthan, c. 19th century. Ink on paper.*

models of the doctrine of holism: each single element is a whole and exhibits unitariness whatever the mutations and changes to which it is subjected. And always it is the underlying vibrational processes that sustain this unity in diversity. In every part, the whole is present or at least suggested.[14]

A yantra is very often referred to as an energy pattern or a power-diagram. As images of primal energy yantras reveal the varying scales of reality which denote cosmos, infinity, time, space or the play of polarities. Since we interpret infinity in finite terms we are forced to express the limitless in relative terms by creating mathematical patterns of virtual space. The yantras are not only based on mathematical form but also on a mathematical method. The artist must look beyond appearances and penetrate to structure and essence; he must reorganize reality in terms of distinctions and relationships of mathematical dimensions. Here Cézanne's proposition comes to mind: 'To relate nature to the cylinder, the sphere, the cone, all put into perspective so that each side of the object, of a plane, moves towards a central point.'[15] The minimal representation of pervading consciousness is the extensionless mathematical point of zero dimension, bindu, placed in the centre of the yantra. Bindu is the ultimate point of power beyond which a thing or energy cannot be contracted or condensed. By virtue of its nature, it is the repository of all manifestation in its complexity and variety and the basis of all vibration, movement and form: 'Transcending the tattvas [elements] is the Bindu' (*Yāmala*). As a centre, the point controls everything which is projected from it; such a centre is called mahābindu, or Great

Point, and signifies the starting-point in the unfolding of inner space, as well as the last point of its ultimate integration. A point also functions as a 'mental point' or 'mano-bindu', serving as the vehicle of the mind, an area which is the meeting-ground of subject and object.

Unbroken series of points which have length without breadth, moving independently, form a straight line. The straight line signifies growth and development and like time, consists of an infinite number of points, each discreetly in space. Pure linear patterns are drawn lyrically to illustrate sound vibrations, or geometrically in criss-cross manner, to form a certain order of the divisions of space, measures of time and the base lines of the universe. A striking line-form is the Mātrikā Yantra: on a plane of yellow ochre horizontal surface, a sweeping red line evokes tension and divides the picture field. The red line denotes Śakti as the epitome of energy.

The circle occurs very frequently in yantras and maṇḍalas and is derived principally from the motion of the revolution of planets. It symbolizes wholeness or totality and, in a yantra, is normally placed within a square pattern with four re-entrant gates. The square symbolizes the elemental earth or the material quality of nature. The four gates represent the earthly plane which one must transcend gradually to identify with the core of the pattern in which resides the essence.

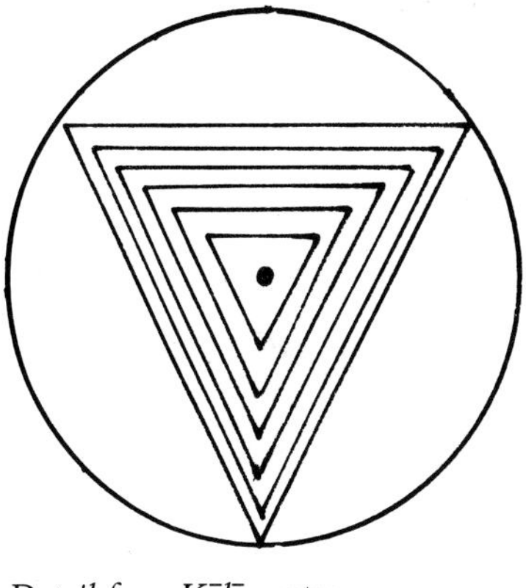
*Detail from Kālī yantra.*

The triangle, on the other hand, or trikona, represents the three worlds, the three guṇas: the neutral, the positive and the negative – Sattva, Rajas and Tamas. The triangle with its apex downwards represents the yoni or female organ, the seat of Śakti, the female energy or nature (Prakṛiti). The triangle pointing upwards is identified with the male principle (Purusha). When the two triangles penetrate each other in the form of a five-pointed star or a pentagon, each of its five points represent the five elements – earth (kshiti), water (ap), energy (tejas), air (marut), and space (vyoman). During contemplation, when the aspirant brings the five elements of his body into harmonious accord with the five constituents of which the energy pattern is constructed, he becomes 'the perfect man' and 'locks the pentagon within him'. The two interlocking triangles in the form of a hexagon, however, symbolize the revolving or kinetic tendency (of Rajas) from the point of view of genesis. Hence the union of two triangles symbolizes the union of Śiva-Śakti manifesting in the creation of the objective universe. When the two triangles are separated and form an hour-glass pattern or the shape of a damaru, the drum of

*Śri Yantra. Rajasthan, 18th century. Bronze.*

Bhairava (the destructive aspect of Śiva), they represent dissolution; time and space cease to exist.

Dynamic colour-form units are created by the spatial integration of these primal forms. A dot appearing in the centre, a line intersecting a plane surface, circles in a square or simply an eye full of etherized colour, create soaring trajectories of the spirit. Innate simplicity of composition is identified with spiritual presence. The projection of the symbol is often direct and bold, so that even a small miniature can create a sense of expansiveness. The dynamism of tantric imagery's abstraction is not 'gestural' but is generated by and strives for a geometric order. It is this quality which gives these psychic improvisations a transcendental quality.

According to Tantraraja Tantra, there are 960 yantras. Śri Yantra, the most celebrated one, projects a very important philosophical segment of tantric thought. It is difficult to determine the exact date of its conception and construction, though it must have been conceived very early and has been transmitted through centuries. Many tantric texts, such as the *Kāmakalāvilāsa,* have explained the nature, significance, construction and application of Śri Yantra, and description of its basic form can also be found in the *Saundaryalahari* traditionally ascribed to Śankara (8th century AD).

The Śri Yantra is a configuration of nine interlacing triangles centred around the bindu, drawn by the superimposition of five downward-pointing triangles, representing Śakti, and four upright triangles, representing Śiva. Because it is a composition of nine (nava) triangles (yoni) it is often called 'Navayoni Chakra'.

The Śri Yantra is a symbolic pattern of Śakti's own form (svarūpa), powers and emanations, the form of the universe (viśvarūpa), symbolizing the various stages of Śakti's descent in manifestation. It is a pictorial illustration of the cosmic field in creation. Like creation itself, the Śri Yantra came into being through the force of primordial desire. The impulse of desire (Kāmakalā), born of the inherent nature of Prakṛiti, creates a throb (spanda) which vibrates as sound (nāda). This manifestation is represented by a point, or bindu. In the first state of manifestation, the bindu is called Parā Bindu, which is the nucleus of the condensed energy, the seed of the ultimate Sound, and the dynamic and static aspects of the two (Śiva-Śakti) in one. It contains all the possibilities of becoming; it transforms into Aparā Bindu when creation begins: 'The essential point in the middle of

*Śri Yantra. Rajasthan, c. 18th century. Gouache on paper.*

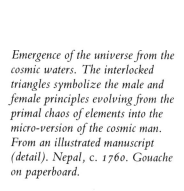

*Emergence of the universe from the cosmic waters. The interlocked triangles symbolize the male and female principles evolving from the primal chaos of elements into the micro-version of the cosmic man. From an illustrated manuscript (detail). Nepal, c. 1760. Gouache on paperboard.*

the Yantra is the Supreme Sakti, when it swells it evolves into the form of a triangle' (*Kāmakalāvilāsa*). The point assumes a radius, the polarization of Śiva-Śakti takes place, the dynamic and static energies interact and two more points emerge to form a triad of points – the primary triangle or the Mūla-trikona.

The three points are represented by Sanskrit syllables and the three basic vibrations emanate from one primal sound substratum. The triangle with its apex down represents the first form pattern of primordial desire in the process of creation. It indicates the sign of evolution and represents the zone or kinetic principle of creation. The static principle predominates in the Parā Bindu, so that it represents the male principle. All of creation is the outcome of these two principles, the point and triangle, and the bliss of their union. Hence 'the Śri Yantra is the one body of the Śiva couple' (*Yāmala*).

The primary triangle stands for three aspects of Śakti: Trividha-Bāla, the young one, Tripurā-Sundarī, the beautiful one, and Tripurā-Bhairavī, the terrifying one. It also represents the threefold process of creation (sṛisṭi), preservation (sthiti) and dissolution (saṁhāra).

The expansion of space and time, sound and energy, continue in the process of creation, and the primary triangle is transformed into a series of lines, triangles, circles and squares to form the Śri Yantra. The various patterns are the modifications of an original primal vibration, and at each stage contain the interplay of the static and kinetic energies in varying degree of concentration.

The Śri Yantra is called 'Nava Chakra' since it is composed of nine circuits, counting from the outer plane to the bindu. Through contemplation on the Śri Yantra, the adept can rediscover his primordial sources. The nine circuits symbolically indicate the successive phases in the process of becoming. They rank from the earthly plane and rise slowly step by step to the final point, the state of supreme joy. By entering into the élan vital of the yantra, the adept reintegrates with it. The nine circuits within Śri Yantra move from the gross and tangible to the sublime and subtle realms.

The outermost periphery consists of a square, with four gates, coloured white, red and yellow. This is the Bhūpura, the ground-plan, of the Śri Yantra.

Inside the square are three concentric circles, girdles (mekhalā). The space between the square and three girdles is the Trailokya-mohana, or the Enchantress of the Triple World, chakra; at this stage the adept is infatuated by aspirations and desires.

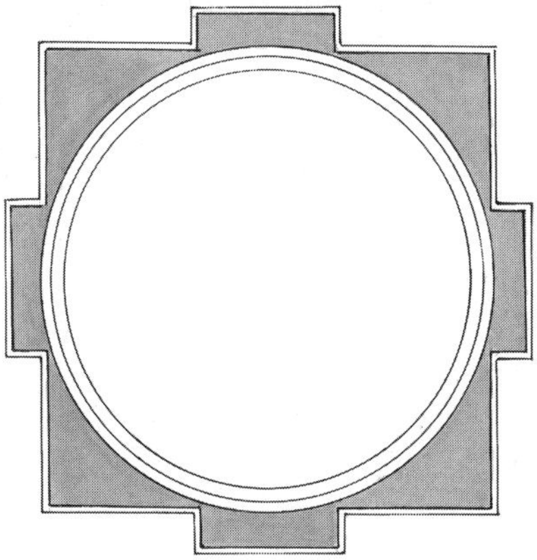

*Trailokya-mohana chakra.*

Next are two concentric rings of sixteen and eight lotus petals, respectively. They are called Sarvā-śāparipuraka chakra and Sarva-śaṅkshobhaṇa chakra, indicating fulfilment of desire.

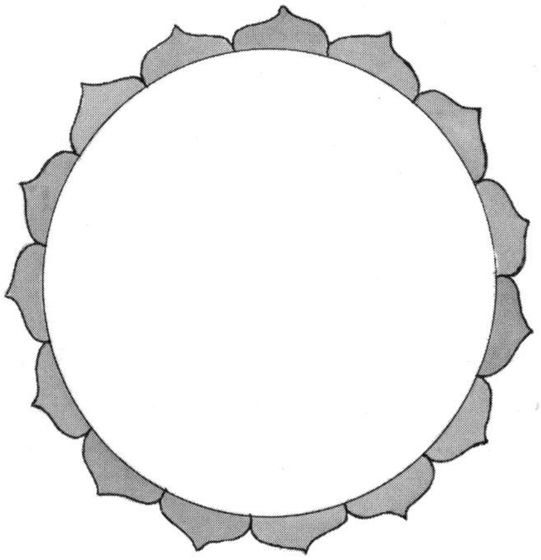

*Sarvāśāparipuraka chakra.*

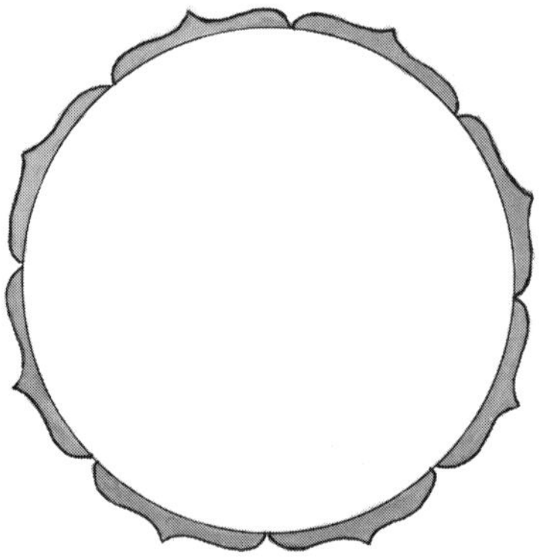

*Sarva-śaṅkshobhaṇa chakra.*

The fourth chakra, Sarva-saubhāgyadāyaka, or Giver of Auspiciousness, projects the realm of possibilities in spiritual ascent; it consists of the fourteen triangles forming the outer rim of the complex interlocking of triangles.

*Sarva-saubhāgyadāyaka chakra*

The next two chakras are each constructed of ten triangles. Called Sarvartha-sādhaka and Sarvarakshākāra, Accomplisher of All Purpose and Giver of Protection, they indicate a stage when inner realization begins to dawn.

*Sarvartha-sādhaka chakra*

*Sarvarakshākāra chakra*

The seventh chakra, consisting of eight triangles, is called Sarva-rogahara, Remover of All Desires and Ills, and represents the stage when the adept is free from earthly bonds and is at the threshold of the inner circle of realization.

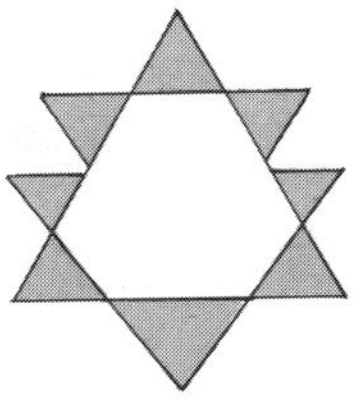

*Sarva-rogahara chakra*

An inverted triangle is the eighth chakra, Giver of All Accomplishments, of Sarva-siddhīprada; it denotes a stage before the consummation of realization. All the triangular chakras are coloured red, to represent radiant energy or the dynamic and fiery element of the cosmos.

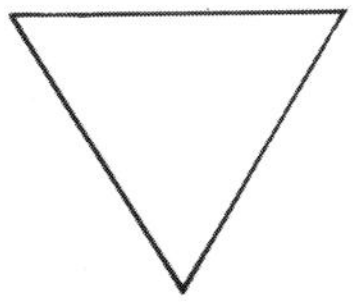

*Sarva-siddhīprada chakra*

The last chakra, the Bindu, is known as Sarva-ānandamaya, Full of Bliss. It is the *sanctum sanctorum,* abounding in joy, in which the adept participates in union. The point is light itself, beyond all colours, and is therefore represented as colourless.

*Bindu: Sarva-ānandamaya chakra.*

The nine circuits of the Śri Yantra are also associated with forty-three presiding deities, nine classes of yoginīs (female yogis), sound syllables or mantras, and gestures or mudrās, each having a distinct characteristic and explicit symbolic function. During the performance of rituals, identity is sought between these various aspects in order to create a cosmic link through a visual equivalent which projects the whole of existence. Most yantras, if not all, have a similar symbolic meaning, though some are specifically applied to a particular creative force portrayed in a particular deity or mantra. The Śri Yantra is distinguished from the rest since it projects 'All'. Its diverse symbolism may be understood conceptually by careful analysis, and its kine-visual aesthetic of symmetry and proportion may be experienced at once, but its subtle meaning and the power it manifests cannot be grasped instantly. Its understanding grows gradually, till one identifies and enters into its circumference to grasp the wholeness it enshrines. For this reason, perhaps, it has been accurately described as 'the vast dense mass of consciousness [leading to] bliss' (*Yogini Hṛidaya*). Bearing witness to the truth of André Malraux's 'every masterpiece is a purification of the world', the Śri Yantra, in its formal content, is a visual masterpiece of abstraction, and must have been created through revelation rather than by human ingenuity and craft.

Whereas a yantra is a linear form, a maṇḍala especially of the classical Tibetan tradition, is a composition of complex patterns and diverse iconographic images. Though there are countless variations and configurations of maṇḍalas, in most of them the formal structure, comprising few elemental forms, remains constant. The predominant shape is the circle, or concentric circles, enclosing a square, which is sometimes divided into four triangles; this basic composition is itself contained within a square of four gates. Painted in fine brush-strokes between the spaces in hot reds, evanescent emeralds, soft terracottas and pearly whites, are labyrinthine designs, serene and static images of deities in meditative postures or terrific deities spewing out aureoles of smoke and flame. Lacy intertwining floral patterns on the outer rim of the circle very often encircle celestial palaces, fortresses built round the four portals, many-armed deities curled about by celestial fires and swirls of clouds, all with symbolic meaning. The centre of the maṇḍala projects the cosmic zone; it may be represented by a ring of lotus as the seat of the Vajrasattva, embodiment of the supreme wisdom, immersed in union with his Śakti in a fathomless ocean of joy.

*Maṇḍala diagram. Nepal, c. 1700. Gouache on cloth.*

The maṇḍala indicates a focalization of wholeness and is analogous to the cosmos. As a synergic form it reflects the cosmogenic process, the cycles of elements, and harmoniously integrates within itself the opposites, the earthly and the ethereal, the kinetic and the static. The circle also functions as the nuclear motif of the self, a vehicle for centering awareness, disciplining concentration and arousing a state conducive to mystic exaltation. Each of the five component parts of the maṇḍala – the four sides and the centre – is psychologically significant; they correspond to the five structural elements of the human personality and the five Buddhas of the Diamond Vehicle: Vairochana, 'The Brilliant One'; Akshobhya, 'The Unshakable'; Ratnasambhava, 'The Matrix of the Jewel'; Amitābha, 'The Infinite Light'; and Amoghasiddhi, 'The Infallible Realization'. Through contemplation on the maṇḍala, the adept can tap higher levels of integration and realize cosmic communion, a micro-macro unity:

The five Buddhas do not remain remote divine forms in distant heavens, but descend into us. I am the cosmos and the Buddhas are in myself. In me is the cosmic light, a mysterious presence, even if it be obscured by error. But these five Buddhas are nevertheless in me, they are the five constituents of the human personality.[16]

Tucci further observes that 'Pure Consciousness assumes five faces of different colours from which derive the five directions which correspond to the five "families" of the Buddhist Schools. White Sadyojatā to the West, Yellow Vāmadeva to the North, Black Aghora to the South, Red Tatpuruśa to the East, all grouped around the central face which is that of the Green Īśāna.'[17] The five colours also correspond to the five cosmic elements: white water, yellow earth, red fire, green ether and blue space.

The maṇḍala is a psychic complex which conditions the return of the psyche to its potent core. Hence the initiation process is often referred to as a 'march towards the centre' so that the adept can interiorize the maṇḍala in its totality, counterbalance the opposing dimensions projected in its symbolism and finally be reabsorbed in the cosmic space represented symbolically in the inner circle. The process of interiorization is a matter of orderly progression, wherein each inner circuit marks a phase in spiritual ascent. The outer border denotes a 'barrier of fire or metaphysical knowledge which burns ignorance'. Next comes the ring of diamonds suggesting illumination or the quality of unchangeability, never lost once knowledge is attained. In maṇḍalas dedicated to terrifying aspects of divinities the iconographic motif of a cemetery is drawn within the girdle of diamonds and outside the

*A contemporary ground-plan of a temple based on a maṇḍala. Gouache on paper.*

inner circle. Symbolizing the 'eight aspects of disintegrated consciousness', these are what bind the adept to the common run of the world and they must be conquered during one's spiritual pilgrimage. The four portals which open up in the middle of each side of the maṇḍala are usually flanked by awe-inspiring divinities, obstructive forces in the unconscious which must be overcome before realization is sought.

The next stage is usually represented by a girdle of lotus petals, leaves or intertwining floral patterns, symbols of 'spiritual rebirth'. Finally, in the centre, or the 'vimāna', is the seat of the deity or the cosmic zone, the last stage of spiritual integration.

Like all tantric activity, the process of drawing the maṇḍala is an exercise in contemplation, an act of meditation accomplished by following definite aesthetic principles and strict visual formulae. To evoke the universe of the maṇḍala with its wide-ranging symbology accurately, the artist has to practise visual formulation, sometimes beginning from an early age. The image, like a mirror, reflects the inner self which ultimately leads to enlightenment and deliverance. In Tibet, the actualization of this awareness is known

The Kuṇḍalinī Śakti, symbol of coiled up psychic energy. Illuminated manuscript page. Rajasthan, c. 18th century. Gouache on paper.

as 'liberation through sight'. The act of seeing, which is analogous to contemplation, is in itself a liberating experience. In earlier times, mineral and vegetable pigments, such as crushed gemstones, rock, gold, silver, turquoise, lapis lazuli, etc. were used for paintings; contemporary artists use gouaches which give their work a brighter appearance but lose the subtle colours and tones of earlier works. During festivals and ceremonies in India, popular forms of maṇḍalas, drawn and coloured in a variety of decorative patterns, are often made on floors and walls. They are also traced in miniature, simple forms by women on their palms as auspicious signs and for protective purposes.

In the West, the maṇḍala as an archetype released from the primordial collective unconscious is much discussed in the works of C. G. Jung, who studied it as a basic therapeutic art form created by patients in their quest for self-realization. In this respect, the maṇḍala is a psychological representation of psychic totality and suggests a form of stability in the process of individuation, unifying opposite forces in the psychic matrix to form the totality of an integrated personality. Such individual maṇḍalas contain an unlimited variety of symbols and contents, whereas ritual maṇḍalas are restricted to defined styles and motifs. Another such similarity exists between maṇḍalas and the Navajo sand-paintings used for ritual healing. In the latter, the basic structure is quite similar: the circle indicates the centre of the cosmos, around which at various points are drawn symbols designating elements, the seasons and the four directions, the outer periphery and the inner motif being mutually inter-dependent.

By extension, the universality of the holistic concept of the maṇḍala can be observed in organic nature and human consciousness alike. From atom to star, each particle's structure represents a wholeness in potentiality which becomes manifest in space and time relative to its nature. It is possible that the inspiration to portray the cosmos in the art form of a maṇḍala came from this basic source.

## The Subtle Body and its Representation

In the symbology of tantric art, the structures of the various psychic centres in the subtle body are represented in lotus forms known as chakras, and the paths of the energy currents are mapped visually in the form of spirals. These are known from both miniature paintings and scrolls. Whereas the maṇḍalas and yantras are ritual motifs with a utilitarian value to the adept, these

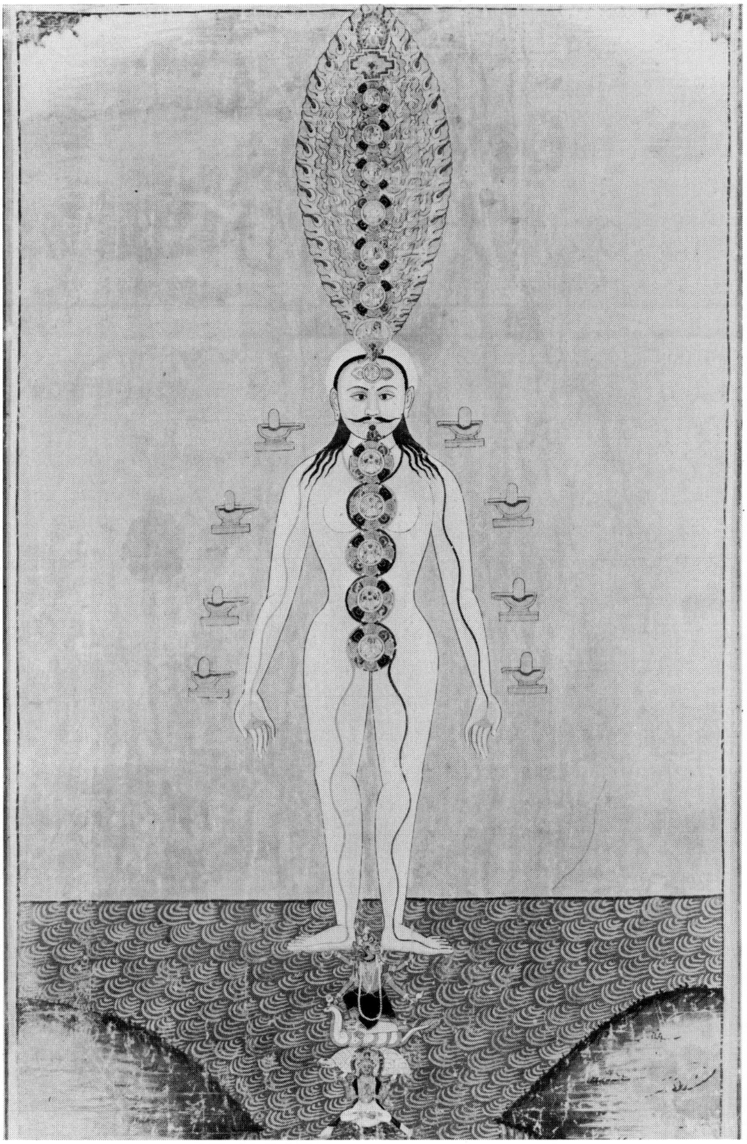

*Chakras, or psychic centres, in the etheric body of the yogi. The energy centres are points of contact between the psychic and the physical body. Of the thirty chakras mentioned in the texts, the principal seven, from bottom upwards, are: Mūlādhāra, Svādhisṭhāna, Maṇipūra, Anahata, Viśuddha, Ajñā and finally Sahasrāra, conceived as lying above the head. Rajasthan, c. 18th century. Gouache on paper.*

paintings are more like instructional charts which convey, in a visual language pregnant with symbols, the inner structure of the subtle body as conceived and visualized by the yogi artist.

The lotus is an archaic symbol:

> When the divine life substance is about to put forth the universe, the cosmic waters grow a thousand-petalled lotus of pure gold radiant as the sun. This is the door or gate, the opening or mouth, of the womb of the universe. It is the first product of the creative principle, gold in token of its incorruptible nature.[18]

Potent as it is, in tantric art the lotus is a symbol of the unfolding of the self and expanding consciousness, which cuts through psychic opacity and ultimately raises the aspirant from the dark depths of ignorance to the radiant heights of inner awakening. Just as lotus plants grow in the 'darkness of mud' and gradually blossom out to the surface of the water, unsullied by the mud and water which nourished them, so the inner self transcends and transforms itself beyond its corporeal limits uncorrupted and untarnished by illusion and ignorance.

Whereas in yantra patterns a ring of lotus petals generally denotes a stage in the actualization of the spiritual process and hence reflects a wave of optimism, in the symbolism of the chakras, or psychic centres of the human body, lotuses denote experience of the upward movement of energy in successive stages, each petal signifying the blossoming of a quality or mental attribute until finally one reaches the acme of spiritual perception symbolized as the thousand-petalled lotus placed above the head, the Sahasrāra Chakra. Thus the lotus form in the subtle body qualitatively indicates a kinesthetic dimension. Its kinevisual nature is further strengthened by the fact that the lotus forms in each chakra are mostly represented with the symbol of the spiral, signifying the flow of energy. Both therefore, are kinetic symbols. Each chakra has its equivalent petals and corresponding colours: Mūlādhāra, red lotus of four petals; Svādhisṭhāna, vermilion with six petals; Viśuddha, sixteen petals of smoky purple; Ājñā, two white petals resembling the shape of the third eye; and finally, the thousand-petalled lotus of the light of a thousand suns.

The lotus also represents the ubiquitous subtle element, space; the infinity of space and consciousness are identical. The Chandogya Upanishad says: 'Verily what is called Brahman [Pure Consciousness] that is what the space outside the person is . . . that is what the space within the person is. . . .' When the adept becomes conscious of the immensity of space outside himself, he simultaneously experiences this through the vast space in his heart, symbolized by the lotuses.

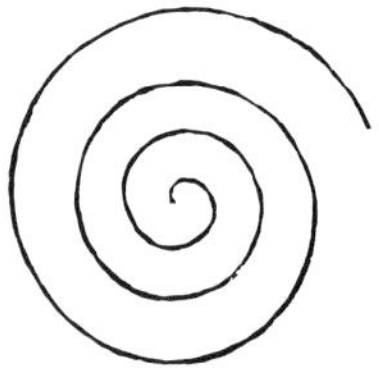

*The creative spiral, Kuṇḍalinī.*

The spiral represents growth or spiritual ascent in the act of becoming. The creative coilings of the feminine energy, or Kuṇḍalinī Śakti, and the flow of the energy current symbolically assumes the supple, undulating form of a spiral. The unmanifested Kuṇḍalinī is symbolized by a serpent coiled into three and a half circles with its tail in its mouth and spiraled around the central axis, or Svayaṁbhu-liṅga, ready to ascend upwards and unite with the cosmic consciousness. The sinuous movements of the energy currents around the Sushumṇā, the central subtle nerve, and their contraction and expansion when the Kuṇḍalinī awakes, are depicted in spiral form. The spiral symbolically projected in the inward odyssey is a microcosmic reflection of cosmic rhythms.

At a cursory glance, most symbolic forms in tantra seem hypothetically based images, but it would not be surprising if these spontaneous and authentic signs afford clues to the nature of the universe. Jung cites the striking example of the 19th-century chemist Kekule who owed his scientific discoveries to the sudden pictorial revelation of an age-old symbol of a snake with its tail in its mouth (symbol of the sleeping Kuṇḍalinī energy) and interpreted it to mean that the structure of benzene was a closed carbon ring, which it is.

The stone forms of the ovoid Brahmāṇḍas, or Śiva-liṅgas, and spheroid Sālagrāmas symbolize the totality in which the male and female principles are eternally united. In the vast expansiveness captured in a single curve in an oval or a circle, matter is made to yield its intrinsic nature so that the inert becomes alive. There is no flamboyance or associative corruption. Its broad universality of impersonal form and content, and close relation to nature, guarantee to it mass recognition and general acceptance.

Tantric imagery reaches its highest level of abstraction in the expression of Pure Consciousness pervading the nuomenal universe. These paintings depict the absolute by a total absence of form, whose spiritual presence is indicated by a saturated coloured field which induces a resonance of the infinite. The 'a-logical immensity' of colour is Śakti's power-field in its pure existence when the cosmic process has reverted to entropy. All forms, shapes, structures have dissolved; only the primordial essence of the exhilarating presence of energy as a reference of the absolute remains. Such paintings also embody the highest ideal of meditative soliloquy and therefore signify the last stage of spiritual realization, often accompanied by an intense perception of the experience of light.

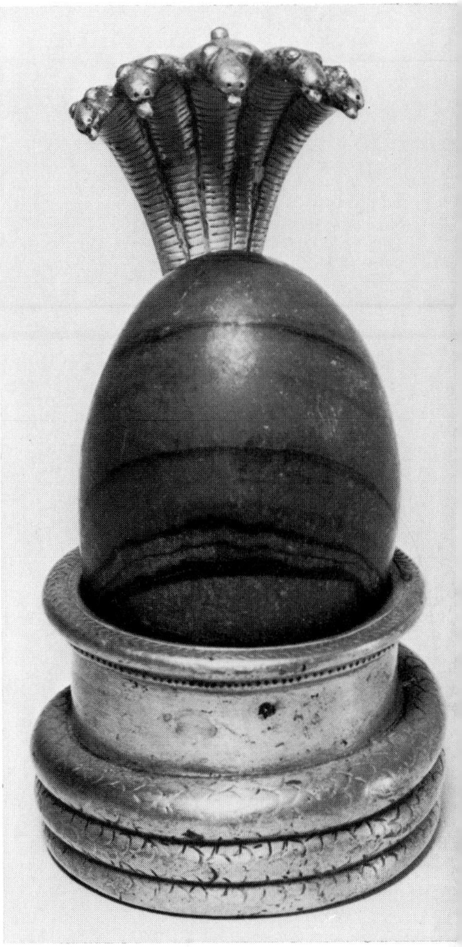

*Five-hooded serpent-power enclosing Brahmāṇḍa. South India, c. 19th century. Brass and stone.*

## *Cosmograms*

Scattered through the annals of tantra are descriptions of the origin of the universe; its various characteristic features have been illustrated on a scale from miniatures to murals. Especially interesting are cosmological and astrological charts, astronomical computations and observations of natural phenomena. These representations are philosophical constructs of a world image and

*A cosmographical schema showing Jambu-dvīpa, the island continent, in the centre with its energy fields and atmospheric zones. Rajasthan, c. 18th century. Gouache on cloth.*

provide a background to sādhanā, concretizing solar and planetary visions: a shimmering gold sun emanating primal flames, stellar orbs or a waning moon, a small central globe placed in concentric atmospheric zones and energy fields. In another series these images culminate in the magnificent conception of the cosmic man, of Purushakāra Yantra, whose body is filled with a checkered pattern resembling some of Paul Klee's abstract paintings. Yet more enigmatic than these, and throbbing with pictorial symbols, are the diagrams of Jambu-dvīpa, the innermost of the island continents in the system of cosmology.

Tantric cosmograms are based on intuitive insight rather than posterior knowledge, and some of them may not have accurate analogies in the phenomenal world. They are in the nature of a celestial mirror which reflects the imaged universe. In these figurations, the artist's main concern is to give form and structure to cosmogonical ideas. The cosmos is order incarnate, and nature's diverse manifestations are held together by a mathematical framework. Like the world in general, these abstract configurations are also based on mathematical relationships. But the cosmos of giant stellar galaxies and planetary systems is not always depicted as a cold intellectualized mass; some paintings include cryptic symbols derived from mythology. Whatever their visionary appeal, the treatment of form is devoid of grandiloquence or emotional fervour. Thus, for instance, according to cosmographic and cosmogonical notions, the universe has three zones, or lokas: in ascending order, the subterranean region, the earth and the heavenly bodies. Dominating the centre of the universe is the mythical Mount Meru around which is the earth, or Jambu-dvīpa, the island continent with seven concentric circles symbolically representing cosmic fields, spheres, atmospheric zones. Bordering the outermost circle is the cosmic sphere separating the visible world from the non-visible, and finally, beyond it, the region of non-universe space, or aloka. The diagram of this idea is a circular disc within seven concentric circles or vertical currents, all of which have an ascetic simplicity indispensable for transmitting the message. For tantra, Philip Rawson observes that 'one should gather the outer world into a single contemplative act. The Mount Meru at the axis should be identified with the centre of the inner body through which runs as axis a subtle spinal tube called "Merudaṇḍa" or "Sushumṇā". The implication of the diagram is thus that the Possible Universe each man knows is a flat "circle" radiating from his own axial centre.' [19]

Many cosmograms have come from Jaina sources, and an interesting concept appears in the diagram of Cosmic Purusha (*Purushakāra Yantra*) depicting the immense potentiality, no less than the size of the cosmos, contained within the body of man. From another point of view, it also depicts the man who has become the universe or is, metaphorically, the perfected one. The cosmic man in his monumentality stands erect. The image contains the entire replica of the universe: the categories and substances, space, time, motion, rest, matter, its cosmographical schemes and the spheres of the dense and subtle realms of the world. The whole cosmos is epitomized in the grand micro-macro vision. In the Jaina

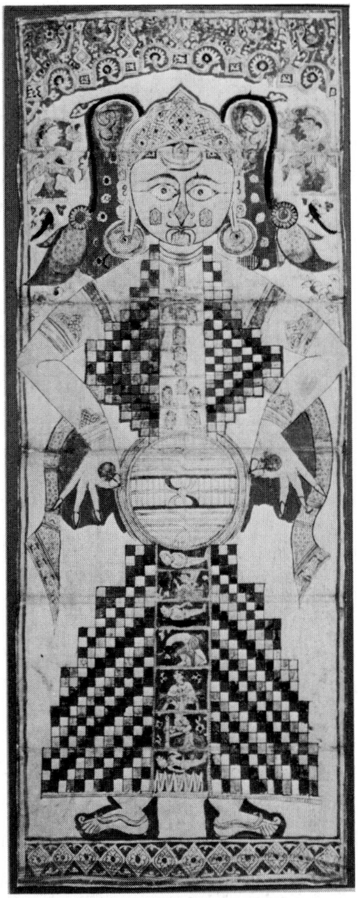

*Purushakāra, the Cosmic Man Yantra. The ascending planes of experience are called lokas, and the descending planes are known as talas. The centre of these planes is the 'earth-plane' (bhūrloka), shown here as a circle. A manuscript page from Gujarat, c. 16th century. Gouache on paper.*

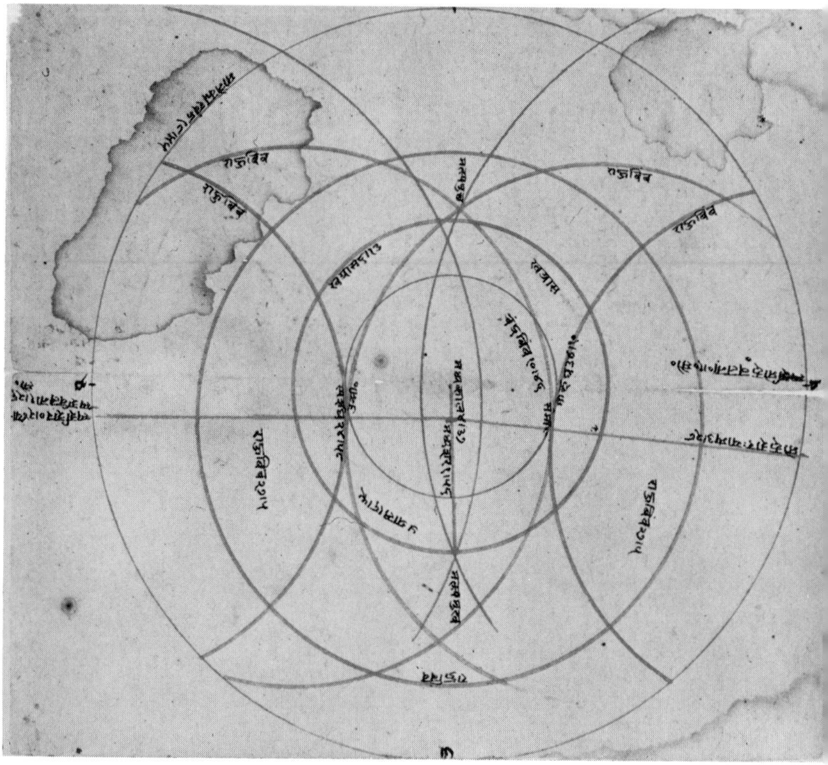

*Cosmogram: an astronomical computation. Rajasthan, c. 19th century. Ink on paper.*

texts the shape of the universe is depicted analogously as a human being standing with feet apart and the arms akimbo. The upper region consists of 16 heavens of 63 layers. The middle world, which coincides with the earthly plane, contains innumerable concentric rings of continents and oceans around the Jambu-dvīpa. The lower realm, in the shape of a half-drum, consists of 7 earths and 49 layers of the subterranean regions. Various elements combined according to a hierarchy of order assume architectonic structure when form and colour introduce rhythms into the composition. Thus the homogeneity of the cosmos is expressed in the combination of red and ochre squares which chart the body of the cosmic man. By means of their monumental size these scrolls have a majestic power: the onlooker is drawn into their living space to apprehend the hidden totality. In them, the function of form is purely analytical and it demonstrates that what is taking place within one's own body – persistently implying that man alone is the measure of all things. We must sink into our own wombs to find ourselves.

Astronomy, the science of celestial bodies, had a decisive influence on tantra. Celestial tides and the movement of planets determine the time for various rites. As an inevitable consequence,

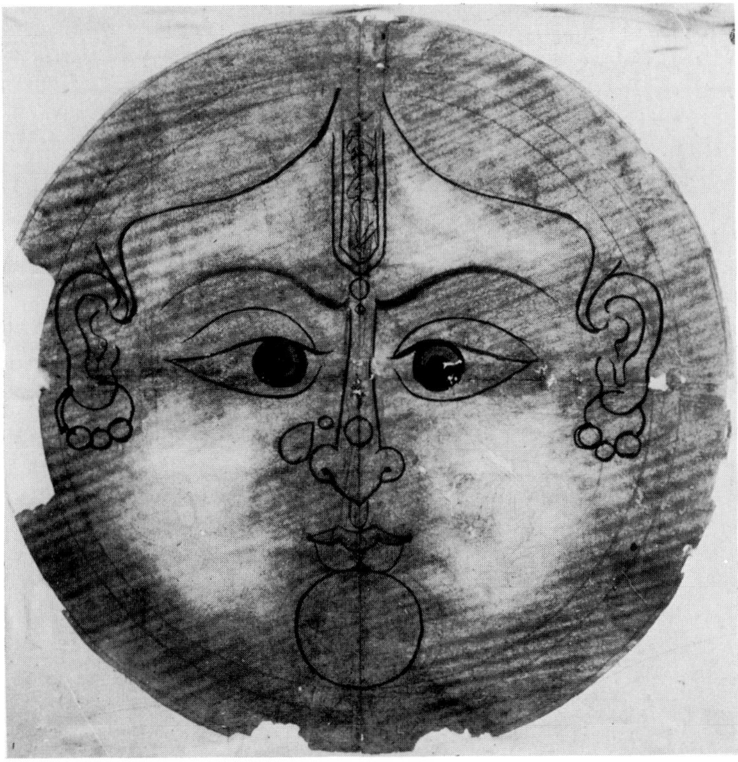

*Sūrya or Sun-maṇḍala. Rajasthan, c. 19th century. Ink on paper.*

planetary signs found their way into cosmograms, giving tantric diagrams a great diversity of geometric patterns. As astronomical charting crystallized, there was a total denunciation of pictorial imagery and a shift of emphasis to the delineation of the elements of natural phenomena. Space, time, light and motion were conceived of against the background of atmospheric phenomena. Astrological computations, like most tantric diagrams, are also marked by mathematical proportions: grid patterns of flat colours have a mosaic-like simultaneity; kinetic curves encircling solar and lunar orbs create powerful gestalt sensations. Planetary signs abound: the sun as a red solar disc; the moon as an opalescent crescent; Mars represented as a vermilion triangle; Mercury as a sap-green droplet; a yellow straight line represents Jupiter; a blue five-pointed star denotes Venus; and Saturn is represented as purple, the densest of all colours. Innumerable other biomorphic shapes and voidal spheres resulted as a fusion of primary shapes in an attempt to record astronomical concepts. Among the observatories, the Jantar Mantar of Jaipur and Dakshina Vṛitti Yantra, engraved in lime plaster on a wall in the Ujjain observatory, built in the early 18th century, not only achieve a functional beauty, but are remarkable examples of abstract forms.

*Cosmographical scheme showing Jambu-dvīpa, the island continent, at the centre. Rajasthan, c. 18th century. Gouache on cloth.*

Cosmograms, in contrast to psychograms, are characteristically outward-directed. They are more like charts mapping natural phenomena, arising from the basic impulse to codify external reality. Just as in contemporary art space, time, light and motion have been directly influenced by modern scientific discoveries such as Einstein's theory of relativity or Minkovsky's non-Euclidean ideas, and other discoveries in nuclear physics, so in the same way tantric cosmograms are primarily interpretations of a reality complex based on scientific norms. On the other hand, a psychogram is inward-directed: through it the adept seeks to find a unification of the self through a symbolic visual mode (yantra, maṇḍala, etc.) until he is completely absorbed in the art symbol. The psychogram is 'in here', within; the cosmogram, as a pictorial model, is 'out there', external to the adept. The Purushakāra Yantra, however, and the diagrams of Jambu-dvīpa are intimately linked with the process of inner realization and are therefore allied to the psychograms.

## *Polarity*

In contrast with the tranquil renderings of abstract forms, the iconographic images portraying the terrifying aspects of Prakṛiti are violent emotional expressions. Tantra's basic philosophy is based on a dualism, and the terrifying image projects the negative aspect of the creative life-force. In the creative aspect, Śakti appears as an enchantress – 'the fairest of the three worlds', exercising her benign powers. In her negative aspect she is demystified and transformed. The image has a naked intensity, so fierce that the incommunicable ceases to be a mystery. Kālī, one of the most important tantric Daśamahāvidyās, in her negative aspect appears as a conglomeration of terrifying elements. Though the picture field is filled with awe-inspiring symbols, their real meaning is not what it first appears; they have equivocal significance. Kālī is the symbol of the active cosmic power of eternal time (Kāla) and in this aspect she signifies annihilation: through death or destruction creation, the seed of life, emerges. Just as the destruction of the seed leads to the birth of the tree, so disintegration is a normal and necessary step of nature moving towards further progress or unfolding. Kālī is the embodiment of creation, preservation and annihilation. She inspires awe and love at the same time. As a disintegrating tendency, Kālī is represented in black: 'just as all colours disappear in black, so all names and forms disappear into her' (*Mahānirvāṇa Tantra*). The density of blackness is also identified with the massive, compact, unmixed, Pure Consciousness. In tantric hymns to the goddess Kālī, she is described as 'digambari', garbed in space – in her nakedness, she is free from all covering of illusion. She is full-breasted, her motherhood a ceaseless creation denoting preservation. Her dishevelled hair, 'elokeshī', forms a curtain of death which surrounds life with mystery. Her garland of fifty human heads, each representing one of the fifty letters of the Sanskrit alphabet, symbolizes the repository of power and knowledge; the letters are nuclear sound-elements symbolizing the power of mantras. She wears the 'girdle of human hands': hands are the principal instruments of work and

so they signify the action of karma or accumulated deeds to be enjoyed in subsequent births, constantly reminding one that ultimate freedom is conditioned by the fruits of one's actions. Her three eyes govern the three forces of creation, preservation and destruction. Her white teeth, symbolic of Sattva, the translucent intelligence stuff, suppress her lolling tongue which is red, indicative of Rajas, a determinate level of existence leading downwards to Tamas, inertia. Kālī has four hands: one left hand holds a severed head, indicating destruction, and the other carries the sword of physical extermination, with which she cuts the thread of bondage. Her two right hands dispel fear and exhort to spiritual strength. She is the changeless, unlimited primordial power (ādyāśakti) acting in the great drama awakening the unmanifested Śiva, a passive onlooker. Their inseparable union reflects non-duality.

This conception of Kālī compares with the magnificent depiction of Śiva as Natarāja, resolving and harmonizing the opposite attributes of creation and dissolution, the very essence of every existence.

These images of destruction incarnate appear to be composed in a surreal reverie. While they blend naturalism and intuition in a

*Kālī. Madhubani folk painting. Bihar, contemporary. Gouache on paper.*

*Sarvabuddha Dākinī. Nepal, 18th century. Bronze.*

*Śiva as Natarāja, Lord of the Dance. Śiva, engaged in the dance of the universe, tramples on the dwarf of illusion, while holding the drum of creation in his upper right hand and the fire of destruction in the corresponding left. His lower right hand is stretched out in a gesture of protection (abhaya), while the gesture of the lower left symbolizes salvation. The outer ring of fire (missing) symbolizes the universe. Tiruvelangadu, Tamil Nadu, 11th century. Bronze.*

*Kālī, represented in her destructive aspect as Chamunda, detail from an album painting. Kangra, c. 18th century. Gouache on paper.*

single impulse, their wrathful appearance can agitate the eye and transport the spectator to a supernatural world. From an aesthetic point of view they suggest a flight from reality and an awareness of a profoundly different world: the poignant, restless and aggressive. These images unveil reality so that it is stripped bare, and have the same mind-altering capability to induce extraordinary experience which arouses intense inward states of rich spiritual content. Their most characteristic feature is that they are images which seem to have sprung from a non-rational source but nevertheless have a rational basis within defined limits. For example, Chinnamastā, the beheaded goddess, holds her severed head; apart from its symbolic meaning, the dismemberment of her body ought not to be confused with actual distortion: the image is not dissociated from its meaning, which underlies and generates the image; where dislocation appears it is to heighten visual impact.

The terrifying aspects of these images are completely dispelled in the tantric āsana forms in both sculpture and painting. In the reliefs of the temples of Konarak and Khajuraho, the sensuous quality is developed to its logical culmination so that it has almost completely shattered aesthetic barriers and forced the ultimate realization that life is art. What is justified and fundamental in life must also be justified and fundamental in art. It is no longer a question of that 'provocative indulgence' of the female figure from which Roger Fry recoils with a puritanical shudder. Here we are confronted with an ecstasy of joy in all its plastic possibilities. These united male and female figures are drawn together in creative force towards the awakening of the inner spirit, new dynamic āsana-forms. Filled with ecstatic conviction, they are no longer torn between the contradiction of life and social existence.

In considering the mithuna sculptures, particularly on the Lakṣhmaṇa Temple at Khajuraho, it is a great mistake to confuse the meaning of the figures carved in the horizontal band running round the base of the temple with those depicted on the upper portion. For instance, the mithuna figures carved at the base of the temple depict the whole gamut of mundane life including various sexual acts; but as one steps upward one is confronted with the interlocking figures representing the antinomic principles; they are symbols of transcendent union, which do not in any way convey the gross sexual intercourse depicted in the lower portion of the temple, which illustrates an earth-bound level of existence.

*Kandariya Mahadeva Temple (detail), Khajuraho. The carvings on the exterior of this temple to Śiva are crowded with hundreds of figures; the interior, on the other hand, is plain and dark – the darkness of the womb (Garbhagriha).* AD *950–1050.*

*Figures on the Sūrya temple in the yoni-āsana (sexo-yogic pose). Konarak, Orissa,* AD *1238–64.*

I *Cosmogenesis. Detail of a scroll painting depicting the evolution of the universe from dense matter, symbolized here by elephants gradually ascending into the ethereal spheres of the cosmos. Kangra, Himachal Pradesh,* c. *18th century. Gouache on paper.*

II *Vishṇu-Pad, the imprint of Lord Vishṇu's feet (upper and lower, left) and Hastakāra Yantra (upper and lower, right) with signs and symbols. Rajasthan,* c. *18th century. Gouache on paper.*

Furthermore, the figures carved on both sides of the upper portion of the temple may be symbolically taken from the tantric point of view as the path of the two psychic nerve channels, Iḍā and Piṅgalā, on either side of the Sushumṇā, the central channel, leading to the inner chamber of the temple. In true tantric tradition, these figures depict the ascendence of sexual energy when it leaves its customary seat in the ordinary plane and moves to a higher level, changing into sublimated energy which awakens the latent Kuṇḍalinī. So eloquent are these interlocking figures that their sinuous curves far surpass mere sensual enjoyment. They clearly suggest tantric yoga āsanas for attaining realization through union with a female partner, Śakti, and that is why, perhaps, the poses are so unconventional and intricate.

The mithuna sculptures of Konarak are equally magnificent, their sculptural values in formal aspect, the fullness of their forms, the highly rhythmic quality, their feeling and three-dimensional quality which perhaps for the first time were shown with complete mastery of the material apart from the ritual values. Thus, both the beatific and the terrifying imagery of tantra art have given to Indian art some of the most dynamic and sublime representations.

The Indian aesthetic theory of 'rasa' developed by Abhinavagupta in the tenth century AD provides a useful key to the understanding of various moods and emotions invoked by tantric imagery. 'Rasa', for which there is no precise English equivalent, means 'flavour', 'taste', 'mood', or 'emotion'. All works of art, however limited, have the ability to evoke certain emotional states. The theory of rasa stresses the importance of this experiential value of a work of art by stressing the very experience itself. When a particular emotion is aroused, a corresponding rasa is experienced. All classical images in Indian art, including those of tantra, can be broadly grouped under one of the nine principal abstract rasa. Terrifying images arouse tāmasik, the quality allied to the emotion of fury and awesomeness; diametrically opposed to these are silence and compassion, associated with sattva, the quality of purity. The ovoid and spheroid Brahmāṇḍas, considered as fragments of spiritualized matter commanding imperishable calm, fall into this class. The rasa of love, valour, laughter and wonder stem from rājasika tendencies. The āsana series, primarily oriented to showing the tendency of the dynamic opposites to union, can be grouped under rājasika. These divisions, though not absolute, emphasize how the wide-ranging aesthetic expressions of tantra are perceivable by our senses since they have the quality to strike our inner moods.

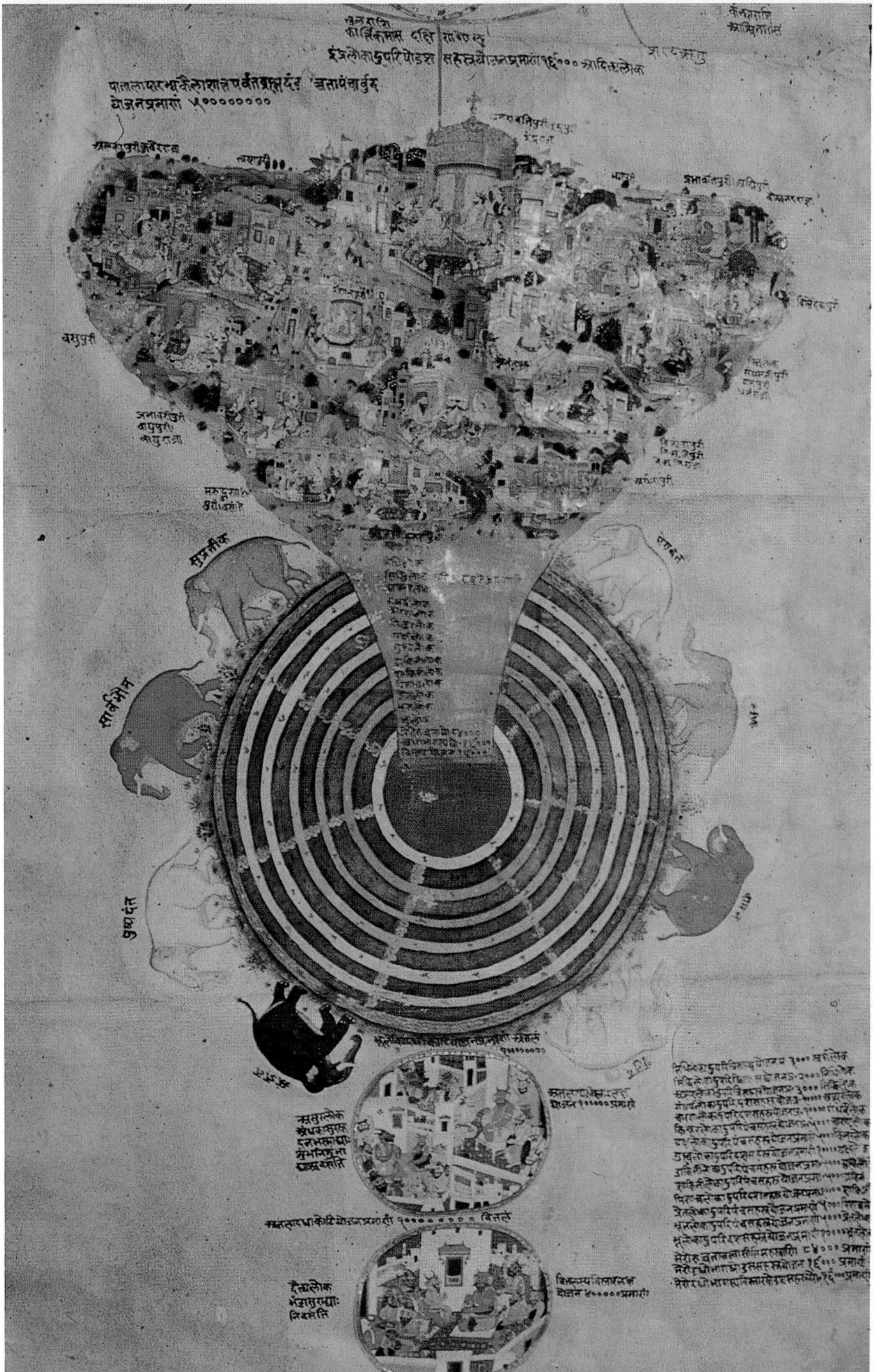

I

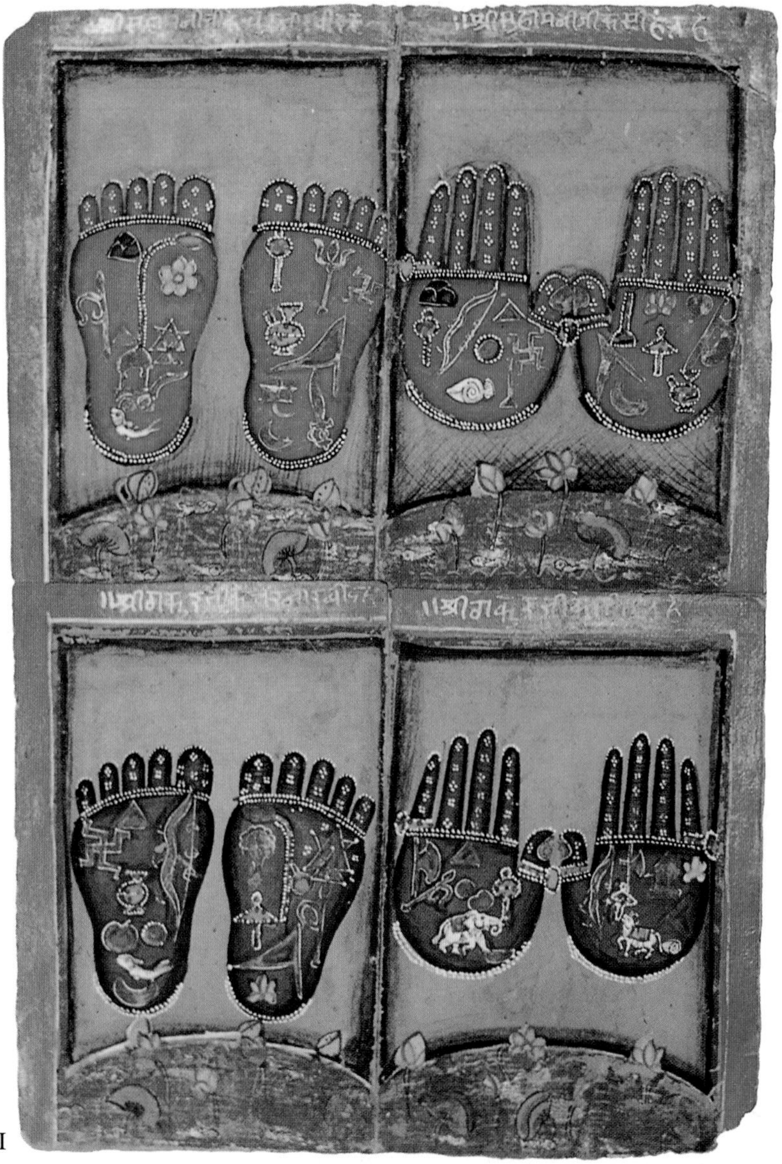

II

IV

*The ceiling of Adi Nath Temple, Ranakpur, is decorated with crystalline patterns symbolizing the unfolding of śabda, the sound element, in a maṇḍala field. Western India, c. 13th century.*

III *Kālī, annihilation aspect of Śakti, standing on Ratī and Kāma, who personify the primordial desire which gives rise to all creation. The garland of human heads symbolizes wisdom and power. Her blood-red tongue signifies the power of Raja-guṇa, the kinetic force which gives impetus to all activities. The sacrificial sword and the severed head are the symbols of dissolution and annihilation directing the Sādhaka to shed his 'ego sense'. The girdle of severed hands signifies one's Karma, action. Kangra, Himachal Pradesh, c. 18th century. Gouache on paper.*

IV *Chinnamastā, representing Devī in her destructive and creative aspects. She is flanked by her two yoginis, Dākinī and Vārninī. Under her Ratī and Kāma, the female and male principles, depict the transcendence of the phenomenal world and the abolition of the experience of duality. Rajasthan, c. 18th century. Gouache on paper.*

Modern research into the compositional pattern of sculpture of the cave temples in western and southern India (6th–9th centuries AD) by Alice Boner indicates that they were based on geometrical principles similar to those on which the yantras are composed. The structural composition of these figures is based upon a central point towards which all parts converge; the principle of centrality as a basis of structural composition is analogous to the tantric concept of Bindu. The nerve-lines intersecting the centre and developing in concentric organization can be seen as yantras whose lines are developed and enlarged into figural compositions. Alice Boner comments:

The analysis of the sculptural panels in the ancient Cave-temples has revealed geometrical diagrams of analogous concentric construction. They have, however, their specific features, different from those of devotional yantras, which make them suitable for figural compositions. The difference consists in this that the circular area, instead of being filled by intersecting geometrical figures, is divided into regular sectors by an even number of diameters and further subdivided by chords running parallel to the diameters connecting their points of intersection with the circle. All forms within the ambit of the circle are placed in correspondence with some of the diameters or with their parallels, and thus they participate, either directly or indirectly, in the concentric lay-out of the diagram. In this way all parts of a composition are connected with the central point.[20]

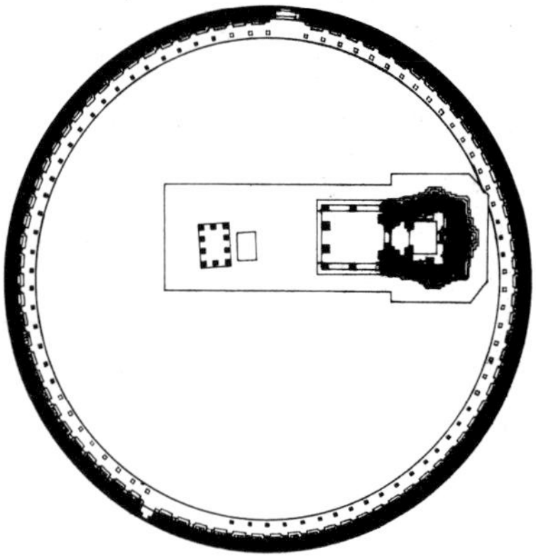

*Ground-plan of the temple of Sixty-Four Yoginis (Chauśatti Yoginī), Bheraghat, Madhya Pradesh, c. 12th century.*

Yantras and maṇḍalas also influenced the ground plans of Hindu temples and the lay-out of the cities. As early as the third century BC, the shape of the Buddhist stupa, originally a monument over the relics of the Buddha, was based on the circle and the square. Ground plans of later temples indicate that they were based on a regular arrangement of squares on a strict grid plan. The three principal geometrical shapes, square, equilateral triangle and circle, on account of their symmetry were related to each other as in a yantra diagram. In one of the earliest references in the manuals of architecture can be found the Vāstu-Purusha maṇḍala which according to that treatise can be drawn in thirty-two ways. The simplest one consists of a square, while all the others can be made from the division of the square into four, nine, sixteen, twenty-five and so on up to 1,024 small squares. In accordance with tantra's original thesis, the spatial orientation of the temples served to create a microcosm in the image of the macrocosm and its governing laws. While these are few examples of tantric influence on Indian art, further research has yet to bring to light all the aspects in which the tantric doctrines left a mark in this field.

## *Image-making*

In tantric art, the image must correspond to the original canonical text; any omission, error or oversight is attributed to imperfect absorption or considered a sign of slackening of attention. In such an event, the image is discarded and the process of composing is deferred. The initial impetus to visualize is invariably provided by the dhyāna-mantra, or the auditory equivalent which enhances concentration and functions as a trance-formula. For example, the trance-formula of the goddess Bhuvaneśvarī, one of the tantric daśa-mahāvidyās, reads:

> I worship our gentle lady Bhuvaneśvarī, like the rising sun, lovely, victorious, destroying defects in prayer, with a shining crown on her head, three-eyed and with swinging earrings adorned with diverse gems, as a lotus-lady, abounding in treasure, making the gestures of charity and giving assurance. Such is the dhyānam of Bhuvaneśvarī.

The artist's visualizations begin with mental construction and there is little attempt to find a syn-visibility in external models. For example, Shilpi-yogin has resolved the anthropomorphic image of Kālī into a simple geometrical pattern – a triangle within a circle.

'Krīṃ', the bījamantra, almost an equation of this, is a further simplification in which the essence of the concept is latent.

Speaking of the achievement of yoga vision, Sukracharya further teaches: 'When the consciousness is brought to rest in the form [nāma, 'name', 'idea'] and sees only the form, then, inasmuch as it rests in the form, aspectual perception is dispensed with and only the reference remains; one reaches then the world-without-aspectual-perception, and with further practice attains to liberation from all hindrances.' This profound discipline led the artist to visualize the highest degree of abstraction, exposing it in the colour-field abstraction where all images are totally effaced in a patternless visual field.

In this form of discipline, art and worship can only be artificially separated. The process of image-making, involving a complex series of interior activities, among other methods of yoga discipline, provides the psychological condition necessary to

*A young aspirant learning the art of carving traditional icon-images from his guru, a Sthapati of South India. The palm-leaf manuscript contains prescriptions and guidance regarding technique and spiritual attitudes.*

*Incomplete Durgā image being prepared by a Kālīghāt (Calcutta) folk artist. Clay.*

achieve spiritual deliverance. The force of this impulse shifts the objective of art from being an end in itself to being the means to an end. The artist pursues his task as a detached observer free from everything that flatters his individual vanity. His path is one of selfless action, where there is a total annihilation of his ego, since his intention is constantly not to express himself but that which ought to be expressed; that is to reveal a 'thesis'. Art of this nature, where the individual longs to cut through the shackles of egohood in order to merge with the universal consciousness for the sake of spiritual enlightenment, has always remained anonymous. Rarely are the works of Silpi-yogins signed or do they bear any mark of individual identity, for any sign of exhibitionism renders the entire pursuit futile. The impact of the aesthetic discipline on the personality of the artist is itself so strong that many who have passed through it finally and inevitably become saints.

Though separated by centuries, the sign-language of tantra art and the works of many modern abstract artists run parallel. Tantra seems to have anticipated many forms that only recently have been rediscovered in the works of contemporary artists. It is interesting to note that what a modern artist struggles to achieve through a process of distillation by and expression of his individual consciousness, came spontaneously in the aesthetic vision of the tantric artist within the defined collective sign-system.

There is a similarity between the spiritual aspects of tantric art and the works of several twentieth-century abstract artists, such as Klee, Mondrian, Brancusi. For these artists, art was not merely an optical manifestation but a revelation of certain metaphysical concepts. Mondrian's chief concern, for example, was to transcend the particular in order to express the universal. Throughout his life he was interested in Hindu philosophy and was so inspired by mystic ideas that he equated 'plastic' expression with the 'spiritual'. The vertical and horizontal theme in his work reflects

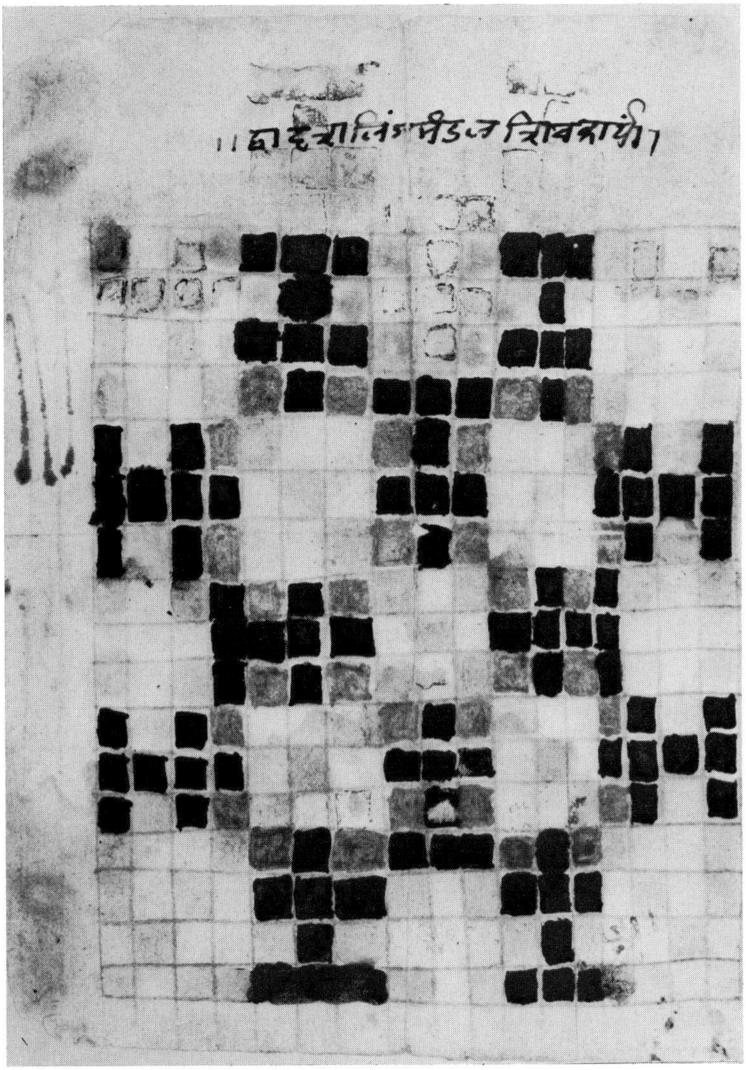

*Liṅga-maṇḍala. The liṅgam as the symbol of Śiva also signifies the all-pervading cosmic space. The diagram is used for ritual and meditation. Rajasthan, c. 18th century. Gouache on paper.*

*Bālā Yantra. Rajasthan, c. 18th century. Gouache on paper.*

the interplay of contrasting forces: male and female, active and passive, spirit and matter; he expressed it himself as the 'static balance' and 'dynamic equilibrium' which constitutes reality. Mondrian identified the vertical with the male principle and the horizontal with the female. In a similar way, Paul Klee explored spatial energy through the concept of polarity: 'A concept is not thinkable without its opposite – every concept has its opposite more or less in the manner of thesis-antithesis.' To express the eternal dialectic of the static and dynamic in its essence, he aligned the notion of polarity to geometry, creating an infinitely variable harmony of coloured planes. These artists' pictorial affinities to tantric art and their metaphysical ideas suggest a link with tantra's dualistic philosophy. A striking sculptural similarity is in the primordial ovoids of Brancusi and the Brahmāṇḍas of tantra. Metaphysically, both forms operate on the same level – the projection of total unity. Indeed, in 1933 the Maharaja of Indore commissioned Brancusi to construct a model for the Temple of Deliverance based on this primordial ovoid form. Kandinsky, too, recalled the sound-form dialectic in the tantras when he said: 'Sound, then, is the soul of form, which comes to life only through sound from the inside out.' More recently, Delaunay, Rothko, Reinhardt, Newman, in the West, and particularly Biren De in India, have demonstrated a striking visual relationship between tantric art and their own. Like their predecessors, these artists were led by the same interior impulse to transform a dream into a vision.

Can the vision contained in tantra's diverse ideologies help the artist to re-create himself? Any quick and easy answer will lead to self-deception. Living tantra is a matter of certain cultural disciplines, and the creation of its aesthetic forms cannot be divorced from their original intention. Just as history repeats itself through and in many events – wars, peace, socio-political upheavals – from deep within it new patterns evolve, new situations arise. In essence, however, they retain a thread of unity whose 'genus' is never lost. In this way, a cross-fertilization of tantric ideas with the contemporary art world may generate a new vision, whose outer structure and rhythms may vary though the underlying insight will be the same. Tantra art has opened the doors of our perception and given to the world, like all great epochs, a vision-inducing-aesthetic-creativity. Some of the art forms which have come down as an anonymous legend will remain unparalleled in the history of Indian art and in the larger context of the art of various cultures.

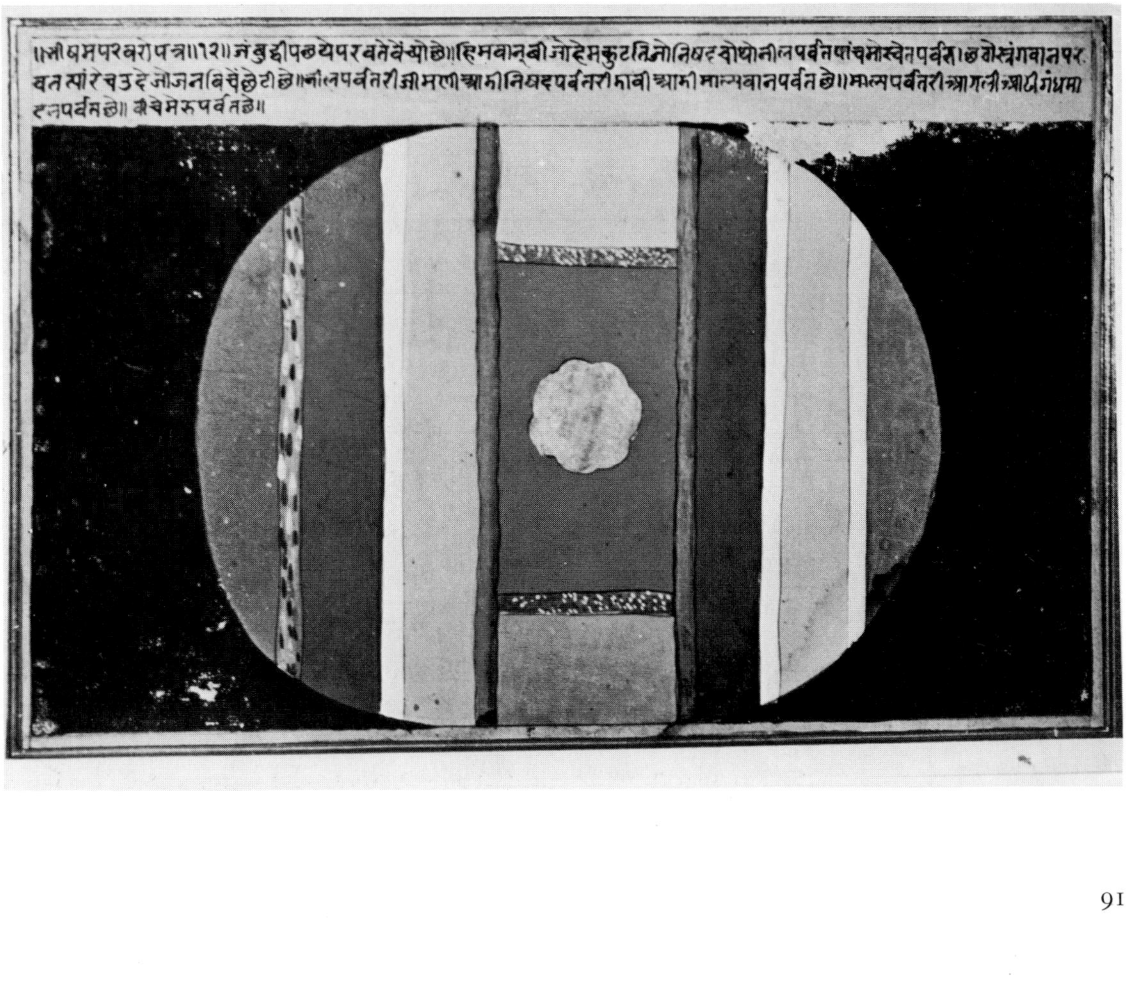

*Goloka, the world-egg with its nine fields. Rajasthan, c. 18th century. Gouache on paper.*

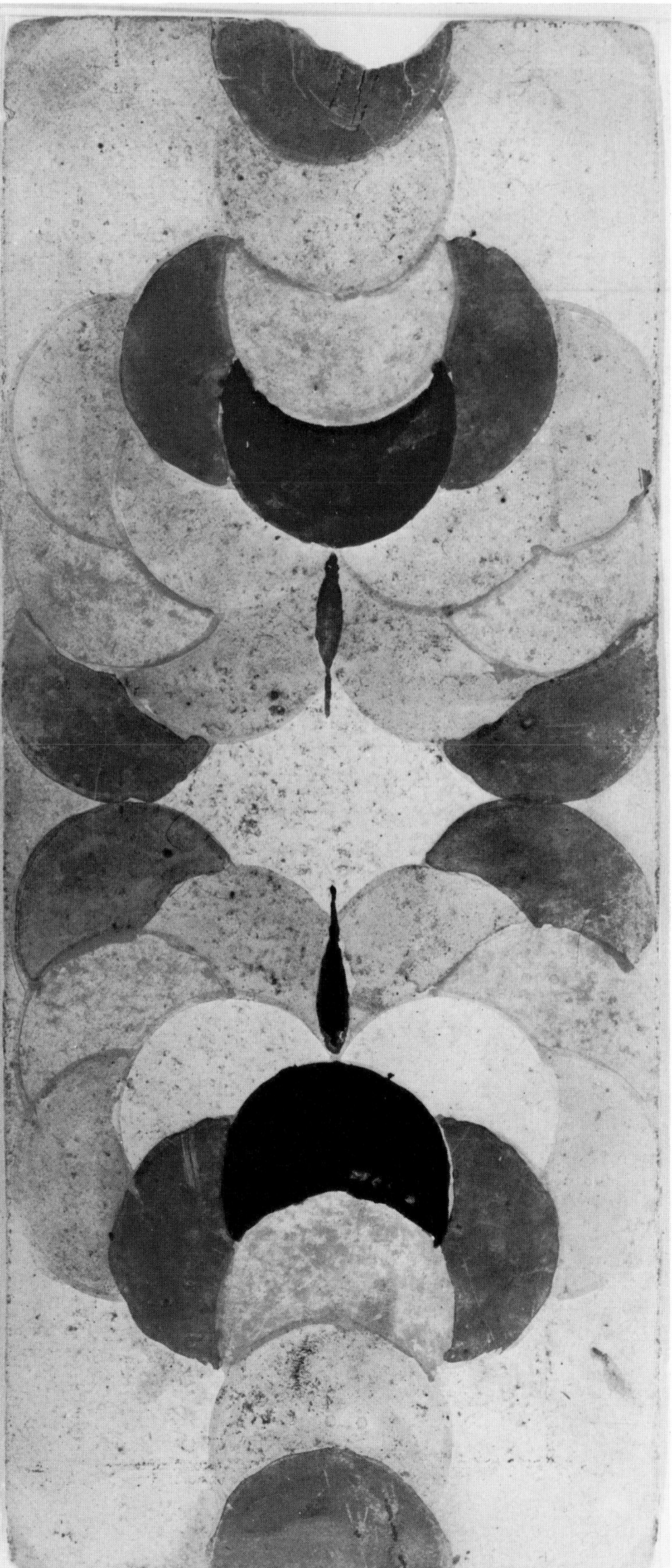

# SCIENCE

*Opposite and above: Creation of the universe showing the energy circles in the course of evolution emanating from a single transcendent source. Gujarat, c. 18th century. Gouache on paper.*

The scientific concepts of the tantras run parallel to the metaphysical. While the latter provide an inherent teleology and ontological framework grafted mainly on the Sāṁkhya system (*c.* 500 BC) of Vedic and Vedantic thought (*c.* 2000–1000 BC), within which ritual and art were assimilated, science helped to free dogmas and gave tantric rituals an empirico-experiential dimension. The tantrikas conducted experiments mainly in the field of chemical operations, particularly in the preparation of medicines consisting mostly of mercury and sulphur. Otherwise, tantra did not evolve any system of scientific thought independently, but drew freely for its own purposes from the various aspects of ancient Indian scientific knowledge. Those aspects of science which had a practical ritualistic interest were of utmost importance. Thus, astronomy and astrology, which revealed the movement of the vast spectrum of celestial bodies and their interaction on man, mapped out the heavens and determined ceremonial periods. Similarly, notions of molecular and atomic structure in the Nyāya-Vaiśeshika system were useful for the preparation of chemical formulae; and the polarity principle of tantra was supported by the theory of cosmic evolution derived mainly from the Sāṁkhya-Patañjali system. Mathematical and geometrical knowledge provided useful keys to the construction of various kinds of yantras. This syncretic trend made tantra an elastic and assimilative system and a fusion of many disciplines.

Men's age-old questions about the origin and nature of the cosmos are not new; only the contexts and the methods of the search for conclusive answers can be unique. Science, by the very definition of its pursuit, bases its investigations on observations and experimental methods susceptible to verification. It is the realm of posterior knowledge based on empirical facts, and in diametrical opposition to it is another domain of knowledge which pursues its search principally along a priori lines of knowing. Paradoxically, the empirical and the intuitive disciplines share a common denominator: both transcend the appearances of the phenomenal world and go into the realm of the unknown to unravel the mysteries of the universe. Both these methods were applied by the ancient Hindus. Some inferences were drawn on the basis of a systematic method: facts were observed, instances were subjected to careful analysis and classification, and their results were verified by empirical means. This method was particularly the source of the Hindu physico-chemical theories and certain astronomical generalizations, which reached a remarkable degree of approximation to the figures of Laplace's table. Their similarity can only be justified by the fact that results were obtained by a process of verification and correction by comparison of the computed with the observed. There were exceptions to this systematic approach, especially when quasi-empirical explanations were sought.

In early times, philosophical doctrines were blended with scientific theories: as a consequence, many scientific pronouncements were based on intuitive insight. A sudden impression or a fleeting imagery of subliminal experience may emerge into the conscious mind; uniquely personal as they may appear, these impressions are correlated to objective facts before any systematic empirical investigation can take place. Thus, for instance, according to Manu (*c.* 300 BC), 'Trees and plants are conscious and feel pleasure and pain' (VII); later this attitude was exemplified by Udayana as well as by Gunaratna, in his declaration (*c.* AD 1350) that plant-life, apart from its infancy, youth and age, or regular growth, is characterized by various kinds of movement or action connected with sleep, waking, expansion and contraction in response to touch, special food favourable to its impregnation, and so on. These statements were taken as 'occult fantasy' or myth until scientifically proved by the physicist, J. C. Bose, in his discovery of the sensitive reactions and physiological processes of the living plant. Using the crescograph, an instrument devised by him to measure the reaction of plants to stimuli, he was able to detect that plants have a sensitive nervous system, and that they 'feel' pleasure and pain.

Instances such as this one indicate that there are other ways of knowing qualitatively different from the scientific method. Like science, the intuitive experiential method postulates certain facts; but, unlike science, it relies on spontaneous supernormal conditions, the result of which may be applied universally though the method be tested in individual cases. Further, discovery may also be recognized as a process of inference which is not subject to any precise rules.

From the tantric point of view, the efficacy of scientific norms does not rest mainly on empirical verification but on the basis of psychological experimentation, by working on one's self. The varied hypotheses which are advanced to explain the world with the help of scientific investigations are the way-stations along an aspirant's spiritual search. They are conceived to be postulates which help the entire edifice of ritualistic techniques cohere as a theoretical framework. To a tantrika their validity rests on the efficacy of the ritual. If the adept attains the core of realization, for him the axioms are *ipso facto* 'true', and there is no longer any need for speculation or hair-splitting experimentation under laboratory conditions. An adept's experimental field is always himself and his body. But even so, opposing attitudes coexist: for instance, the Tamil Siddhāi tantrikas explain their supernatural power 'as a kind of game with anti-matter', a view very similar to contemporary scientists' that there may be an entire universe of anti-matter; other tantrikas may offer a different explanation for the same feat, seeing it as caused by the power of a mantra. These two different frames of reference, describing the same event, are to be understood as complementary to each other.

## *Cosmogenesis*

The history of cosmic evolution, according to Sāṁkhya, which profoundly influenced the tantras, may be regarded as possessing all the characteristics of a scientific hypothesis based on the principles of conservation, transformation and dissipation of energy. Before examining the theory, however, we must review some of its salient features in simple terms. A broad cosmogonical view holds that grosser elements of the tangible world have evolved from finer elements; the finer elements in turn are seen as having been compounded from still more subtle homogeneous substances. Furthermore, this broad view formulates a psycho-physical parallelism and postulates that matter and mind evolve simultaneously. Finally, it lays down the theory of the recurring cycles of the universe, according to which destruction amounts to a mere reversal of the evolutionary process to its primary sources. For instance, the universe evolves in stages 'layer after layer'; the first to emanate is a vibratory element of Ākāśa, which gives rise to heat, heat turns into gaseous substance and liquefies, and finally the gas is turned into solid matter. When the cycle is complete it reverses itself: solid matter disintegrates into liquids, and finally dissolves into vibratory state; the cycle of expansion, contraction and dissolution starts again. Thus, this view proposes the possibility of a steady birth of matter and continuous creation of the universe.

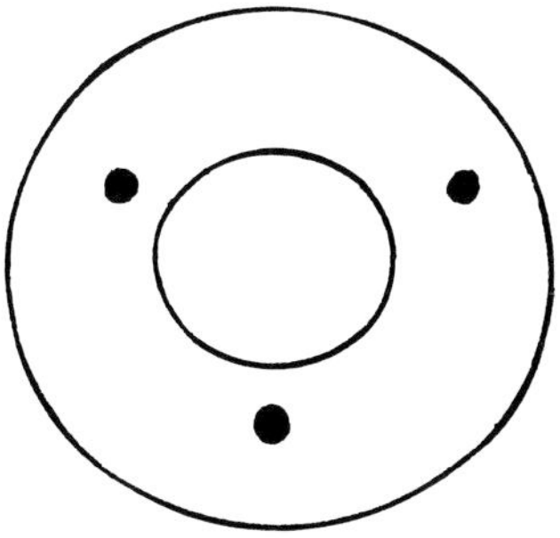

*Guṇas: sattva, rajas, tamas.*

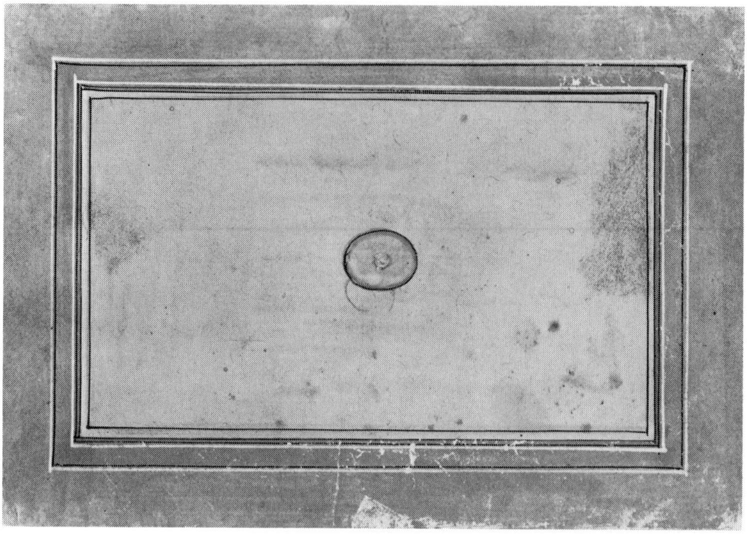

*Bindu. The universe in its unmanifested form is conceived as the most minute point from which the expansion of the world takes place and into which, completing the cosmic cycles, it recedes. Rajasthan, c. 18th century. Gouache on paper.*

The cosmos is evolved of an unmanifested ground, called Prakṛiti, which is conceived as a group of three indeterminate continua of categories technically known as guṇas. Literally, guṇa means quality, but as quality and substance are identical in Sāṁkhya, the guṇas are therefore substantive entities. They are sattva, the essence or intelligence-stuff, the principle of conscious manifestation; rajas, the energy-stuff producing motion, force, quantum, extension, and overcoming resistance; and tamas the matter-stuff is mass or inertia that offers resistance to opposing force. At the commencement of a cosmic cycle the process of evolution is at rest. The three guṇas exist together in perfect equilibrium or uniform diffusion in the infinite continuum, Prakṛiti. They neither interact nor manifest their existence. In that state, both the energy and the matter-stuff, according to Sāṁkhya, possess the attributes of quantum and continuity, a description which is in keeping with modern notions of energy and matter.

Evolution begins with the disturbance of this primordial balance by the transcendental or magnetic influence of Purusha, the Universe of Consciousness, on Prakṛiti which is in a state of equipoise or equilibrated trance. Disequilibration breaks up the uniform diffusion and impels the aggregation of the guṇas to a state in which one or more is relatively preponderant over the others, a creative transformation accompanied by evolution of motion (parispandana).

The diversity of phenomena results from the special combination of the guṇas which constantly unite and separate. Though they cooperate to produce the world of effects, they do not coalesce. All the guṇas are present in any manifestation in a potent latent or sublatent form: in the material system, for instance, where tamas, or the matter-stuff, predominates mass is potent, energy is latent and the intelligence-stuff is sublatent. The totality of the guṇas, whether actual or potential, always remains constant since they can neither be created nor destroyed, which suggests the principle of the conservation of the energy-stuff and the matter-stuff as well as their transformations.

Evolution is based on recognition of a natural law whose order of succession is 'from a relatively less differentiated, less determinate, less coherent to a relatively more differentiated, more determinate, more coherent whole'. The implication here is that though there are consecutive transformations and developments of categories, there is no change in their substance; in other words, differentiation of categories is within an integrated whole. This stage continues until there is a tendency of the unstable equilibrium to reverse the course of events and the order of succession to return to the original stable equilibrium of Prakṛiti, with the equal diffusion of all the guṇas. This is analogous to a state when there is a total dissipation of energy and mass stuff. Thus, then, the process of evolution is an incessant manifestation of a twofold process according to irreversible cosmic principles.

The Sāṁkhya doctrine postulates that in the process of evolution, matter and mind evolved concurrently from the original flow of energy. The first evolute is the intelligible essence of the cosmos which bifurcates into two coordinated series to make the world of appearances. The two divisions are the 'object series', which gives rise to material potencies and gross matter, and the 'subject series', from which emanate all the modes of the mind, such as intelligence, volition, sense perception, ego-sense, and the like, all of which can be generically termed 'mind-stuff'. In a physicalistic attempt to link matter and mind, an eminent astronomer, V. A. Firsoff, postulates the existence of extremely subtle particles of mind stuff, or 'mindons', of a quasi-ethereal quality. He suggests that mind is 'a universal entity or interaction of the same order as electricity or gravitation, and that there must exist a *modulus of transformation,* analogous to Einstein's famous equality $E=mc^2$, whereby "mind stuff" could be equated with other entities of the physical world'.[21]

After a series of subtle transformations, there is further differentiation and integration which transform the universal energy of the cosmos into various classes of infra-atomic potential units of energy called tanmātras which cannot be seen or measured. The tanmātras result from the action of energy on subtle matter, bhūtādi, which is absolutely homogeneous and inert when the original equilibrium comes to an end. The infra-atomic potential units of energy possess something more than mass, energy or quantum, and they are characterized by powers of pressure, radiant heat, cohesive attraction. They are also charged with specific energies represented by sound potential – the energy of vibration; touch potential – energy of impact on mechanical pressures; colour potential – energy of radiant heat and light; taste potential – energy of viscous attraction; smell potential – energy of cohesive attraction. These subsequently give rise, by a process of 'condensation and collocation' from the corresponding tanmātras, to the five grosser atoms: space (vyoman), air (marut), fire (tejas), water (ap), and earth (kṣhiti).

The cornerstone of this view is that the universe does not evolve out of atoms but the atoms are the tertiary state in the formation of the universe. Each kind of infra-atomic potential becomes charged with the grosser element which together with the original action of energy over bhūtādi in turn generates the next infra-atomic potential. For example, the first to emanate is the sound potential, which generates the proto-atom of space; then the atom of space together with the original action of energy generates the tanmātra of touch potential and the atom of air; the atom of air together with the original action then generates colour potential, and so on. The grosser elements should not be confused with elementary substances; they represent abstract principles on the basis of their properties.

A bird's-eye view of the successive stages of cosmogenesis has been provided by Dr B. N. Seal:

Out of the all-pervasive rudiment-matter (Bhūtādi) appeared Ākāśa (ether), first as a Tanmātra (subtle matter) charged with the potential energy of sound (vibration potential), and then as an atomic integration of mono-Tanmātric structure (the Ākāśa-atom) also ubiquitous and all-enveloping. In the next stage we find a new kind of Tanmātras, systems of the infra-atomic vibratory particles, so arranged as to manifest a new form of Energy, that of impact or mechanical pressure, and these Tanmātras combining with the vibration potentials (Ākāśa-Tanmātra) produced a new kind of atom, the di-Tanmātric Vāyu-atom, which by aggregation formed a gaseous envelope composed of impinging (driving) vibratory particles (Vāyu). Next appeared the third class of Tanmātras, infra-atomic systems of the impinging vibratory particles, which by their collocation developed a new form of Energy – the energy of radiant heat-and-light. These Tanmātras, combining with the potentials (Tanmātras) of vibration and impact, produced a new kind of atom – the tri-Tanmātric Tejas-atom, the light-and-heat corpuscle, which by aggregation enveloped the gaseous world in huge flames. In the next stage we have the fourth class of Tanmātras, new and complex infra-atomic systems of the radiant impinging vibratory particles, which evolved the energy of viscous attraction, as well as the potential energy concerned in the taste-stimulus. These Tanmātras, combining with the three previous ones, gave rise to another class of atoms, the tetra-Tanmātric Ap-atom, and the flaming gases were thus precipitated into cosmic masses of viscous fluid matters (Ap). Finally appeared the fifth class of Tanmātras, infra-atomic systems of the viscous radiant impinging vibratory particles which developed new forms of Energy – the energy of cohesive attraction, as well as the potential energy concerned in the stimulus of smell. These Tanmātras, uniting with the four other kinds of infra-atomic subtile particles, formed another class of atoms, the penta-Tanmātric Earth-atom. Thus the viscous fluid matters were condensed and transformed into the Earth-Bhūta, comprising the majority of the so-called elements of chemistry.[22]

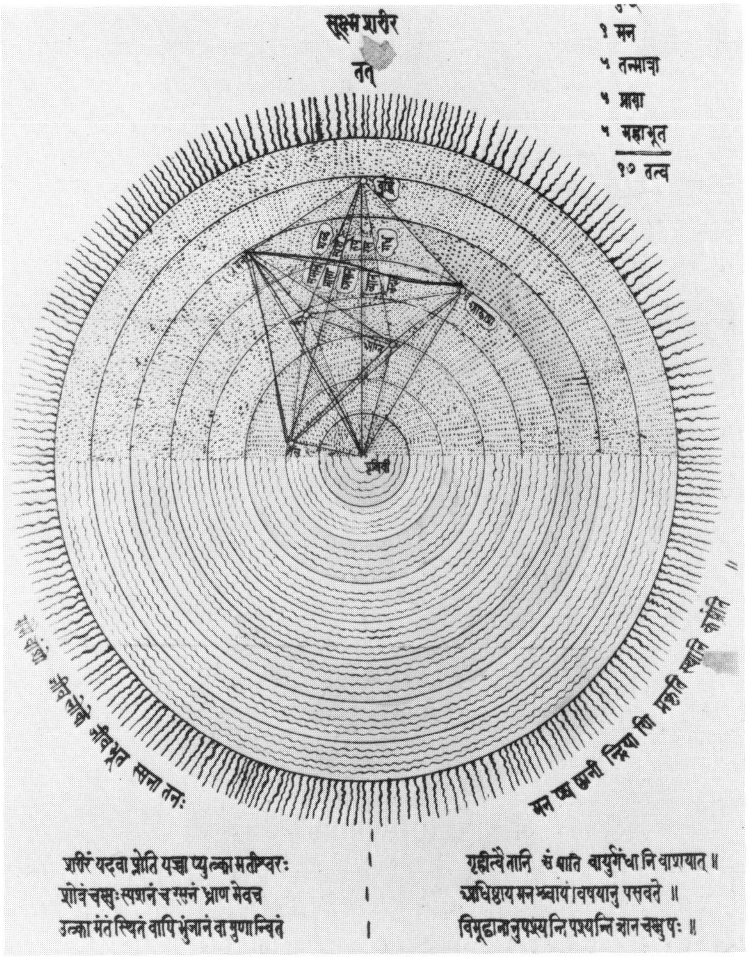


*Cosmic plan representing the interaction of elemental forces on the energy circles surrounding the earth. Rajasthan, early 19th century. Ink on paper.*

The process of evolution of the material universe is always conceived in relation to space, time and causality. Time is a continuum of one dimension which distinguishes 'then' and 'now'. A moment or an instance is the ultimate irreducible unit of this continuum. A moment also represents the ultimate moment of change or an instantaneous transit of an atom from one point of space to the next. In the time sequence only a single moment is real, and the whole universe evolves in that single moment; the rest, past and future, are potential or sublatent phenomena. Time is relative and has no objective reality, being always conceived in relation to its antecedents and sequence. Space, like time, is also considered to be only relative, constructed on the basis of relation or position. Both these categories are forms of intuition of our empirical consciousness and are real only in finite terms. The contradictions and inconsistencies of the old scientific theories forced Einstein to ascribe new properties to the space-time continuum. According to him, space and time are not absolute quantities imposed on the universe but have significance only when relations between events and systems are defined. The ancient Indian thinkers also stressed this aspect.

In Sāṁkhya, cause and effect are more or less evolved forms of the same ultimate energy. The sum of effects exists potentially in the sum of causes. Production of effects only means an internal change in the arrangement of atoms already present in potential form in the cause. The material universe, which is a product, is only a change of appearance of Prakṛiti and the three guṇas. According to the physicist Joseph Kaplan, the principle involved is identical with what is known in Western physics as the principle of superposition:

In our modern description of nature, we proceed as follows: Let us say we are describing a molecule of nitrogen. Instead of giving a completely detailed account of its structure, as we might do in describing a chair or a house, we say that the molecule is adequately described for experimental purposes by giving all the possible energy states in which the nitrogen molecule can find itself, and then assigning to each such state a number which gives its relative weight, that is, the relative number of times that state appears compared with other states. Thus the molecule is not something which takes on successive states, but it is the states themselves. So dice are the sum of possible ways in which they can fall. The principle is known as the principle of superposition. So the three guṇas represent the universe, and as the three occur in various relative intensities, so the properties of things are determined.[23]

V *Astronomical equations, based on time units, used to determine the mean position of a planet. Rajasthan, c. 18th century. Gouache on paper.*

VI *Astrogram. This painting represents how astronomy blends with astrology. The symbols depicted on the various parts of the body map out the interaction of the twenty-eight Nakshatras, or lunar mansions, on the micro-self. The body, depicted in the shape of a bow or Dhanu-āsana, represents the energized unit of the vast macrocosm. Rajasthan, 19th century. Gouache on paper.*

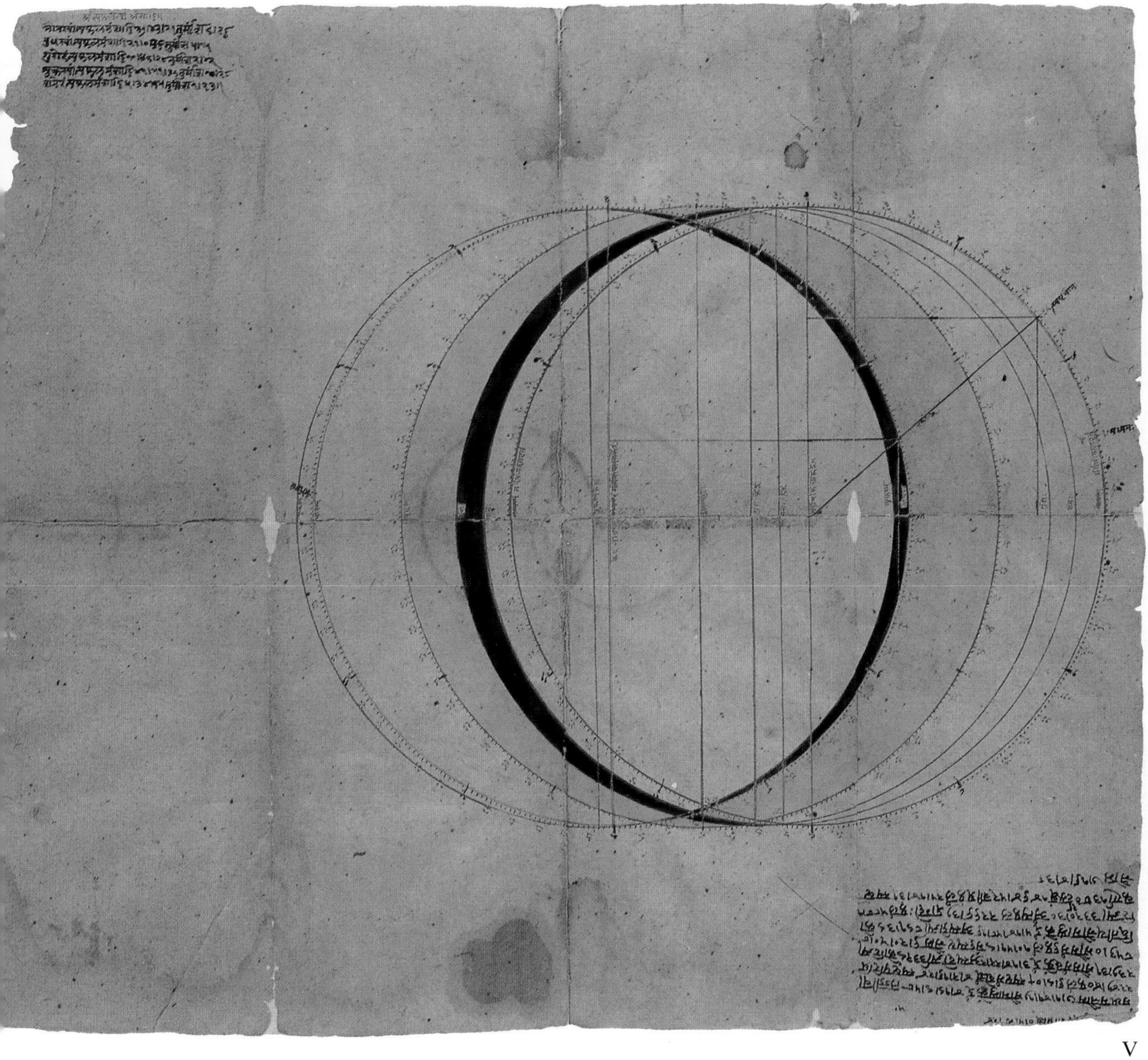

V

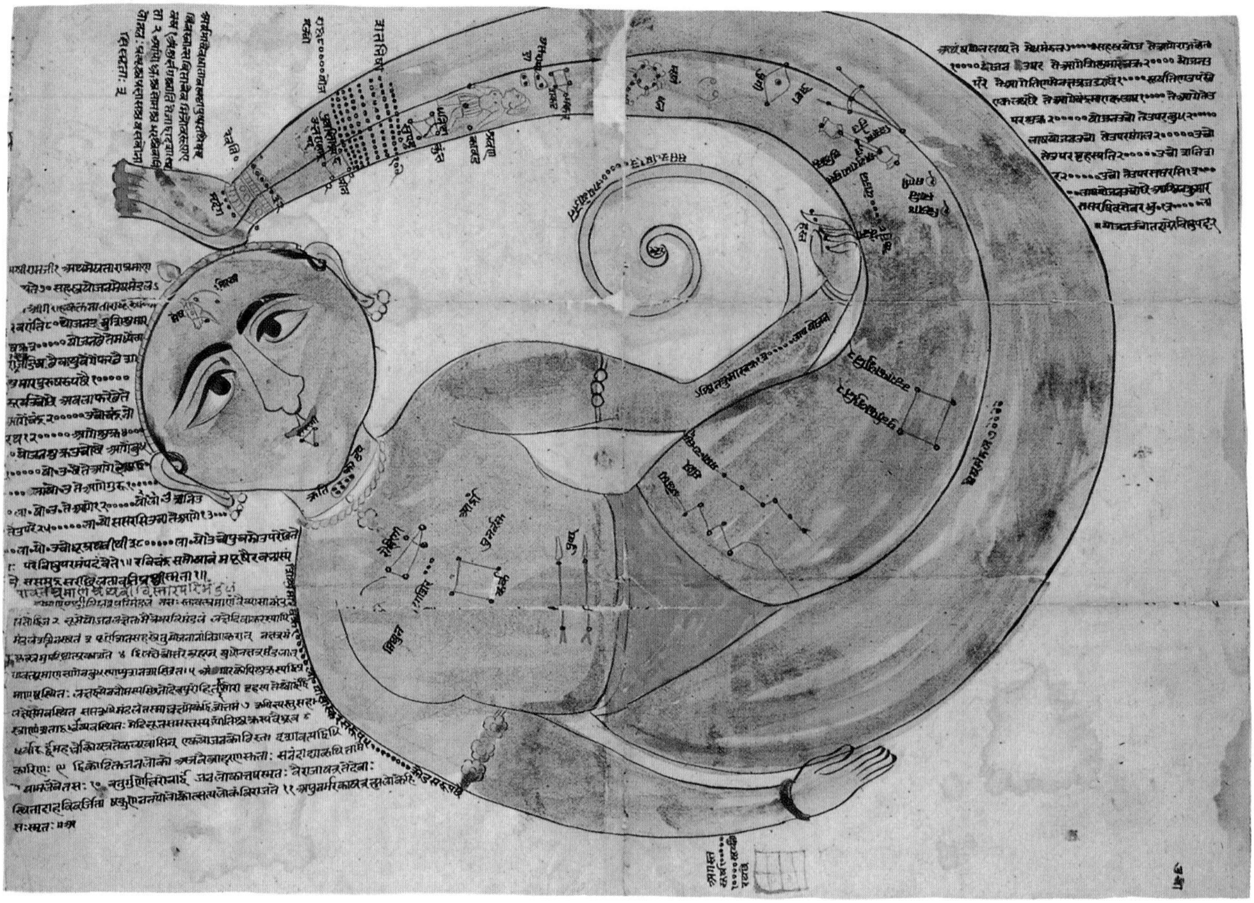

VI

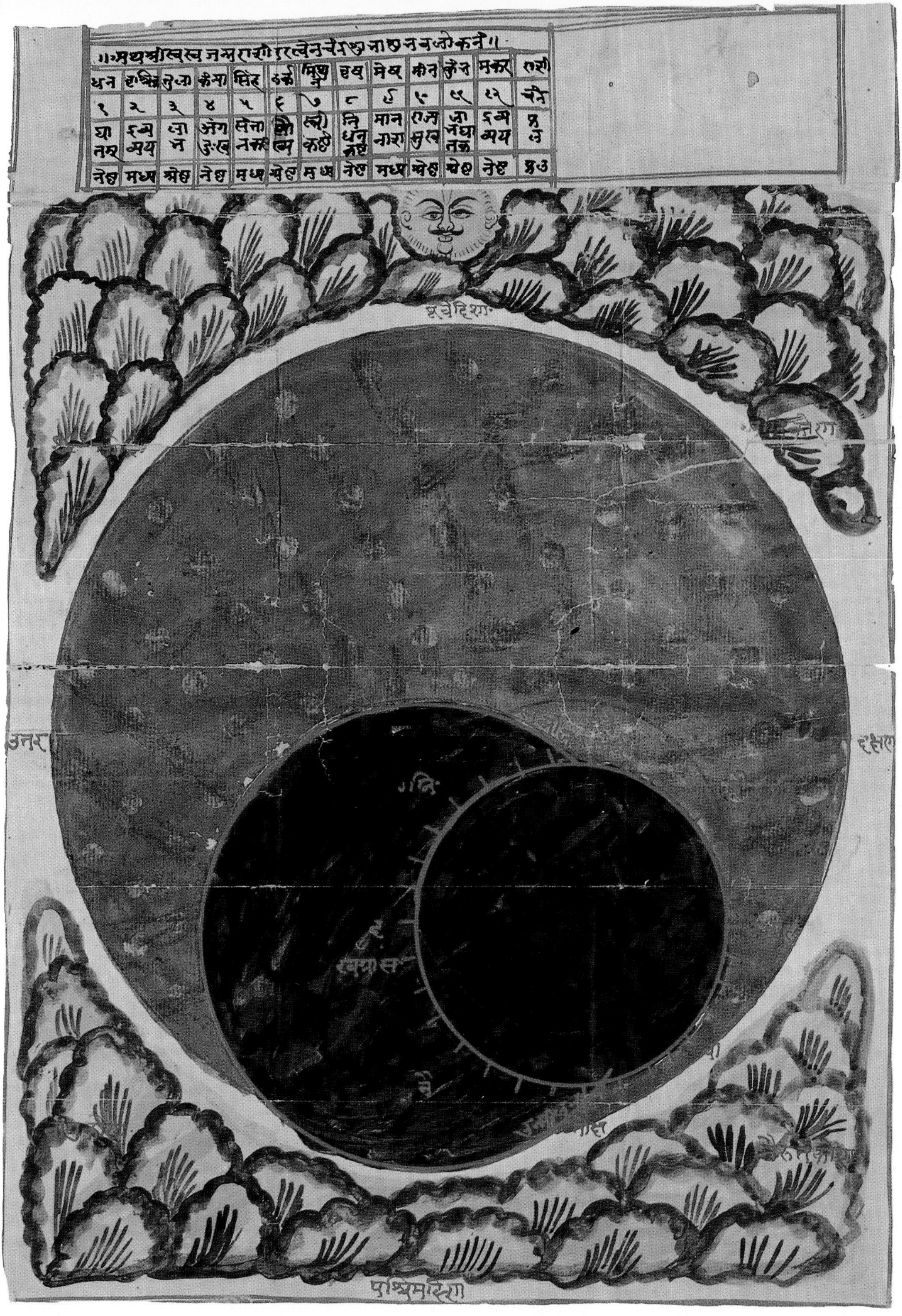
धन वृश्चिक तुला कन्या सिंह कर्क मिथुन वृष मेष मीन कुंभ मकर राशी
१ २ ३ ४ ५ ६ ७ ८ ९ १० ११ १२
नेष्ट मध्य श्रेष्ठ नेष्ट मध्य श्रेष्ठ मध्य नेष्ट मध्य श्रेष्ठ श्रेष्ठ नेष्ट
पूर्वदिशा
उत्तर
दक्षिण
पश्चिमदिशा

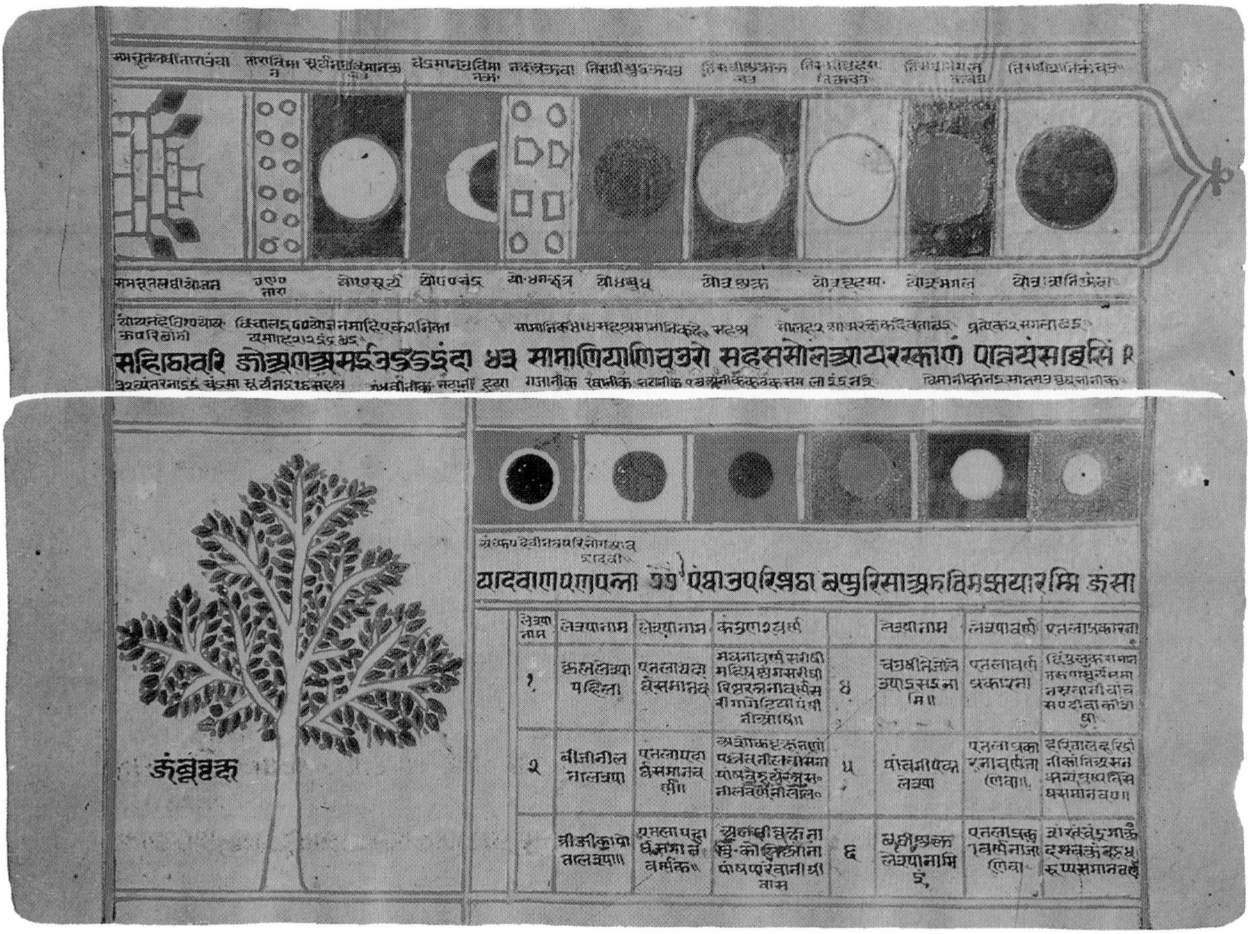

VIII

Sāṁkhya's view that it is possible for one element to change into another also tallies with modern physics. Kaplan further comments:

The transmutability of the elements has been shown in many ways. For example, it is possible, by bombarding certain elements with extremely rapidly-moving electrical particles, to change them into others, and to even produce elements which do not occur in nature because they are unstable (radioactive). We go even further. It is possible to produce matter, such as electrons, from radiation (light). Thus the ultimate constituent of the universe of the physicist is energy of radiation – that is, light. Thus the Sāṁkhya theory is in absolute agreement with the latest results of physics. It is interesting here to make the following comment. The atomic theory is the product of the Western mind. In his naive way the Western scientist generalizes the experience that one can subdivide matter until one meets an ultimate particle into an atomic theory assuming many elements. The Hindu philosopher goes much further and reduces everything to one element.[24]

## *Sound*

The importance of sound and its basic vibrations has been investigated and explained with considerable detail in Indian thought. The Nyāya-Vaiśeshika's hypothetical analysis of sound in its physical aspect and the mode of its propagation centres round the following: sound is conceived to be the specific quality of space. The physical basis of sound is traced to a mechanical impact which generates vibrations in the molecules of the object struck, which in turn impinge against surrounding molecules of air to produce sound. Sound expands in space as waves propagate in an ocean, and it is said to increase in successive concentric spherical layers of filaments which emanate from one another. Further, it is maintained that sound can be distinguished into decreasing orders of subtlety: Sphoṭa or transcendental sound; Nāda or supersonic sound which can be but is not necessarily heard; and Dhvani or audible sound. The articulate sound we all experience is Dhvani.

The basis for this concept of sound is a central doctrine described in tantras as Sphoṭavāda, the foundation of tantric mantras which form an important aspect of ritual. By repetition of sound syllables, vibratory rhythms are created in the body to awaken the psychic fields. Everything from the subtlest idea to gross forms of matter is a product of the coagulation of simple or complex combinations of vibrations. Every object has its norm of sound as an accompaniment of its energy. Vibration, therefore, is one of the numerous results of sound and not, as it is commonly held, its cause.

VII *Conjunction of the sun and the moon with zodiacal divisions. Rajasthan,* c. *19th century. Gouache on paper.*

VIII *Cosmological charts from an illuminated manuscript. Gujarat,* c. *16th century. Gouache on paper.*

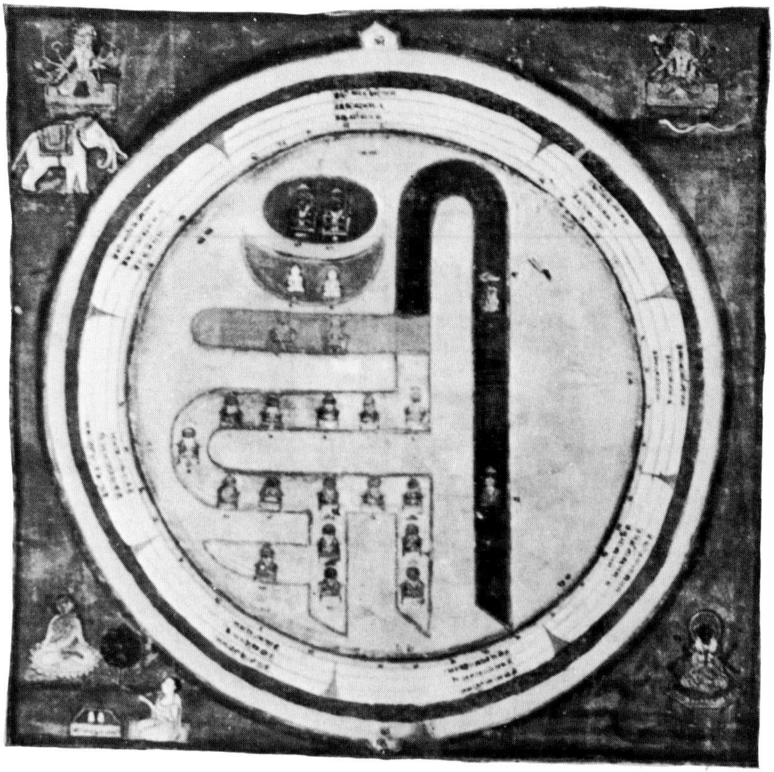

*Oṃ. Rajasthan, c. 18th century. Gouache on paper.*

The doctrine of Sphoṭavāda postulates the inexplicable notion that there is transcendental sound without vibration of a supersonic order which is therefore inaudible to the normal range of the physiological ear. This non-vibratory sound is variously designated as 'silent sound', 'static sound', 'unstruck sound' or anāhata-dhvani. This postulate leads us to the assumption that there is no vacuum anywhere. The universe is a continuum of unfragmented plena, a stage in the vibratory scale which can be equated with the pre-creative stage of Prakṛiti. The primary sound created by a causal stress is known as 'Parā-śabda'. The doctrine also holds that though the ultimate quality of the sound potential is 'silence', at the finite level it generates different degrees of vibration that create light and dimension. Every vibration has its own volume and structure which vary in accordance to the density of sound. Sound is said to become more and more differentiated in relation to pitch, rhythm, volume, frequency, speed, and harmony. Hence, if the right chord of the octave of an object is struck, it can be animated, remodelled or destroyed. It is around these concepts that techniques and processes of sound syllables and their visual equivalents are built up in the mantra and yantra rituals.

# *Atoms*

The atomic hypothesis of the Nyāya-Vaiśeshika explains the properties of matter and the nature of atoms and molecules. The atom, in Sanskrit aṇu, is invisible and intangible, but is called paramāṇu when it assumes a state of tangibility. The paramāṇu, or the smallest possible dimension of an elementary particle, is generally calculated as between 1/1,000,000 and 1/349,525 of an inch. Aggregations of atoms produce the molecule, or 'sthūla bhūtaṇi', which produces the visible universe. Four kinds of atom are distinguished in the Vaiśeshika system, each possessing certain characteristic properties such as number, quantity, individuality, mass, gravity, fluidity, velocity, and certain potentials of sense stimuli. The four types correspond to the grosser matter of material phenomena: earth, water, fire and air. (The other, fifth, element, ether or space, is considered to be non-atomic in structure, serving only as a receptacle of sound.) Spherical in shape, atoms have a characteristically vibratory or rotary motion. Atoms have an inherent impulse to unite to form molecules, and as long as they are not subject to the influence of corpuscles of heat, atoms of the same elementary substance unite to form homogeneous binary molecules. Under the impulse of their basic tendency to unite into larger aggregates, binary molecules then combine to form ternary and quarternary molecules. In this way the variety of substances belonging to the same element class results from the molecular combination and configuration of atoms of that element. On the other hand, polybhautic compounds are formed by the union of atoms of heterogeneous substances belonging to the various classes of bhutas or gross matter.

The atomic theory of the Jaina system offers an interesting hypothesis about the formation of chemical combinations. According to this theory (*c.* AD 40), mere contact between two atoms or molecules is not sufficient to produce a compound. Such composition is, rather, based on an interlinking which must precede the compound's formation. This interlinking can only take place between two particles of opposing character, though no linking is possible if the opposing qualities are feeble or defective. On the other hand, particles of homogeneous quality can only unite to form molecules if the strength and intensity of one particle is at least twice as great as the other's. This linking forms the basis of all qualitative transformations in atoms. This view is very like the dualistic hypothesis of chemical combination propounded by the Swedish chemist Berzelius.

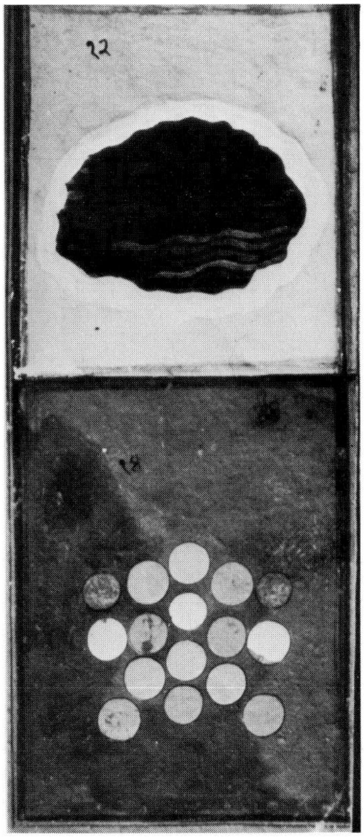

*Payodhi-jala, the Primordial Waters. The force of the manifested universe, whether primordial water or primordial atoms, is the source of all being. Rajasthan,* c. *18th century. Gouache on paper.*

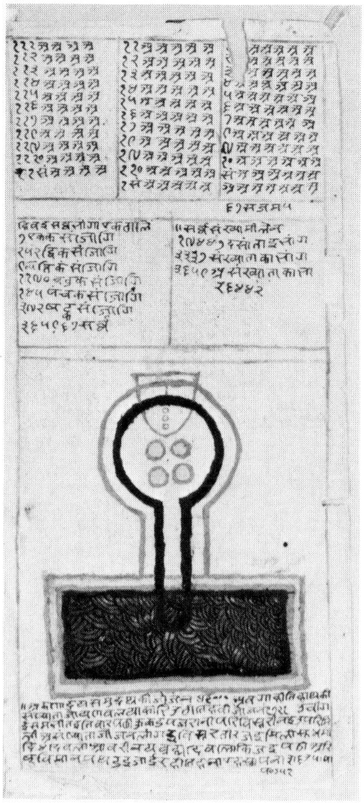

*Diagram of an astronomical computation. Rajasthan, c. 18th century. Ink and colour on paper.*

Different systems of Indian thought, then, developed various theories of the origin, constitution and structure of matter. This diversity contributed significantly to the work of constructing scientific concepts which were freely applied to the methods of investigation of the material universe and in the development of such disciplines as, among others, chemistry, alchemy and medicine.

## *Alchemy*

Alchemy and medicine originated as necessary aids to the fulfilment of spiritual objectives. The chief pursuit of alchemy, besides transmutations of substances, was to preserve the vital elixir of life and thus effect a state of physical balance and immutable duration, so that all the energies of the body were unified. In addition, the psychic changes following the intake of alchemical preparations were not induced for their own sake but for higher spiritual goals.

Hindu alchemy can be traced back to the Vedic period. The Ṛig Veda describes the Soma Rasa, or the juice of the Soma plant, as amṛita, which is akin to the Greek ambrosia. In spite of the divergence of views as to the attributes and properties of Soma, it is generally agreed that it must have been an extremely potent euphoriant. Authorities agree that it was a milky climbing plant, most probably Asclepias Acida or Ephedra or a type of uncultivated vine. For the extraction of juice, Soma herbs were crushed between two stones or pounded in a mortar; the extracted liquid was then filtered through sheep's wool and subsequently mixed with milk, butter or honey. The texts describe its reaction on the body as no less than a 'roar of a bull'. Soma was an inexhaustible source of strength and vitality: it increased sexual energy, stimulated speech and possessed healing properties.

Though alchemical knowledge was widely cultivated in ancient India, it reached its zenith in the tantric renaissance period (AD 700–AD 1300). The tantrikas intimately understood the body and its cosmic affinities; they were well aware of the various techniques of attuning the body by the use of mercury, medicaments, breathing exercises and helio-therapeutic meditation.

Alchemical experiments were concerned mainly with the reduction of elements and their use in their primary forms. There is, it was believed, an original stuff, or ultimate substance, out of which the whole universe has been formed. This primal element could be reduced or precipitated as powder – the ash form of matter or the remaining sediment of liquid – and could be made manifest by burning or heating the element so that extraneous additions could be dispersed. This reduction of substance into ashes, therefore, was regarded as a form of purification, and ash is the basic cohesive element for the preparation of elixir vitae. For further purification, ash has to be dissolved in a still more elemental substance called rasa, or liquid. The primeval form of all things was linked up with the cosmic sea, or the wet element, and almost all forms of fluid – sap, juice, water, blood – were used as medicine.

The chemical theory of organic and inorganic compounds of the prevalent medical schools, particularly of Charaka (AD 80–180), provided useful knowledge about the combination of properties of substances. The physical characteristics of the five subtle elements and their isomeric modes were classified as follows:

*Earth-substances:* heavy, rough, hard, inert, dense, opaque; exciting the sense of smell.
*Water-substances:* liquid, viscous, cold, soft, slippery, fluid; exciting the sense of taste.
*Fire-substances:* hot, penetrative, subtile, light, dry, clear; rarefied and luminous.
*Air substances:* light, cold, dry, transparent, rarefied; impingent.
*Ether-substances:* imponderable (or light), rarefied, elastic; capable of sound (vibrations).

Each of the substances, it was believed, is a fivefold ultra-compound, and in this sense is penta-bhautic, or a combination of the five original subtle elements, each of which can be found in a lesser or greater proportion in a particular substance. Thus ether is the vehicle of air, heat, light and water; air, the combination of water vapour, light and heat, and even five particles of earth, held in an indeterminate state. The colour and sensible qualities of a substance result from its structure, the arrangement of its atoms and its physico-chemical properties resulting from the relative preponderance of a specific substance in its composition.

The most fundamental, and indeed the quintessence, of all substances was mercury. In all tantric alchemical treatises the term rasa means mercury; their medicinal preparations consist mainly of mercury. Although it was considered that mercurial compounds should, in theory, be prepared by amalgamating mercury and air, mercury and blood, mercury and semen or mercury and various ashes, several other ingredients, such as mica, sulphur, orpiament, pyrites, cinnabar, calamine, various alkalies, bitumen, and metals

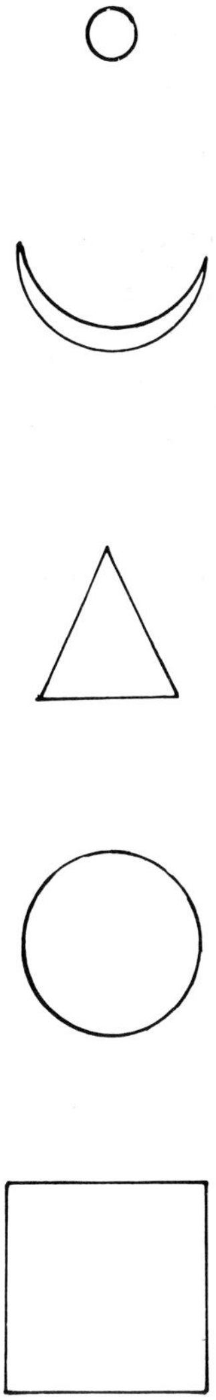

*The five elements, in ascending order.*

like gold, silver, zinc, copper, arsenic, were also used, as well as various acids.

An important tantric treatise, *Rasaratnākara,* ascribed to Nagarjuna (*c.* AD 800) is a repository of much chemical information and many alchemical recipes. The text provides valuable information about the various preparations of mercury, including red crystalline sulphide of mercury, and techniques for extracting mercury and zinc from zinc ore. It also describes more than two dozen apparatuses for experiments in physico-chemical processes. Another significant tantric treatise, *Rasārnava* (AD 1200) has important information on chemistry and is a direct precursor of iatrochemistry. An elaborate description of the location, construction and equipment of chemical laboratories is available in *Rasaratna-samuccaya,* an iatrochemical treatise of the 13th century. A later work, *Rasasāra* (whose name literally means 'sea of mercury'), is a purely chemical work and describes eighteen mercurial processes.

Several special operations involving mercury and examples of chemical composition and decomposition, by processes of calcination, distillation, sublimation, steaming, fixation, and so on, were elaborately discussed in the texts devoted to alchemy and chemistry, as also were various metallurgical processes – extraction, purification, killing, calcination, incineration, powdering, solution, precipitation, rinsing or washing, drying, steaming, melting, casting, filling. Here is a typical example of a recipe, for a mercury potion, and the apparatus for reducing it to ashes:

Mercury is to be rubbed with its equal weight of gold and then [the amalgam] further admixed with sulphur, borax, etc. The mixture is then to be transferred to a crucible and its lid put on, and then submitted to gentle roasting. By partaking of this elixir [i.e., the sublimate] the devotee acquires a body not liable to decay. . . . [The apparatus, the Garbha-Yantram, is described thus:] Make a clay crucible, 4 digits in length and 3 digits in width, with the mouth rounded. Take 20 parts of salt and one of bedellium and pound them finely, adding water frequently; smear the crucible with this mixture. Make a fire of paddy husks and apply gentle heat.

One text speaks of 'killed mercury':

When the mercury assumes colours after having given up its fluidity, it is known as 'swooned'. Killed mercury is that which does not show signs of fluidity, mobility or lustre. When the quicksilver, which has acquired the colour and the lustre of the rising sun, stands the test of fire [i.e., is not readily volatilized], then it to be regarded as fixed. (*Rasaratnākara* of Nāgārjuna.)

The *Siddhayoga* of Vṛinda is an Ayurvedic-Tantric treatise which discusses the external and internal uses of mercury. A preparation called parpatitamram, which contains mercury and was taken internally, was prepared by pounding sulphur and copper pyrites together with mercury and roasting the mixture in a closed crucible. The product thus obtained was administered with honey. This process probably produced sulphides of copper and mercury. Sulphide of mercury was also the main ingredient of another preparation called rasāmṛita-churan. To make it, one part of sulphur and half its weight of mercury were rubbed together and then administered with honey and clarified butter. Killed copper, blue vitriol, rock salt and a few vegetable ingredients compounded together formed a collyrium for the eyes.

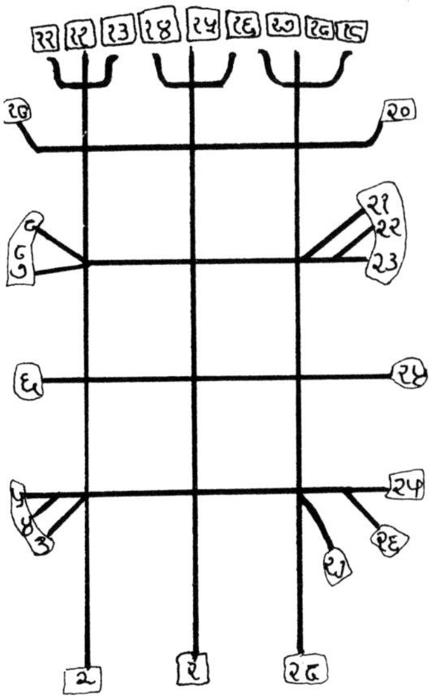

*Sūryakālānal chakra.*

Many foreign travellers to India, notably Marco Polo, Al-Bīrūnī and François Bernier, recorded their observations on the remarkable uses of mercury as a restorative and stimulant. Marco Polo, describing 'the chugchi [yogis] who live 150 or 200 years', wrote: 'These people make use of a very strange beverage, for they make a potion of sulphur and quicksilver mixed together and this they drink twice every month. They say this gives them long life, and it is a potion they are used to take from their early childhood.'

Despite the apparent simplicity of these recipes and procedures, it should not be assumed that the mere mechanical mixture of compounds will yield immediate results. Indeed, the effectiveness of these formulae is not the literal interpretation of the alchemical texts but lies within a body of closely guarded secret processes and considerations. Researches of the contemporary alchemist Armand Barbault have met with scepticism based on a simplistic view:

> Armand Barbault, a contemporary alchemist, achieved after twelve years what he calls in his book *L'Or du millième matin* (Paris 1969) the 'vegetable gold' or Elixir of the first degree. This elixir was thoroughly analysed and tested by German and Swiss laboratories and doctors. It proved its great value and efficacy, especially in the treatment of very serious heart and kidney ailments. But it could not be fully analysed nor, therefore, synthesized. Its preparation required such peculiar care, and took so long, that eventually all hopes of commercialization were abandoned. The scientists who examined it declared that they were in the presence of a new state of matter having mysterious and perhaps deeply significant qualities.[25]

This is not an isolated case. Dr P. C. Ray, in his *History of Hindu Chemistry*, emphasizes the inscrutability of alchemical preparations and records that Nāgārjuna, (*c.* 8th century AD) the father of Indian alchemy, had to undergo twelve years of asceticism to know the hidden secret.[26]

# *Astronomy*

Like other disciplines of Indian thought, astronomy and its origins may be genetically related back to the Vedas. The Vedic Aryans were well acquainted with the natural routine cycles of heavenly bodies. The vault of the sky, for example, was seen as being governed by the eternal ordinances of an inherent universal principle, Rita (literally, the course of things), which determines the paths and phases of the moon and the planets, the day/night cycle and occurrences of eclipses.

The *Jyotisha Vedāṅga* and the *Sūrya Prajñāpati* (*c.* 400 BC–AD 200) record the earliest Hindu astronomical statements. In early times, astronomy developed out of pragmatic speculations which were necessary and therefore of paramount importance for the careful calculation of appropriate times for rituals and sacrifices. The important treatises on Indian astronomy were the *Gārgī-saṁhitā* (*c.* AD 230), the *Aryabhattiya* of Aryabhaṭa (AD 499), the *Siddhānta-śekhara* of Śripati, and the Siddhānta-śiromaṇi of Bhāskara II (AD 1114–1160).

By the beginning of the Christian era, a great upsurge in the astronomical search was formalized in a number of methodical studies; many works of great importance, such as the five *Siddhāntas,* of which the *Sūrya Siddhānta* is probably the best known, were compiled and later summarized by the sixth-century astronomer and mathematician Varāha-Mihira in his *Pañcha-siddhāntikā* (*The Five Astronomical Systems*), written about AD 550. In his outstanding work, the *Bṛihat-saṁhitā* (*The Great Compendium*), he describes the motions and conjunctions of celestial bodies and their significance as omens.

The classical period of ancient Indian astronomy is considered to have ended with Brahmagupta who wrote the *Brahma-siddhānta,* in AD 628, and the *Khaṇḍakhadyaka,* a practical treatise on astronomical calculations, in AD 664. Aryabhaṭa's new epicyclic theory, and his postulates regarding the sphericity of the earth, its rotation upon its axis and revolution around the sun, as well as his formulae for the determination of the physical parameters of various celestial bodies (such as the diameters of the earth and the moon), and the prediction of eclipses and the correct length of the year by means of mathematical calculation, were significant achievements which anticipated and agree with the modern ideas. Aryabhaṭa also gave the first fundamental definition of trigonometric functions and was responsible for pointing out the importance of zero.

*Astronomical computation, based on the Sarvatabhadra Yantra, composed of nine fields, each of which represents an aspect of the universe. Kangra, Himachal Pradesh, c. 18th century. Ink and gouache on paper.*

The science of mathematics was closely allied to astronomy. To ensure accurate predictions, astronomical data had to be compiled on the basis of sophisticated mathematical calculations, and the ancient Indians devised an efficient system of computing so that they could deal with highly complex astronomical calculations. Modern numerical script and methods of computing originated primarily from Indian sources and were based on the combination of two fundamental factors, the place-value given to the digits and the zero-sign. Ancient Hindu mathematicians recognized number as both abstract and concrete, and were, consequently, well acquainted with the numerical quantity of objects and spatial extension, necessary to develop algebra. They posited the notions of 'possession' and 'debt' quantitatively to discriminate positive from negative in order to concretize the existence of opposite quantities. They also developed a wide application of word numerals as well as symbols and arithmetical signs. In this system, astronomical tables were condensed in verse and numerals were expressed by means of objects, concepts, and so on. Thus, the number one could be denoted by the moon or earth; two by any pair (eyes, hands, etc.); zero by the sky, void, etc. This method was predominantly used to connote large numbers in astronomical works. For greater concision, the use of chronograms was later replaced by an alphabetical system of notation which was sometimes applied to descriptive astronomy.

Indian mathematicians have long worked with number of the order of billions, even conceiving of infinity as a unit. The smallest measure of time mentioned by the Indian astronomers is the truṭi, 1/33750 second. The unit of time required for the passage of the sun over an atomic object is mathematically calculated in the *Siddhānta-śiromaṇi* to be 17,496,000,000 paramāṇus; paramāṇus,

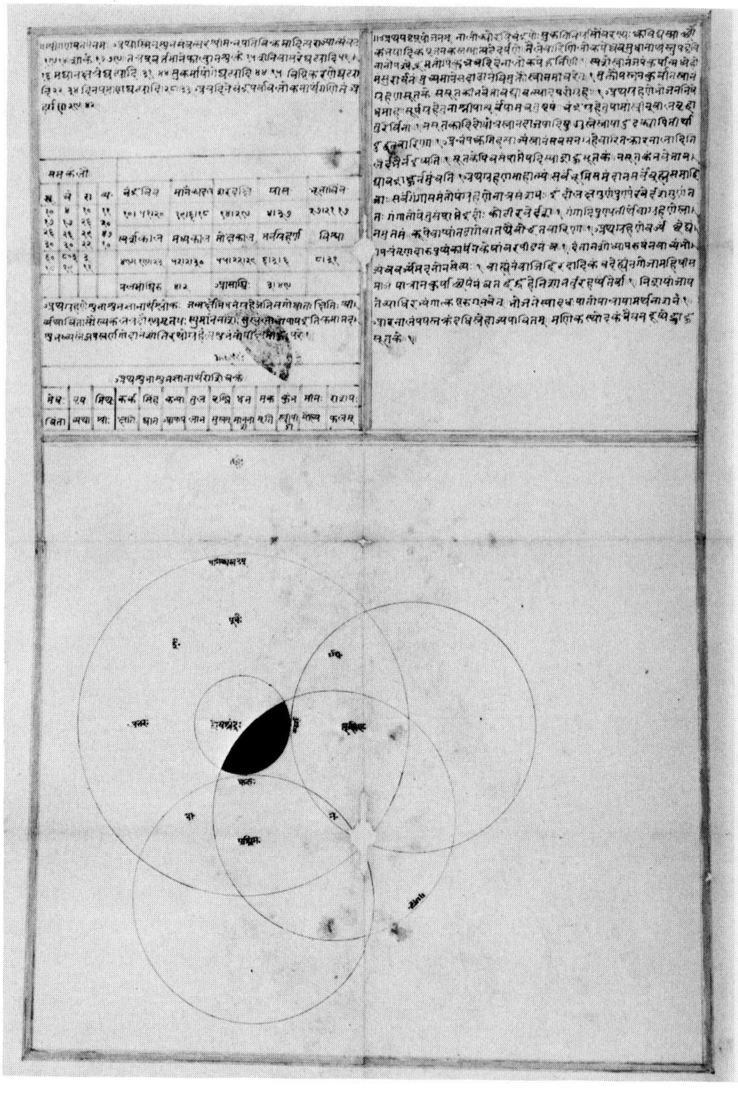

*Astronomical diagram used to ascertain the mean position of a planet. Rajasthan, c. 18th century. Ink and colour on paper.*

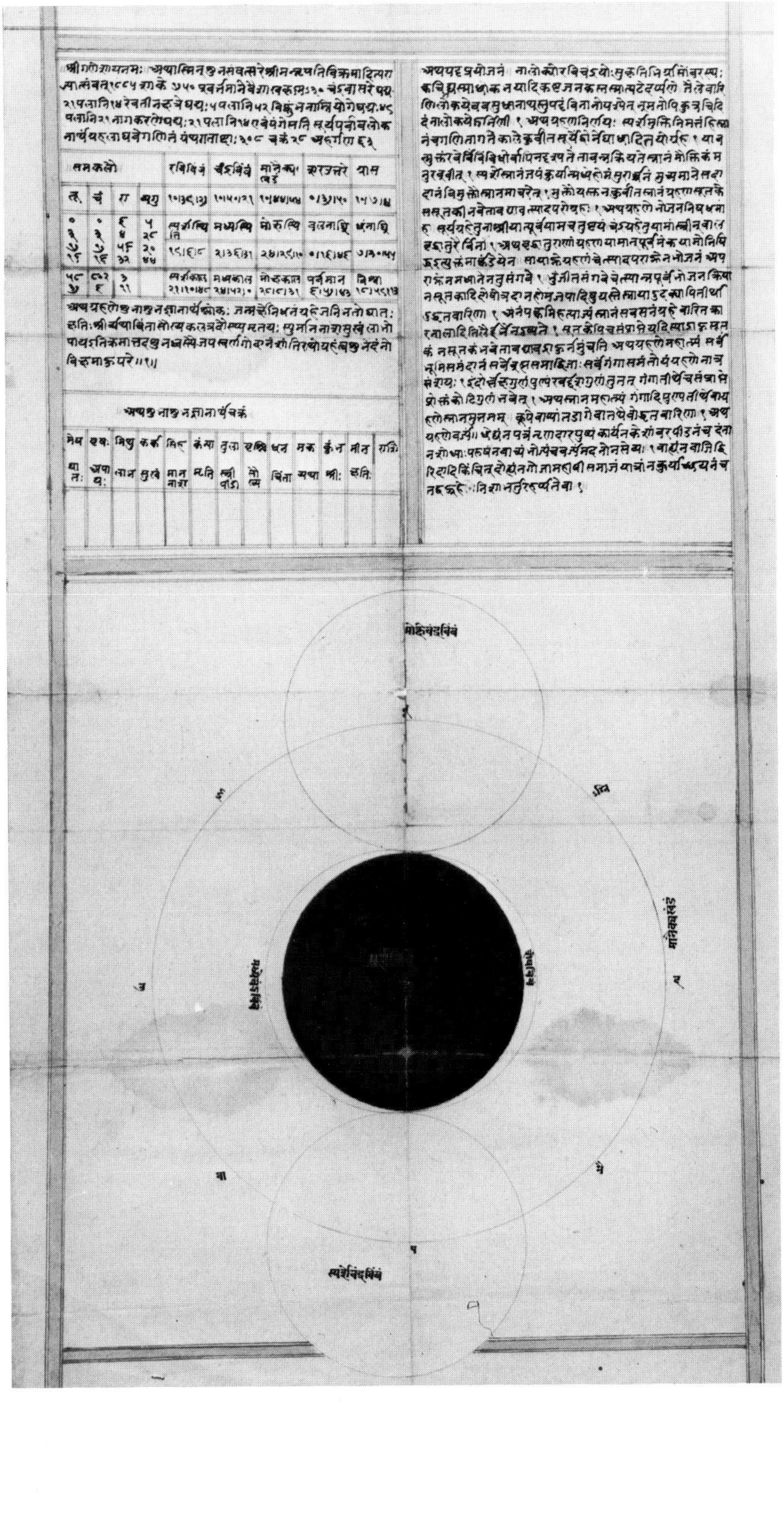

*Solar orb. An astronomical chart used to determine the sun's altitude, zenith, distance and declination, principally for ascertaining correct hours for rituals. Rajasthan, c. 18th century. Ink and colour on paper.*

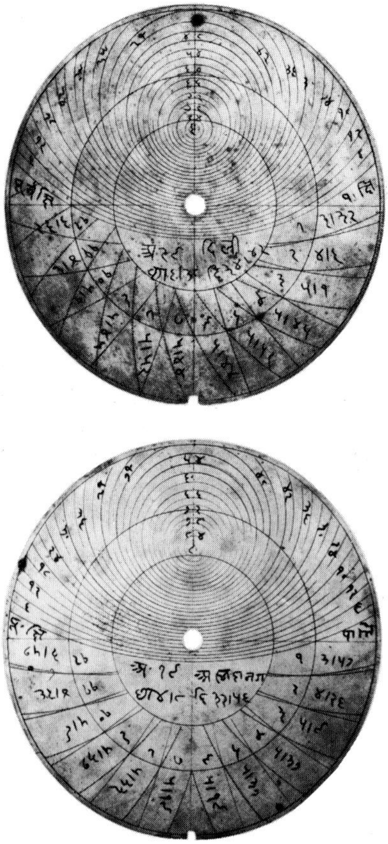

*Astrolabes. The two discs or tablets are engraved with azimuth circles, hour circles for various latitudes, etc. Jaipur, Rajasthan, c. 18th century. Brass.*

'extreme atoms', are generally measured as being between 1/1,000,000 to 1/349525 inch.

Mathematical units of time were considered an integrated category for recording observations of a constellation correct to one second. There were three ranks of time. The first, cosmic or epochal time, is referred to the eternally recurring cosmic ages. The four ages, or yugas, are calculated to be in the order of ratio of 4:3:2:1, each of which precedes the other until the universal cataclysm. The first cosmic age, called Kṛita or Satya-yuga, is 1,728,000 solar years, the second, Tretā-yuga, is 1,296,000 solar years long, the third, Dvāpara-yuga, is 864,000 years long, and the last, Kali-yuga, the present age of mankind, is 432,000 solar years long. We are passing through the sixth millennium of the Kali-yuga, and so there are still about 427,000 years for it to run, after which the cycle will be renewed and the four ages will commence once again. The second range of time is the solar or lunar calendar which determines the days, weeks, months and seasons. The third rank, the smallest unit of duration, is horologic time. To achieve accuracy in calculation, the span of a day was converted into smallest atoms of time. Thus, a day is conceived of as lasting for 86,400 seconds and is further divided into 46,656,000,000 moments, a number arrived by the following time-scale: 1 day = 60 Ghatika (or 24 hours comprising 60 units of time); 1 Ghatika = 60 Vig-Ghatika; 1 Vig-Ghatika = 60 Lipta, 1 Lipta = 60 Vilipta; 1 Vilipta = 60 Para; 1 Para = 60 Tatpara; therefore, 1 day = 46,656,000,000 Tatpara or moments.

Among various methods to ascertain the mean position of a particular planet in its revolution, one of the most frequent of the Hindu calculations, known as the equation of the centre, is perhaps the most illuminating. The calculation entails considerable skill, but can be explained simply as being determined on the basis of assuming epicycles. The mean position of the planet is calculated in relation to the number of revolutions during a yuga, or age. In order to find the 'true place' of a planet certain epicyclic motions were assumed, that is, the planet was hypothesized as moving in a second circle whose centre is carried round the circumference of the mean circle. Errors were further corrected by obtaining results from combining two equations arrived at from two separate epicycles. They were the equation of conjunction (when two bodies have the same celestial longitude) and the equation of 'apsis' (the point of greatest or least distance from the central body). In this way the average is obtained by combining the results of these two equations and correction could compensate for discrepancy.

*Jaiprakāsh Yantra, the crest jewel of all yantras. The sun's position can be calculated by the shadow of the intersecting wires on its concave sides falling on its surface. Jaipur observatory, Rajasthan, 1728. Bronze.*

Extant astronomical charts were used to ascertain the sun's altitude and zenith distance and its declination; to find the declination of a planet or star; to find the degree of azimuth of a planet or star; to determine celestial latitudes and longitudes; to calculate position during eclipse. For the same purposes, astronomical observatories, or Yantras, were also built, at a comparatively later date, by Jai Singh II (AD 1699–1744). Their equipment included the mural quadrant, a meridional wall set in the plane of the meridian, sloping up to point to the North Pole, charts of the celestial sphere and a huge gnomon.

Astronomical findings greatly influence the whole gamut of tantric ritual. All practices, including the preparations of alchemical products, are preconditioned by time, planetary positions and the observance of the calendar. Astronomy also laid the theoretical foundation for the practical application of astrology, the science of the influence of the stars on human and terrestrial phenomena, which flourished in logical sequence to other disciplines.

## *Astrology*

Hindu astrology is predominantly an extension of astronomy, to such an extent that many ancient treatises on astronomy incorporate a section to astrology. The *Sūrya-Siddhānta* devotes a chapter to astrology, but two major works, *Bṛihad-jātaka* and *Laghu-jātaka,* which are ascribed to Varāha-Mihira, deal

*Hastakāra Yantra, with auspicious signs on the palms. Rajasthan, c. 18th century. Gouache on paper.*

exclusively with astrology. Many significant notions, such as the twelve signs of the zodiac, the seven days of the week, the division of the day, show a remarkable affinity to modern Western concepts; it is generally considered that a number of these topics are based on the Greek system.

The celestial sphere, with its infinite constellations, has always been a principal life-force in the Indian way of life in general and the tantric way in particular. Recourse is had to astrology for every conceivable operation, however trivial, from drawing a birth chart and making prognostications to setting out propitious months, days, hours and moments. The same method was used for a great enterprise or for casting a personal horoscope. It usually involves computation of time by mathematical calculation, from which the results of complex planetary combinations are drawn. In operation, it is so closely related to horometry that astrology became a system for the measurement of time in relation to the stellar and galactic rhythms and their interaction on behavioural patterns.

The practice of astrology was not concerned so much with esotericism as with the pragmatic aim of determining the fruitful results of any event. Every operation, it was believed, must have a favourable outcome, and one of the most powerful means of ensuring it is not to isolate the event but to integrate it with every mode and rhythm of life including those of the distant asterisms, or lunar mansions. This belief was based partly on the notion of micro-macro correspondence and partly on the persuasion that every object in nature, thought, matter, or action, radiates a certain degree of cosmic force; various cosmic forces must be combined in harmony and at the right moment if they are to interact favourably. A typical example is the tradition of pilgrimages, or yātrās, which are an important astrological subject and event in that it is desirable to commence such a journey at an auspicious hour. The *Yoga Yātrā* texts provide many astrological conjunctions which supply the proper and useful knowledge to make pilgrimage a success. A yātrā was recommended at specific positions of the 9 Nakshatras (lunar mansions), viz., Aśvini, Punarvasu, Anurādhā, Mṛigaśiras, Pushyā, Revatī, Hasta, Śrāvaṇā and Dhanisṭhā. In his *Bṛihat-Saṁhitā,* Varāha-Mihira devoted 1,100 verses to the subject and also composed important independent works, such as *Brihad Yoga Yātrā, Yoga Yātrā* and *Tikkānikā,* which deal exclusively with the same topic.

In calculating the precise 'time', many factors are taken into consideration, among which the most important ones are the conjunction of the planets, the lunar mansion, the fortnight (beginning with the new and full moon), the season, the day of the month and the exact time, or auspicious moment, known as muhūrta. (There are thirty propitious muhūrtas in a day and 10,800 in a year.) All these calculations are derived from the Indian almanac which lays out methodical combinations of days, months and years for registering astronomical and astrological phenomena. In India there are numerous calendars in use based on the data of ancient manuals, and much of the numerical data they provide has been corrected, made uniform and adapted in relation to up-to-date information based on observed facts.

The most significant hypothesis of astrology is that in the course of their natural rotation the planets release their magnetic force, which impinges upon the animate and inaminate world. We, in our human terms, describe these effects as the 'influence of the stars'. The range of influence, according to Hindu belief, is never caused by a single planet but is invariably the result of the effects of various planetary conjunctions including those of the twenty-eight lunar mansions or asterisms, called nakshastras, in the zodiacal belt. Each of the planets is in relationship with the zodiacal signs in septenarious, novenarious, duodenarious order. Their relative influence is understood as beneficent when they are in harmony and malific when in disharmony. Furthermore, Hindus, like the Greeks, have also assigned certain characteristics to each planet and fixed the maximum period of any particular planetary influence. Benjamin Walker summarizes these notions as follows:

The maximum span of a planet's influence is also rigidly determined according to astrological laws. The full extent of all planetary influences over a man is said to last 108 years. Out of this any man may be influenced by each planet for not more than a fixed number of years.

| | |
|---|---|
| Surya, the Sun, for wealth, fame, success | 6 years |
| Chandra, the Moon, for religion, philosophy, mysticism, writing, asceticism, madness | 15 years |
| Maṅgala, Mars, for warfare, strife, litigation, quarrels | 8 years |
| Budha, Mercury, for travels, business, agriculture, wealth | 17 years |
| Śani, Saturn, for worries, troubles, death, mourning, tragedy | 10 years |
| Bṛihaspati, Jupiter, for domination, power, authority, rule, justice | 19 years |
| Rāhu and Ketu, the ascending and descending nodes of the moon, for greed, anger, jealousy, defeat, setbacks | 12 years |
| Śukra, Venus, for pleasure, love, women, lust, and voluptuary delights | 21 years |

In theory, the maximum bad luck period possible for a man to have would be a succession of the worst aspects of Mars, Saturn and Rāhu, i.e., 30 years.[27]

A planet's strength is determined in relation to its place, direction, activity and time, and a planet in transit is spoken of as affected in nine ways: 'blazing' when it is in exaltation, 'at ease' when in its house, 'glad' when it is in its friend's house, 'quiet' in its auspicious position, 'powerful' when it is shining brightly, 'oppressed' when overwhelmed by another planet, 'frightened' when in depression, 'impaired' when its light is lost in sun's light, and 'malefic' when in the midst of negative force.

Indian astrology's main concerns are the range and influences of the twelve zodiac signs, the planets and the twelve astrological houses, of which the last is an important doctrine in the Indian system of casting horoscopes. Horoscopes are drawn in a square or a circle of twelve divisions, and are based on the lagna, or the sign rising on the horizon at the time of birth. Each of these houses indicates a specific function. A horoscope, however, is not an exact blueprint of an individual's future, but only forecasts the direction in which the events of his or her life might evolve.

Astrological principles were also used in gem therapy. Gems are regarded as reservoirs of the energy concentrated from cosmic rays. As crystallized products of invisible rays, gems have the magnetic power to transmit cosmic rays through space and, in this way, they are on a par with the planets. However the planets may influence the human body, gems also exert such power; as condensations of energy, they constitute benefic forces to counteract the effect of badly aspected planetary conjunctions, and thus each of the planets is assigned its corresponding gem. It is said that by wearing certain gems the negative influence of planets can be substantially reduced or abated.

Running parallel to astrology many different methods of divination, such as palmistry, different body signs, prognostication by observing the oneness in nature's phenomena, and others, were also practised, but astrology alone has withstood the weakening of time and is beginning to be considered as a science.

If we are to comprehend scientifically the relationship between extra-terrestrial radiations and environs and biological and human life, it is essential that we have a complete picture of the invisible forces at work. Science has only very recently discovered the electro-magnetic spectrum to which our naked eye is sensitive in a very limited way. The discovery of the earth's magnetosphere, with its various layers which act as a screen against solar and cosmic vibrations, is also recent. The 'Van Allen Zone' placed between 3,000 to 10,000 miles above the earth was discovered in 1958. Similarly, intense bursts of radio radiation from Jupiter were

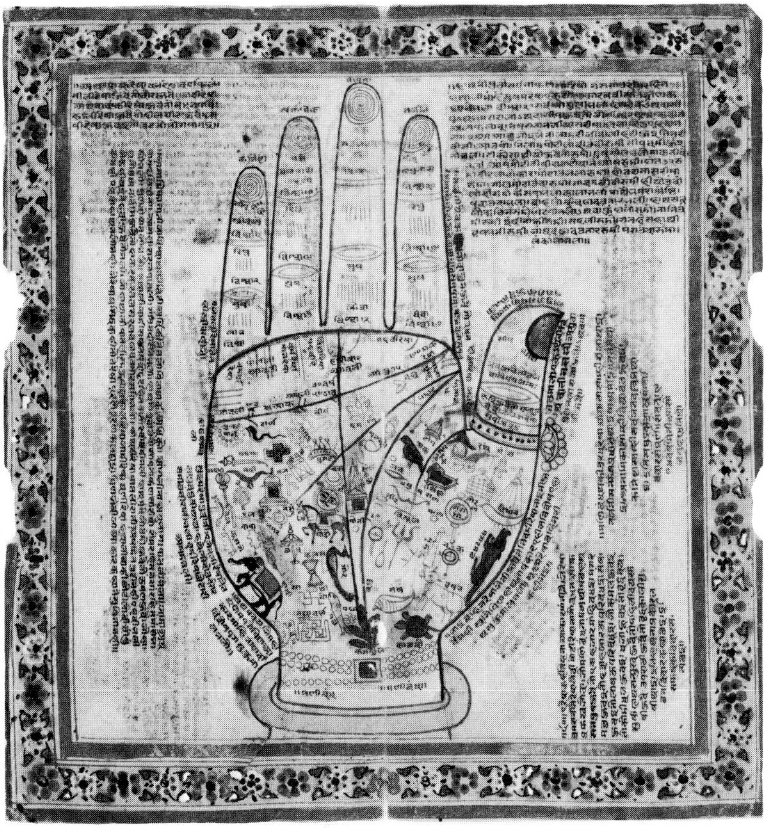

*Hastakāra Yantra. The auspicious signs on the palms indicate the integral relation between interplanetary rhythms and the human organism. Rajasthan, c. 18th century. Gouache on paper.*

recorded in 1954. Though science has made tremendous progress towards a clear-cut view of the vast panorama of cosmic vibrations, the unknown still eludes us. Nevertheless, evidence is increasing that shows that solar and lunar progressions influence many vital physiological functions, such as breathing and reproduction, in the human and animal species. A Czech scientist has established with statistical evidence that fertility periods of women can be determined on the basis of the sun and the moon's position in their birth charts. Solar clocks have been found to deter the migratory pattern of the birds, and lunar rhythms influence the movement of oysters. It has recently been proposed that astrological effects are based on wave patterns:

The universe, whether at cosmic, biological, or molecular level, is a complex of wave forms whose periodicity may range from nanoseconds to millions of years, and objects, events, people, nations and even planetary systems may be linked together in ways incomprehensible in terms of traditional astrology and physics, but explicitly discoverable through astrology.[28]

Such findings have gone a long way to give astrology an empirical footing.

## *The One*

Of all the varied formulations, one of the central concepts of Hindu thought which influenced the tantras considerably is the notion of a universal energy known as Prāṇa, the source of all the manifestation of various forces. All forces in the universe, all motion, attraction, even thought, are only different manifestations of Prāṇa. In the human body, its gross manifestation is the life-breath, and though Prāṇa is often misinterpreted as breath or air, it is something more. Breath is only one effect of Prāṇa; similarly, if Prāṇa were caused by air 'it would be possible for the dead man to breathe'. Prāṇa acts upon the air, not the air upon it. Prāṇa, then, is a vital bio-motor force which governs and manipulates the functions of the body. While this vital principle exists in the human organism, life continues; with Prāṇa's departure, life ceases in that human body. All living organisms, from a speck of protoplasm to plants to animals, are animated by the combined activity of Prāṇa, the life-force, and matter. Though all systems of Hindu thought recognized the potency of Prāṇa, the adepts of tantra-yoga elaborated the whole science of metamorphosis of Prāṇa and applied it as an instrument to arouse the latent psychic force in the human body. Prof. C. F. von Weizsäcker, the eminent physicist, writes:

> The concept of prāṇa is not necessarily incompatible with our physics. Prāṇa is spatially extended and vitalizing. Hence above all it is moving potency. The quantum theory designates something not entirely remote from this with the term 'probability amplitude'. The relationship may become clearer when we consider the possibility as a strictly futuristic concept, that is as the quantified expression of that toward which the flow of time is pressing to evolve.[29]

In the cosmic hierarchy, however, Prāṇa is neither the ultimate nor is it a radical construct; it is a derivative of an ultimate reality. The fundamental thesis of tantrism is that though the universe evolves out of the interacting forces of two principles, in the ultimate analysis both these emanate from the One. Behind the entire phenomenal world, matter and thought, there is the Eternal One, without a second. This monistic principle is all-pervasive: all things, physical and biological, are finite versions of the One. The nature of that reality is described in voluminous terminology, negating all attributes and relations, yet its real nature eludes description.

The One, therefore, should not be confused with any theistic expression, like the notion of a benign father or a super-earthly

Being residing in heaven. The real nature of the One is that it is attributeless, undefinable yet omnipresent, and at best it admits only of approximate explanations. It can be summarized as an eternal continuum of extremely ultra-subtle cosmic reality which gives rise to the grosser elements in nature. In tantra, it is termed as Parā-Prakṛiti. The quasi-monistic form of Prakṛiti, or Śakti, appears in rich ritualistic imagery, but its real nature is more than empiric existence: though it embraces everything, it transcends all. Into this primordial reality which bridges the cleavages of dualism, all things return.

As this century approaches its end, contemporary physical researches tend more and more to demonstrate that what we term gross matter in the world at large is simply an appearance of a more refined substance. In its quest for unity, science is drifting towards a monistic explanation of the universe. Classical physics regarded mass and energy as two independent realities. The theory of relativity resolved the dualism and demonstrated that mass and energy are proportional and interchangeable. The diversity of phenomena is attributed to the mere rearrangement of a single common 'essence' which scientists have called energy. Although modern science has dematerialized the atom and shown that it is divisible, still the smallest conceivable ultimate entity, the neutron with zero mass and no electric charge or magnetic field, cannot be divided further. Heisenberg's comments allude to the paradoxical notions of the illusoriness of the basic particle (atom) when he states that any attempt to explain it in visual terms is to 'misinterpret' it: 'All qualities of the atom of modern physics are *derived*; it has no immediate and direct physical properties at all, i.e., every type of visual conception we might wish to design is *eo ipso* faulty.'[30] Thus we find that on the cosmic and sub-atomic level, the property called 'mass' turns out to be an illusion. Matter is reduced to energy, energy to swarms of wavicles and vibrations in multi-dimensional space. Indeed, atoms, stars, comets, meteors, the moving galaxies, the vast universe of waves are shifting configurations of the same underlying reality. Yet one question remains: what is the essence of this mass-energy substance which vibrates? The scientist's answer is no less puzzling that the metaphysician's, for the fundamental substance is the 'unknown'. The unknown has been described by the scientists as the 'psi-field', an abstract non-material field which defies definition. While not calling it Parā-Prakṛiti, scientists have found that only one substance, or a single unified principle whose nature is equally elusive, is the *causa sui* of the world.

# *RITUAL*

In the preceding discussion, all the factors related to the basic doctrine of tantra, its metaphysics, art and science, are supplemental to this central feature – ritual, or the spiritual science of self-culture. Metaphysics, art and science are the edifice of knowledge which provide the origin and goal of tantric sādhanā; ritual provides the corpus of means. Ritual is based on two basic and interdependent presuppositions: first, that the self is potentially divine and can be developed illimitably; second, and following as a corollary from the first, that reality or the Absolute (Śiva-Śakti), whose inherent nature is joy (ānanda), is the most fundamental and desirable goal to seek. At one pole is the self or individual aspiring to be free or enlightened; at the other pole is the goal. Between the poles is the intermediate state of reaching for the goal by means of effective techniques – this is ritual. Thus ritual here can be defined as a 'link' connecting the individual psyche with the universal noumena. Tantra offers an operational model for psychic liberation and outlines an effective *modus operandi* within its defined conspectus, and tantric ritual, therefore, should be considered a key factor of psychic evolution.

In a theoretical exposition such as this, the purpose is to expound the practical psycho-physical prescriptions of ritual and their significance. This means we are obliged to discuss in terms of concepts and abstractions what in reality is a dynamic translogical unitary experience. It should, therefore, be borne in mind that tools of language cannot do full justice to the actual experience of living in the ritual. The real search begins when language ends and logic-oriented positivism is dispensed with: 'Darkness is not dispensed with by mentioning the word "lamp"' (*Kulārṇava Tantra*). Just so, words are impotent to dispel the darkness of the ego. Self-realization springs from an inner experience – a feeling-sense of something which can never be articulated in words. Tantric ritual is thus both an aid and a psychological experiment which sensitizes and revitalizes the inner experience for higher spiritual awakening. Dr A. V. Gerasimov, a tantric scholar of the

*The supreme Goddess as the Void, with projection-space for Her image. Andhra Pradesh, 19th century. Bronze.*

Moscow Institute of Oriental Studies, aptly observes: 'But what explains its persistence in Indian life is its greater awareness of human psychology.'

Tantra's exclusive concern with practical techniques of self-enlightenment over theory and speculation has given sādhanā (spiritual discipline) a unique place of importance in the whole system. A vast body of tantric literature concerns itself with the systematic attuning of the body and psychic forces for a gradual unfolding, so that the tantras are often considered a way of action, a way of life, a way of joy for the attainment of desired ends. Tantric rituals are an internally consistent code of practices which follow logically from its belief system. They have definite symbolic meanings: though all rituals are performed as symbolic acts, they have the power to bring about alterations in consciousness and therefore when they are efficient they become sources of manifestation of that power. In tantra, ritual assumes the status of much more than mere obeisance to the deity; it calls for unification, an internalization of the personal and specific towards the timeless, abstract and universal. In this way, rituals in tantra become an operational concept uniting theory and practice. Its merit depends upon its correct application, for only then can it become a verifiable experience of a definite state of consciousness.

The various rituals generally practised are basically consciousness-amplifying techniques in so far as they represent psycho-physical experiences touching every aspect of our senses; but when they are practised mechanically for material gains or results, the rites may not necessarily lead to higher results.

A distinction can be made between a single ritual act and a sādhanā. A ritual technique performed in daily life may be artificially separated from the whole discipline and the entire process may remain value-free without being bounded by any specific code, whereas sādhanā implies a total spiritual discipline comprising many concurrent practices of which a particular ritual forms an integral part of the whole belief system.

If tantra is freed from its cult-oriented associations, that is, if not pursued for its wider goals of sādhanā but for its own sake as a device of expansion of consciousness, it can become a key to modern needs.

There is a multiplicity of techniques employed in tantric rituals through the medium of sound (mantra), form (yantra), psycho-physical postures and gestures (nyāsas and mudrās), offerings of flowers, incense and ritual ingredients, breath-control (prāṇā-yama), sexo-yogic practice (āsana), concentration (dhyāna).

These various forms of inner illumination are not mutually exclusive but interpenetrate one another. They are always performed in concert so that, for instance, a single ritual act may include the use of mantra, mudrā, āsana, prāṇāyama, dhyāna, drawing all senses into participation.

Ritual forms can be external as well as internal. External media are stimulus-bound, that is, their mediation is only possible through externally symbolic objects such as yantra, nyāsa, mudrā, or offerings. Contrariwise, the internal orientation is stimulus-free; it does not have recourse to any external symbols but requires an active participation of the aspirant so that he is receptive to a programmed spontaneity achieved through formless media such as the recitation of mantras and concentration.

Tantric sādhanā varies in relation to the end to be achieved, but the prime aim of its major ritual practices is to accelerate the latent forces already in the human organism for a peak experience of joy and unity. The final stage cannot be achieved without the practice of several categories of technique, each of which serves an intermediate end of sādhanā. They form a group of ritual composites which bring together a number of inputs, each of them serving a definite purpose. The sādhaka should not deliberately omit even a single one of these techniques, as they constitute the necessary preliminaries for the final goal. They are:

*Tantric yogi, Lākshmaṇa Temple, Khajuraho. Meditation is perfect concentration of mind. An appropriate āsana, or yogic posture, creates physical and mental equilibrium.* AD *1059–87. Stone.*

(1) *Purification and sanctification:* The first step of deconditioning a heavily imprinted and programmed attitude towards one's body consists of a hypothetical transformation of the gross body into the subtle body, so that the obstacles besetting it are lifted. The body is mobilized by physical training and the use of bodily postures in order that it may consciously emerge from the inert state and become 'cosmicized', 'purified' and 'sanctified' in the image of the divinity. The purification may operate on the mental level when the impurities obstructing the subtle bodies are removed by rituals such as nyāsa, āsana-śuddhi, bhūta-śuddhi with the help of proper intonation of mantras.

(2) *Identification and internalization:* This step consists of the experience of integration, a condition in which, by an intimate unconscious relationship, the initiate becomes the 'thing'. Identification consists in an introjective process as a consequence of which the object of worship is treated as a part of the self. The rituals which promote identification are mudrās, meditation, visualization, mantric concentration, prāṇāyama, etc.

(3) *Harmony and equilibrium:* In harmony lies the precondition

of realization. Harmony is the intermediate equalizing point between two extremes, a bridge between opposites. It is to be sought between the higher and lower energy centres, between the positively-charged solar and the negatively-charged lunar currents, between the plus and minus forces manifesting as male and female, conscious and unconscious, in the body. One might say that a balance is to be attained at several levels and planes of human consciousness. On the physical plane the gross body should be regulated by physical postures; on the mental and psychological levels, the internal vital processes are harmonized by the regulation of breath, the cerebral centre by the repetition of mantric sound, and the variously directed mental operations by the practice of concentration, meditation. The greater the synergistic fusion of polarized energies within us, the greater the experiences of unity.

(4) *Unity-merging:* By balancing polarized interaction, a third quality is born: unity. Unity can also be described as indivisibility, or becoming a whole after the process of self-actualization has been completed. With the experiential awareness of the peak state and of the complementary interplay of the plus and minus forces in the body, the adept achieves his *summum bonum.*

## *ORIENTATION AND PREPARATION*

## *The Guru*

An essential prerequisite to the world of tantric sādhanā is the guidance of a competent spiritual preceptor, the guru, who can initiate the aspirant into the correct application of methods commensurate with his temperament and competence. Just as an unknown journey becomes easier with the help of a competent guide, in the same manner the best way to commence the spiritual journey is with the help of a guru. As cosmonauts undergo severe physical and mental disciplines under strict observation before their journey into the unknown depths of space, similarly an adept has to undergo a long and arduous process of training and guidance for the gradual unfolding of his potentialities.

A guru is one who has already lived through the discipline and has experience of various stages of spiritual development in his own life. In ascending order, the first step in initiation is the mantra given by a guru, Paśyācāra (ordinary); this is followed by, second, Vīrācāra (rājasik); third, Mahāvidyās (higher knowledge); and finally, Brahmayoga – the highest, knowledge of the Absolute. All

*Brahmā, reverently begging his spiritual vehicle, Haṁsa, the goose or swan, to bestow upon him supreme knowledge. Rajasthan, c. 19th century. Gouache on paper.*

these degrees of initiation may be imparted by different gurus each competent for one degree only. It may, however, happen that a single guru of high order is competent to impart the secret knowledge to all levels of sādhanā.

The guru sometimes indicates the ways and means along the path by his silence or casual words; the aspirant must discover for himself what he needs. Many meditative and ritual techniques are difficult and often dangerous, and require extensive orientation under experienced guidance. The guru's aim is always to observe

*Symbolic marks painted on wooden manuscript cover. Orissa, c. 19th century.*

the aspirant and the effect of the 'how' and 'what' of techniques on him and to identify when the effects of the training are beginning to be felt. On the other hand, it is imperative that an aspirant should not turn into a blind follower of a guru but have an open mind, a fact testified to by many instances of the guru-disciple relationship throughout Indian spiritual tradition. An old proverb says that the guru will appear when the sādhaka is ready. No guru, however, can help a sādhaka unless he helps himself by his own efforts and willingness. Having learnt what he can learn, the sādhaka should be prepared to question and if necessary introduce experimental verifications by working on himself. In this context the role of a guru may be compared to a 'therapeutic alliance' or a task-oriented collaboration between patient and therapist in an emotionally involving relationship. In this case, however, the adept is not 'sick' but has the mental preparedness to go beyond the defined modalities of his being. He is searching for an experiential realization of his innermost subconscious self, in which he has had a glimpse of a wider and truer reality. The task of the initiate is not merely to grasp the mechanics of various techniques involved in rituals but 'how to be'. It is precisely when the adept moves beyond the arena of utility that he is said to have the correct mental disposition.

A seeker remains a disciple as long as he has not achieved his spiritual goal. Once he has attained what he has been seeking, he is 'born anew'. The proverbial relationship to the guru as initiary master ceases, since there is no need for further instruction of, guidance.

*Kuṇḍalinī-yoga. A painting illustrating various practices of Kuṇḍalinī-yoga around the central Female Principle, Śakti. Kangra, c. 18th century. Gouache on paper.*

## *Initiation*

Before the adept can participate in the whole gamut of tantric ritual, it is essential that a consecration, in a ceremony known as dīkshā, or spiritual initiation, take place. The word dīkshā comes from the Sanskrit root do- (dyati), meaning to cut or destroy; in the initiation all negative forces are destroyed in order to gain the supreme state of existence. Dīkshā involves one-to-one interpersonal contact between a guru and a disciple. The most popular form of this ritual is initiation with the guru giving the aspirant a personal mantra, known as mantra-dīkshā. The desired guru selects an auspicious day and hour, and in certain instances the horoscope of the prospective aspirant is matched with that of the guru to determine precisely the time when the mantra should be imparted. The guru also ascertains the aspirant's 'ishṭa-devatā', the chosen deity or the divine aspect which is in consonance with his personality, so that by concentrating on it the aspirant will be in rhythm with that deity while attaining unity. The guru normally sits facing the east and the disciple sits in the lotus posture close to him. In order to purify the process of initiation the guru first recites his basic mantra and invokes his own 'chosen deity' and then three times whispers the dīkshā-mantra into the disciple's right ear. The mantra must be kept secret and it should not be divulged; indeed, it is considered that even a written mantra loses its impact. Once the mantra has been given, the basic stage of mantra initiation ends.

## *INSTRUMENTS OF TRANSFORMATION*

## *Mantra*

The oldest and perhaps most widely used concentrative technique is the mantric sound. Mantra is primarily a concentrated 'thought form' composed of nuclear syllables based on the esoteric properties believed to be inherent in sound vibrations. Tantra has developed a system of sound equations which may vary from simple to complex, exerting its power not so much through expressing meaning as we normally understand it but more deeply, through its emphasis on a 'phonic element'. For example: the vocables Hrīṃ, Śrīṃ, Krim, Phaṭ, which are found throughout the tantric texts, may seem meaningless, unintelligible and irrelevant to the non-initiate, but to the initiate they have positive symbolic connotations. Whether recited audibly or inaudibly they run through most of the rituals like an uninterrupted symphony. The recitation of the mantra without understanding its proper meaning or the mantra technique is an exercise, and it is said to be inert.

According to Sāradātilaka, mantras may be divided into male, female and neuter; masculine mantras end in 'hūṃ' and 'phaṭ', the female in 'svāhā', and neuter mantras end with 'namaḥ'. The power of a particular mantra lies in a set of inter-connected factors: its pattern of sound waves and the mode of its proper intoning. Generally, it is considered that the mantra is efficacious only when it is 'received' from the mouth of the guru by his disciple. A mantra thus 'awakened' activates vibration channels and produces certain superconscious feeling states which aid the disciple in his sādhanā.

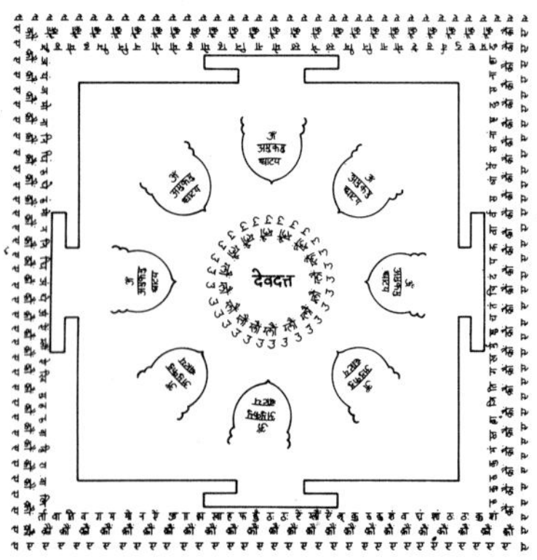


*Yantra with mantra.*

The very sound of a mantra or a combination of them has the capacity to arouse the divine forms or their energies. Each divinity possesses a bīja mantra, or seed syllable, which is its equivalent. Thus the bīja mantra is the root vibration or atomized form of sound representing the essential nature of divinity.

The monosyllabic bīja mantra is to tantric sādhanā what a seed is to a tree: just as the seed possesses the potential of the tree, in the same way a single sound can contain the sum-total of divinity in its vibration. The term bījākshara, 'seed syllable', consists of two words: bīja, meaning seed or germ, and akshara, which connotes both 'syllable' and 'imperishable'. The true bījākshara ends within an anusvāra, or upturned semicircle with a dot in its centre, and in romanized transliteration the anusvāra is indicated with a dot above or below the letter m. The anusvāra is described as a continuous nasal sound without any modification and is an adaptation of an 'unpronounceable vibration'. The dot in the anusvāra represents the bindu, and is the visible form of Śiva-Śakti. Hans-Ulrich Rieker has made an illuminating observation:

*Period (dot).* It does not stand like a tombstone at the end of a Sanskrit sentence, but is the sign for vocal vivification. The dot above the consonant (which is always connected with a vowel) changes a dull ka into a rich kam or kang, a ta into tam or tang, pa into pam, and so on, through all the consonants. It adds vibration to the dull sound. It is especially significant that it raises o from the chest vibration to the Oṃ sound in the head, the higher sphere. Thus it raises the physical sound to the chakra of consciousness, the ājñā chakra between the eyebrows, and gives it meaning. In this way, the dot becomes the symbol for *sense.*[31]

The seed mantra is considered to contain the entire potentiality of full significance of a doctrine. A treatise running to several thousand verses, for instance, may be condensed into few stanzas, and then summarized into a few lines, and finally abbreviated to a bīja mantra which, though the smallest sound unit, will still retain the full power of the doctrine. The manifested bīja mantra creates cerebral vibration, and it is believed that even after the repetition of a seed mantra has ceased, its effect continues. It is further held that the power a particular bīja mantra generates can be stored up in the cerebral centre and activated at will.

*The seed-syllable Oṃ.*

Oṃ, the most powerful of all sounds, is the source of all mantras and a key to realization. It is made up of three sounds, a, u, m, which symbolically represent the three ultimate tendencies or guṇas – creation, preservation, dissolution – and encompass all the knowledge of the different planes of the universe. It is referred to as the 'quintessence of the entire cosmos', 'monarch of all sounded things', 'mother of vibrations' and 'key to eternal wisdom and power'. These are a few examples of seed mantras and their meanings:

*Hrīṃ:* bīja mantra of the goddess Bhuvaneśvarī, the female energy of the spheres. According to *Varada Tantra,* H = Śiva, R = Śakti, I = transcendental illusion; the nasal sound m = progenitor of the universe.

*Krīṃ:* Kālī-bīja representing the power over creation and dissolution; recited mainly for the conquest of limitations. K = Kālī, R = absolute, I = transcendent power of illusion; m = primal sound (*Varada Tantra*).

*Śrīṃ:* Lakshmī-bīja; represents the female energy of abundance and multiplicity; recited for the attainment of worldly joys and gains. S = transcendent divinity of abundance, R = wealth, I = fulfilment; m = limitlessness.

*Klīṃ:* bīja mantra of the procreative desire of Śiva as Kāma; represents joy, bliss, pleasure. K = transcendental desire, L = lord of space, I = satisfaction; m = pleasure and pain.

In a similar way, Kroṃ stands for Śiva, Aiṃ for Sarasvatī, Eṃ for yoni, Phaṭ for dissolution, and so on.

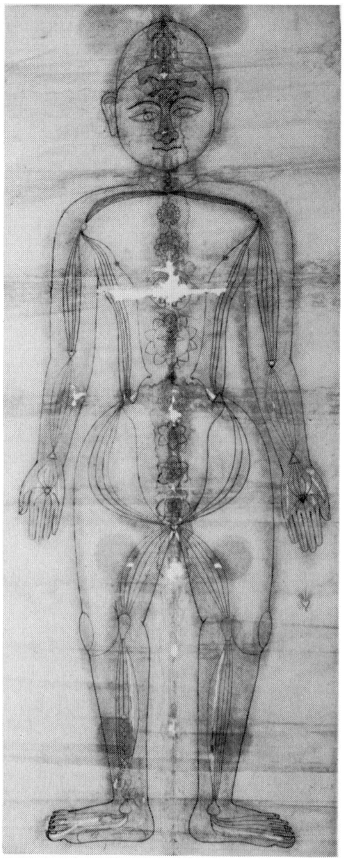

*Chakras in the etheric body. Rajasthan, 18th century. Ink on paper. Running parallel to the organic body of the yogi is the cosmocized etheric body with its astral and vital currents. This invincible and intangible body serves to provide cosmic cross-points at several junctures through the body's seven psychic centres and two main nerve channels, Iḍā on the left side and Piṅgala on the right. The yogi can terminate their separate functions by reconciling them into the central channel, Sushumṇā.*

The bīja mantras are primarily intended for japa, or repetition. They are repeated and counted on the beads of a rosary which consists of 12, 18, 28, 32, 64, 108 or more seeds. The technique of japa involves the synchronization of a sound, the number of rhythmic repetitions and the sound's symbolic meaning. Mantras which are not audibly repeated but are internal are called ajapā-japa; they generate ceaseless vibrations of a monosyllabic sound. The mantric sound of ajapā-japa is assimilated in such a way that with constant practice it is produced effortlessly with the individual's breathing in and out. Incessant repetition of the mantra gathers so powerful a momentum that repetition of a phonic sound like haṃ-sa can make the sound vibrate in an inverted form, i.e.. 'sa-ham' or 'so-ham', 'this am I', or 'I am He.' It is only when all these factors are in accord that a favourable concomitance is achieved.

The main function of the mantra is identification with or internalization of the divine form or its energy. The bīja mantra, when repeated in accordance with the rules of the doctrine, serves as a means of anchoring or centering auditory perception and is a

*Painting representing yogic āsanas. Āsanas, divided into two principal groups, either facilitate concentration or are performed for physical well-being. The one represented here is Pāśanimudra, with the legs wrapped around the back of the head (pāsha), used mainly as a physical posture. Rajasthan, c. 19th century. Gouache on paper.*

tangible 'support' to concentration that helps to attain continuity in awareness. The practice of japa, or silent repetition of the mantra, brings outwardly-directed and diffuse mental currents together in a point or centre. With the condensation of the power-field the sought divine form is, as it were, drawn towards the aspirant until it is totally internalized.

## *Body consciousness and body language*

Tantrikas regard the body as the basis of individual identity: 'He who realizes the truth of the body can then come to know the truth

IX *A practising Tantrika from northern India with the Saiva's symbol on his forehead.*

X *Chakras or psychic centres in the etheric body of the yogi. The energy centres are points of contact between the psychic and the physical body. Of the thirty chakras mentioned in the texts, the principal seven from bottom upwards are: Mūlādhāra, Svādishṭhāna, Maṇipūra, Anāhata, Viśuddha, Ājñā and finally Sahasrāra, conceived to be above the head.*

XI *A Tantrika aspirant in the foothills of the Himālayas.*

XII *Hanumān Yantra. Diagram of Hanumān, the great devotee of Lord Rāma in all his magnificence and power, with inscriptions and symbols. Rajasthan,* c. *18th century. Ink and colour on paper.*

of the universe' (*Ratnasāra*). When the adept accepts his subjectivity as a thinking, feeling, willing individual, he does not limit himself to mental concepts but lives in an existential awareness of his concrete physical entity which is animated in concert with the psychic forces moving it.

In tantras, the body is considered an assemblage of five kośas, or 'sheaths', in order of decreasing density. They are, first, the tangible physical body (Annamaya); the second is life breath, the sheath of vital air (Prāṇamaya); the third and the fourth sheaths, still more subtle, are the cognitive processes (Manomaya and Vijñānamaya); finally, the sheath of bliss (Ānandamaya), the subtlest of all, is identified with the eternal element of joy in man. Thus, the psychic and physical are interdependent since each makes the other more possible.

It is possible to be alienated from the body – to be unaware of its potencies, to reject and negate it completely – but its fullest appreciation will call for an awareness of it as a fact of nature. Since the body is the link between the terrestrial and cosmic, it is as it were a 'theatre', in which the psycho-cosmic drama is enacted. A positive and receptive attitude towards the body is a precondition to sādhanā. The adept must identify with his body and transform it, for his body is the concrete expression of his psyche characterized by its own rhythm and structure. As a material extension of psychic expression the body glows, radiates and animates in the joy of being itself. It is not surprising, therefore, that the tantrikas evolved a system of psycho-physical culture, comprising various kinds of physical posture and gestural body techniques, a body language to render the body obedient to the will in order to animate ritual.

## *Nyāsa*

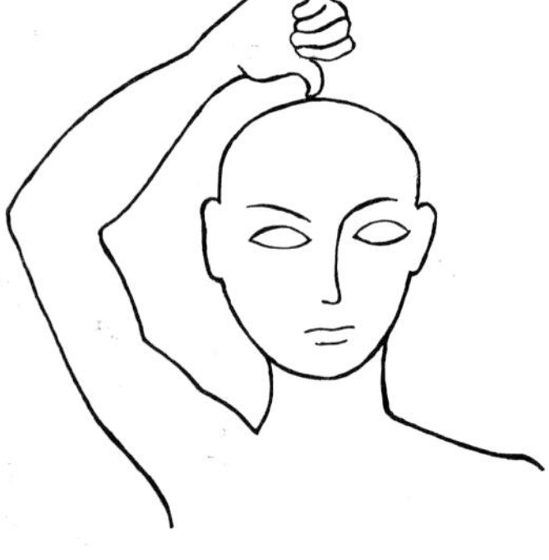

*Nyāsa.*

In the ritual known as nyāsa, parts of the body are sensitized by placing the fingertips and palms of the right hand on various sensory awareness zones. A common practice is to accompany each placing of the fingers on the body with a mantra, so that with the mantra's powerful resonance the adept may gradually project the power of divinity into his own body. The tantrikas believe that the flesh must be 'awakened' from its dormancy, and this rite symbolically 'puts' the power of the vast pantheon of divinities into the various organs of the body. The most popular form of nyāsa, known as saḍanga-nyāsa, is performed by touching various parts of the body in the following manner:

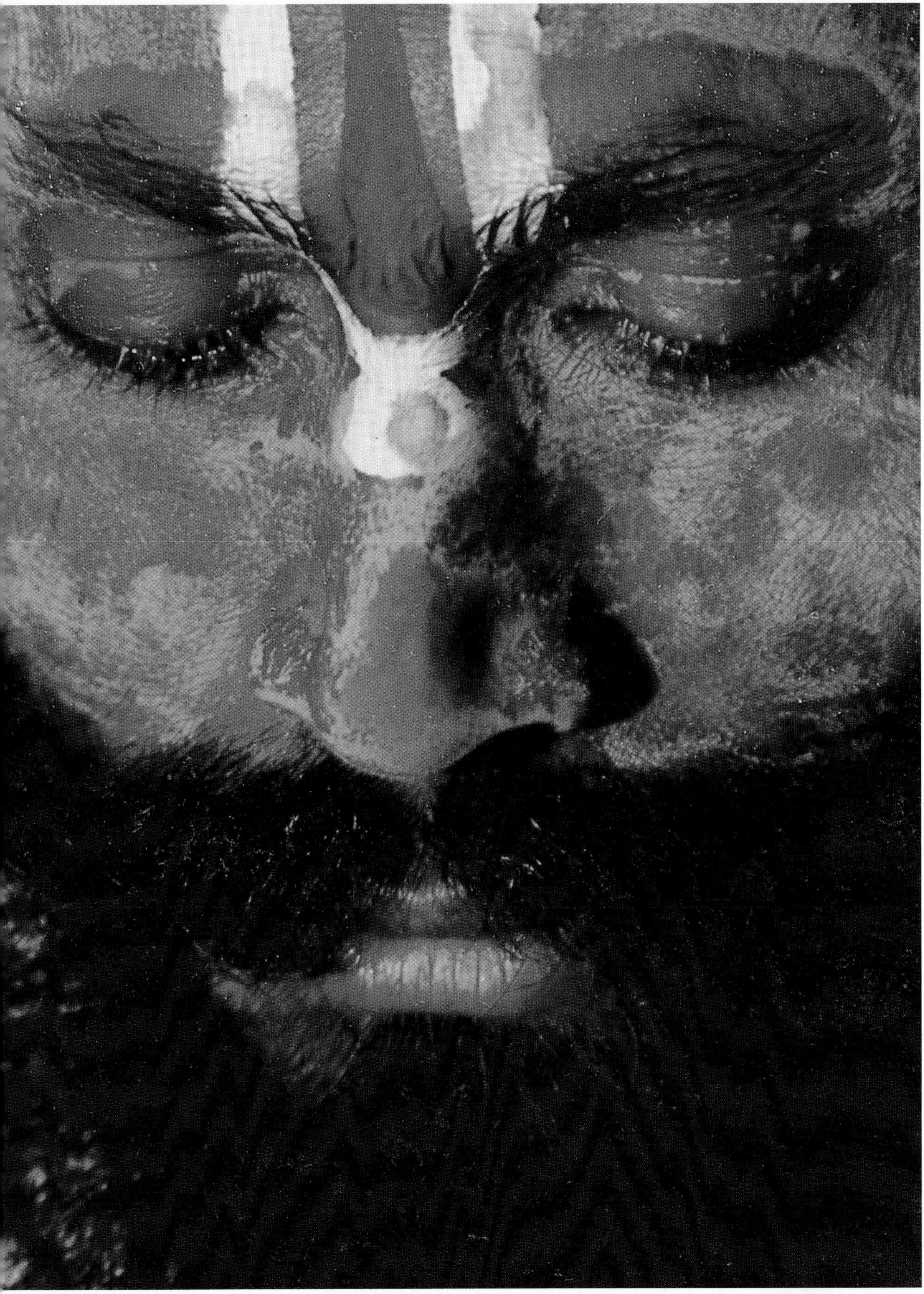

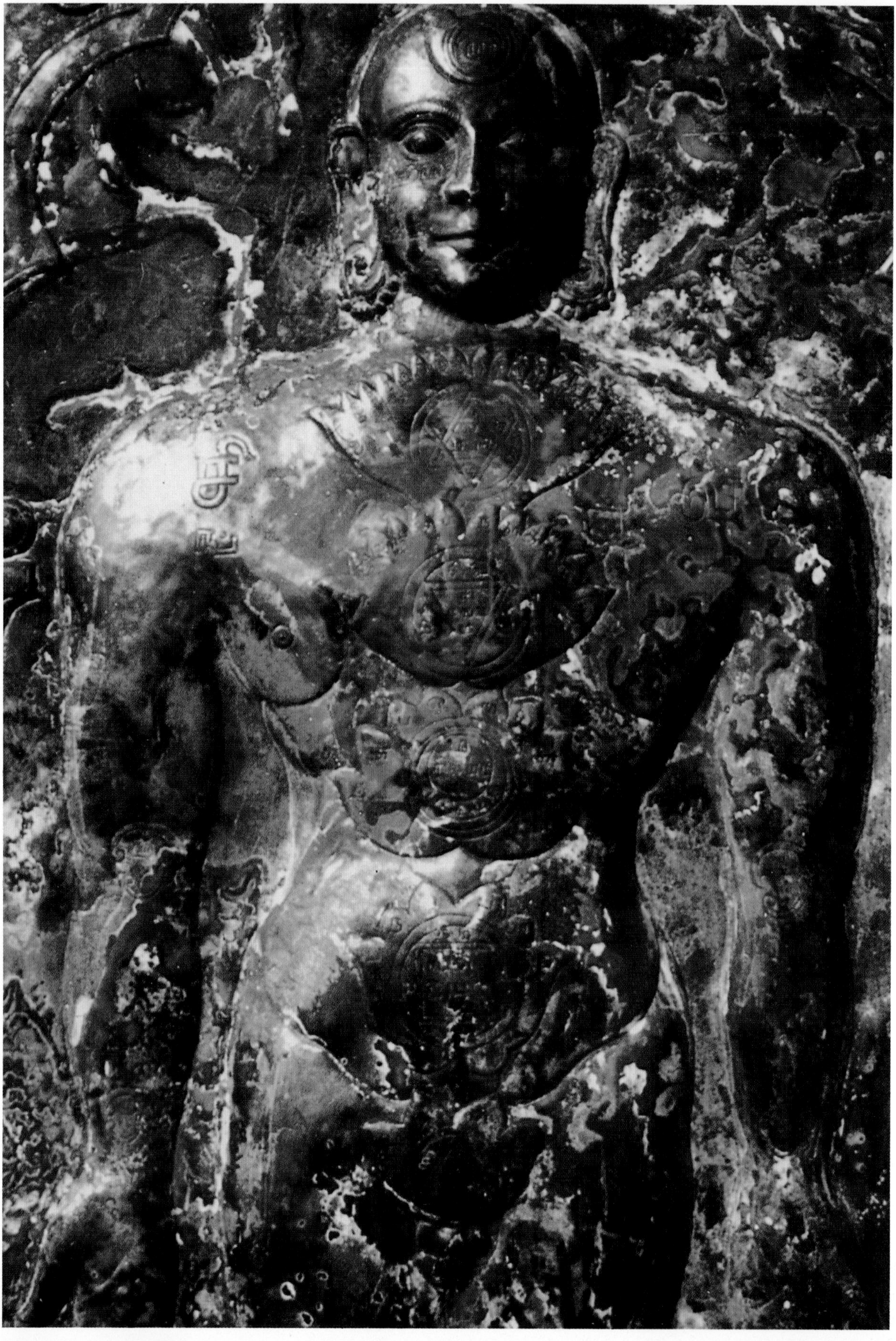

X

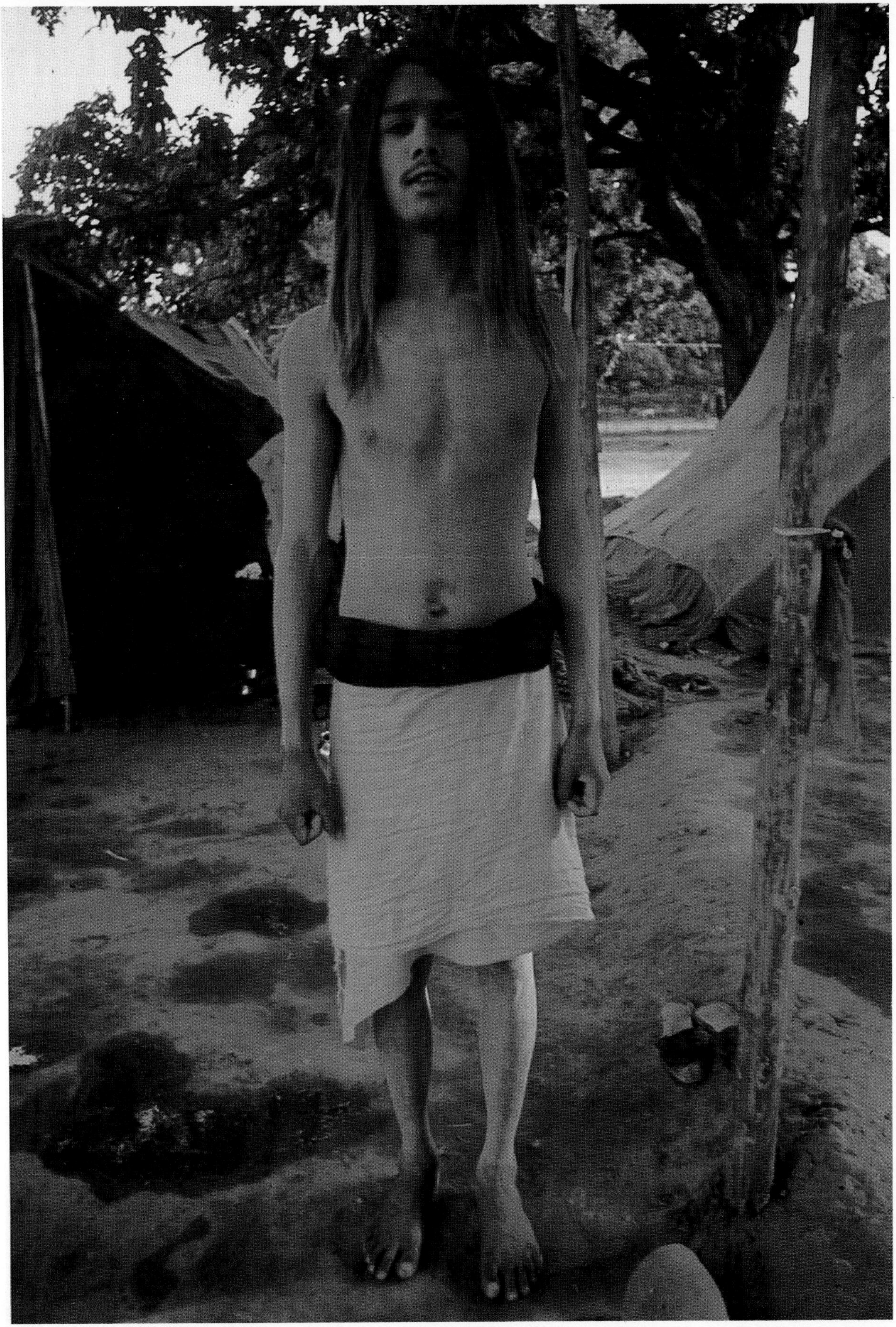

XI

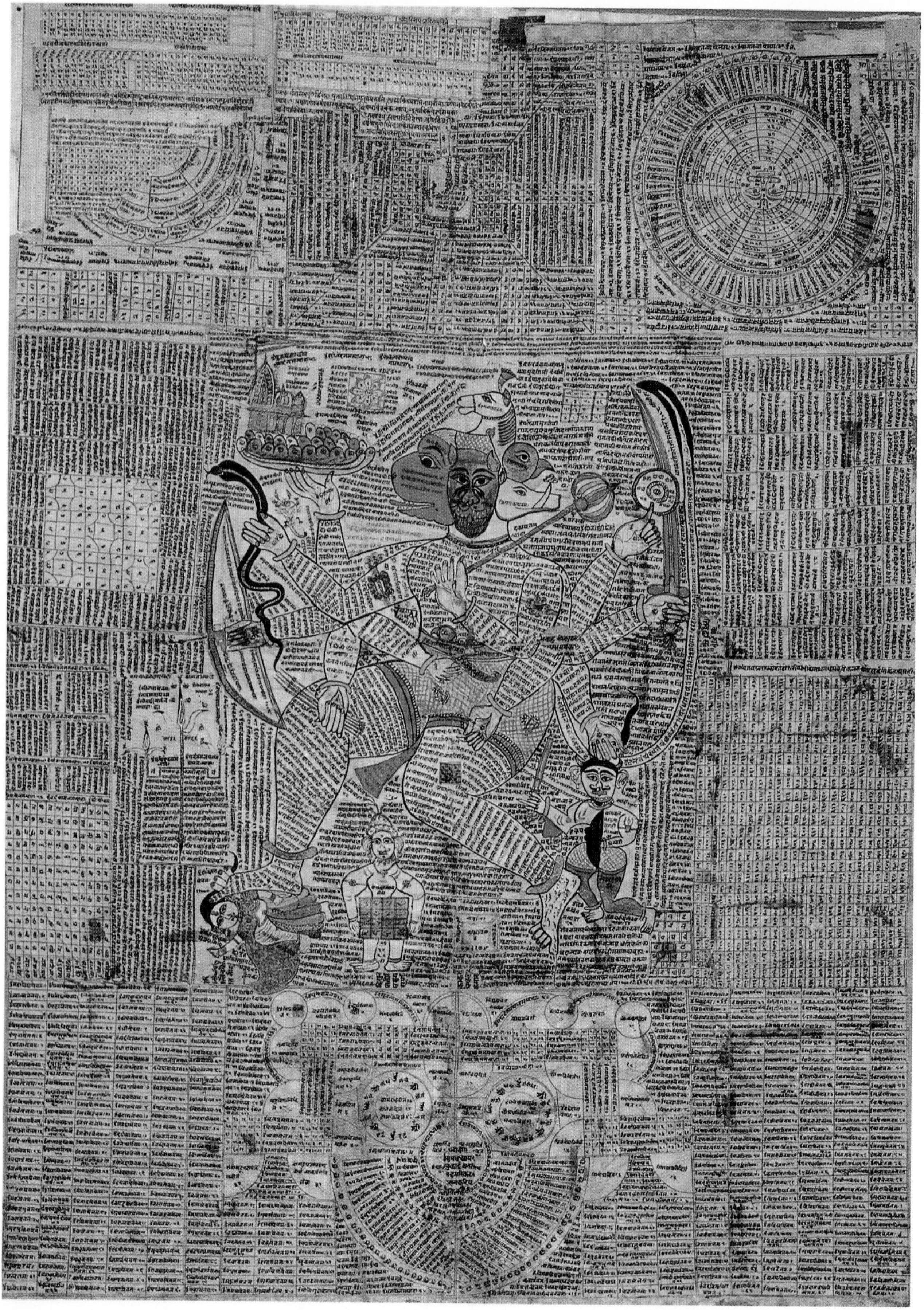

touching the *heart centre* with the palm while reciting:

aiṁ *hṛidayāya* namaḥ

touching the *forehead* with four fingers:

oṃ klīṃ *śirasī* svāhā

touching the *top of the head* with the tip of thumb while the fingers are closed into a fist:

oṃ sahuḥ *śikhāyai* va ṣaṭ

clasping the *upper part of the arms* just beneath the shoulders with hands crossed on the chest:

oṃ sahuḥ *kavacaya* hūṃ

touching the *closed eyes* with fore- and middle-fingers:

oṃ bhuvah *netratroyaiya* vausaṭ

placing those two fingers on the left palm:

oṃ bhur bhuvaḥ *phaṭ*.

## *Mudrā*

Another non-verbal mode of communication and self-expression consists of repetitive gestures and finger postures known as mudrās which are connected with nyāsa in tantric ritual. Ritual postures of the hand provoke a subjective reaction in the mind of the adept. Mudrās are symbolic archetypal signs, based on gestural finger patterns, taking the place, but retaining the efficacy, of the spoken word. They are used to evoke in the mind ideas symbolizing divine powers or deities themselves in order to intensify the adept's concentration. The composition of the mudrās is based on certain movements of the fingers which are highly stylized forms of gestural communication. The yoni mudrā, for example, representing Śakti's yantra, is performed with the sole object of invoking the divinity to bestow her energy and infuse it into the sādhaka. A vivid description of the composition of the yoni mudrā is given by the goddess herself in the *Lakṣmī Tantra*:

Learn how the yoni-mudrā of myself who occupies the place of the gross. Stretching out the hands firmly [and] well pressed together in front [of the body], one should reverse each ring-finger over the back of the other. From their middle and base the [two] index fingers, [each] touching its base, should be nestled in front of them [the ring-fingers]. The two little fingers are first placed in front of the remaining two middle [fingers], touching each other's surface, while the palms are concaved in the middle. The two thumbs should be placed in the direction of the first part of the middle fingers.[32]

*Tattva mudrā.*

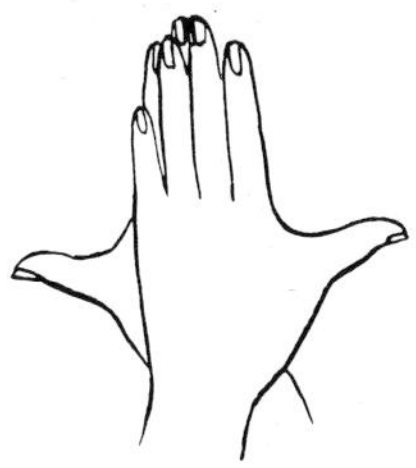

*Matsya mudrā.*

*Śaṅkha mudrā.*

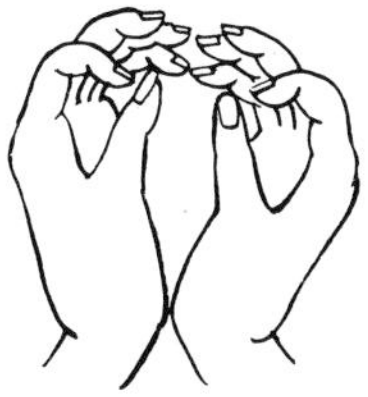

*Padma mudrā.*

*Gadā mudrā.*

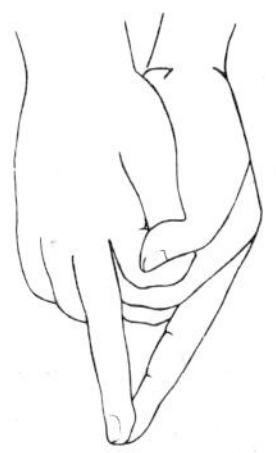

*Yoni mudrā.*

Both mudrās and nyāsas are external expressions of 'inner resolve', suggesting that such non-verbal communications are more powerful than the spoken word. In recent years there has been a growing awareness of the efficacy of such non-verbal communication. A group of scientists studying this form of communication has established that there appears to be an 'alphabet' of gestures, postures, body movements which express much more than words can convey. A recent study by the psychologist Albert Mehrabian based on extensive laboratory measurement of the communication between two persons, concluded that 'only 7% of the message's effect is carried by words, while 93% of the total impact reaches the "listener" through non-verbal means. . . . Feelings are conveyed mainly by non-verbal behaviour.'[33]

## *Bhūta-śuddhi*

Like nyāsa and mudrā, the ritual of bhūta-śuddhi, the 'purification of the elements', is a great aid to the mental process of identification. Performed prior to all tantric worship, the ritual consists of a gradual dissolution of each of the five grosser elements of which the body is composed into ultra-subtle primordial sources. The ritual is carried out by reciting appropriate mantras: 'Oṃ hrīṃ pṛthivyai [earth element] huṃ phaṭ'; 'Oṃ hrīṃ adbhyah [water element] huṃ phaṭ'; 'Oṃ hrīṃ tejase [fire element] huṃ phaṭ'; 'Oṃ hrīm vāyave [air element] huṃ phaṭ'; 'Oṃ hrīṃ ākāsāya [ether element] huṃ phaṭ.' These mantras act on the mind of the adept until the material body is purified, dissolving it mentally step by step. In the various parts of the adept's body exist all the elements and cosmic principles. According to the *Lakṣmī Tantra*:

The place of the earth [element] is considered to be up to the waist; the place of the fire [element] is up to the heart. The place of the ether [element] is up to the ears. The place of ahaṃkāra is up to the hole [the cavity of the mouth or the fontanelle, the hole on the crown of the head]. The place of mahat is up to the brows, and in the space [above the head] is said to be the place of the absolute.[34]

The earth element of the body is dissolved by that of water, water by fire, fire by air, air by ether. Ether, finally, is absorbed into the subtle principles until the source of all is reached. By the dissolution of the five gross elements (mahā-bhūtas), together with the subtle principles (tanmātras) and all the organs of senses and

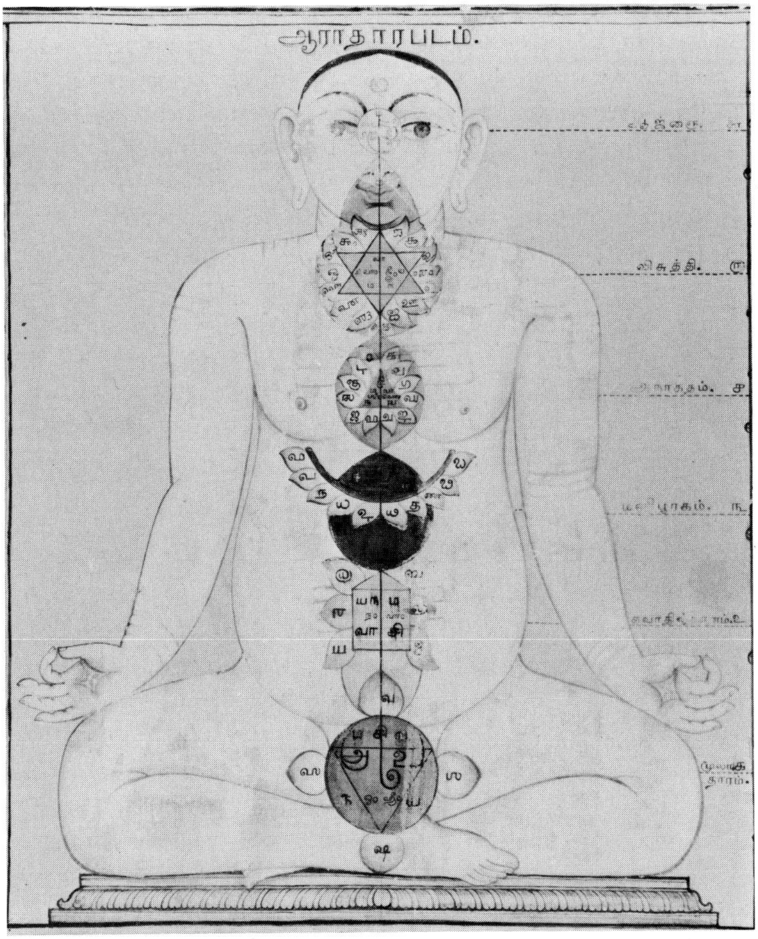

*Opposite: Scroll illustrating various tantra-yoga āsanas assumed before concentration and meditation. Rajasthan, c. 18th century. Gouache on paper.*

*Diagram of the chakras in the body of the yogi. Tamil Nadu, 19th century. Ink and colour on paper.*

intelligence-stuff (mahat), into Prakṛiti, a gradual mental process of involution takes place. After having thus recreated his own body, the sādhaka acquires the capacity for proper ritual worship.

## *Prāṇāyāma, concentration and meditation*

A significant contribution of yoga discipline to tantric ritual is the control of psychosomatic mechanisms by the regulation of breathing. Breath, a constant factor of personality, is a vital point of contact between the self and the body. Prāṇāyāma (the yoga of controlling Prāṇa, or élan vital) is perhaps one of the oldest and most important consciousness-amplifying techniques for controlling the bio-motor force in the human body which manifests itself as Prāṇa. Controlling the breath, and thereby the 'vital airs' in the body, is employed to purify the nerve circuits and to give vitality to the subtle centres of the body; its major aim is to stimulate the centre of paranormal consciousness in the brain centre for the arousal of the Kuṇḍalinī. To achieve this aim yogic discipline has developed a systematic technique, with special emphasis on location, duration, speed, depth and rhythm of breathing. In normal circumstances our breathing is very irregular; not only are the inhalation and exhalation unequal but they lack harmony. Though every individual's respiratory cycle reacts dynamically upon the latent Kuṇḍalinī, this reaction takes place about 21,600 times a day, that is, at a frequency more or less equal to the individual's number of breaths. However, for the majority of people these breaths are both shallow and fast, filling the lungs to only a fraction of their capacity. Under those circumstances, the current of energy flowing downwards to strike the Kuṇḍalinī is inadequate to awaken her.

The first step in Prāṇāyāma is concerned with regulating the breath in a measured way and letting the breath flow in and out rhythmically. Rhythmic control prevents dissipation of energy, and its practice supports concentration and harnesses the impulses of the autonomic nervous system, thereby improving the whole tonus of our body and harmonizing the inner relationships of our psycho-physical organism.

Prāṇāyāma is used in conjunction with other disciplines of yoga practice such as āsana, mudrā, mantra, bandha or internal muscular contraction, and so on. Many variations and combinations have been developed to regulate Prāna for purposive and directive movements. The practice of Prāṇāyāma consists of several phases. Its first and most important goal is to be sensitive and alert to the act of respiration, to be aware of breathing. If we begin to 'feel' the flow of Prāṇic current, we can also begin to control it. Next is bodily posture: Prāṇāyāma, to be effective, should be practised in a special position best suited to promote the desired result. An easy position is either Padmāsana, the lotus posture, when one sits cross-legged with the right foot resting on the left thigh and the left crossed over the right leg, or in Siddhāsana, the posture of accomplishment, with the left heel pressed firmly on the perineum and the heel of the right leg on the left thigh and touching the abdomen. In both these positions one is required to sit upright with the head, neck and spinal column in a straight line in order to lessen the possibility of drowsiness. The eyes are directed towards the tip of the nose and the hands are laid on the knees.

Yogis explain that sitting crosslegged in either of these postures lessens the possibility that the Prāṇic energy will escape. It provides



*Schematic representation of how a yoga posture forms a circuit, the crossed legs protecting against loss of Prāṇic current.*

*Yogi meditating on the bank of the Banaras-ghat.*

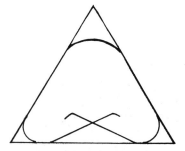

*Āsana schematically analysed to indicate circuits of Prāṇic and psychic energy.*

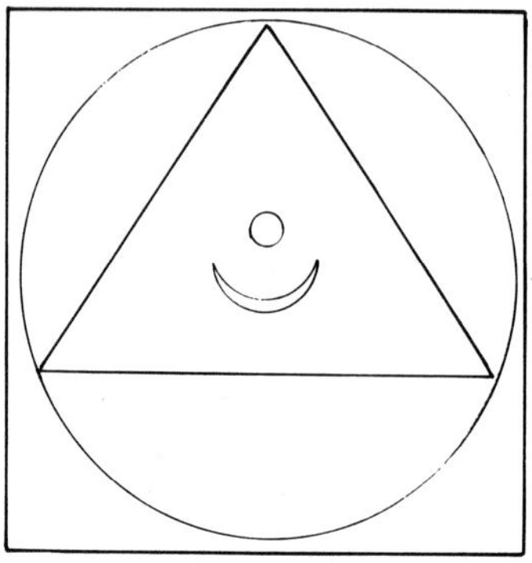

*Āsana-maṇḍala. Diagram of the five elements, Panehabhūta.*

a stable triangular base on which the whole body makes a 'closed circuit' of the energy field so that the currents do not flow out from the tips of the hands and feet but are continually retained or 'locked' within the body circuit while the position is held. After mastery over the posture of the body, the next step is to build energy within the system by taking deeper breaths in order to fill the lungs from apex to base, so as to absorb a maximum quantity of Prāṇa current.

Next, and of equal importance, is achieving rhythmical respiration by striking a correct ratio between the different phases of a breath unit. A breath unit consists of three parts: inhalation (shallow or deep), retention of the breath at any point of inhalation, and exhalation. Rhythm in breathing is a balance, a correct ratio, between these three. The correct timing of inhalation (puraka), retention (kumbhaka) and exhalation (rechaka) is 1 : 4 : 2. Thus the duration of the breath control in degrees enumerated in seconds will be:

| | *Breathing in* | *Inner chalice (retention)* | *Breathing out* | *Outer chalice (repose)* |
|---|---|---|---|---|
| Low | 4 | 16½ | 8 | 1 |
| Intermediate | 6 | 33¼ | 10–12 | 2 |
| High | 8 | 50 | 12–16 | 3 |

The air is breathed in slowly through the left nostril, connected with the lunar channel, Iḍā, while the other is closed with the thumb. The breath is held and exhaled according to a specific rhythm. The exercise is repeated in the same rhythm and timing with the right nostril, which is connected with the solar channel, Piṅgalā. During the exercise the syllable Oṃ or a bīja mantra is repeated to measure the relative duration of inhalation and exhalation; at the same time it is also essential to concentrate on the two nerve currents (Iḍā and Piṅgalā) by their repeated and rhythmic filling and emptying; one feels, as it were, that one is sending the current impulses to strike at the root impulses of Kuṇḍalinī.

After completing a round of Prāṇāyāma, it is necessary to lie flat on the back, like a corpse (known as Śavāsana), to relax and calm the mind. The number of exercises should be increased gradually. When the breath is retained over a longer period more energy is absorbed within the system and a greater voluntary control of Prāṇa is evident. With perfection of this practice the first sign of its effect begins to appear. The body slowly becomes more relaxed, calm, rhythmical and in harmony with inner elements; the face 'glows like the sun'. It is only when the adept has reached absolute perfection that Prāṇa will be felt rising through Sushumṇā (the central channel of the subtle body) by arresting the flow of currents in the solar and lunar channels on either side of Sushumṇā.

Prāṇāyāma is also used extensively to achieve meditative states by concentrating on the inner movements of breath. A common practice is to concentrate on or be aware of that fraction of a moment between breathing in and breating out, that split second when there is no breathing. Emphasis may be put on the turning or 'breath curves', the various regions of chakras through which Prāṇa ascends or, more simply, the sustained awareness of breathing and not the time-gap between breathing in and out.

## *Concentration and meditation*

In tantric ritual the yogic techniques of concentration and meditation play a central role. All identifications, the interiorizations to which tantrism attaches such importance, can be attained by systematically focusing awareness on a stimulus. To identify oneself with the divinity, to merge in the object of contemplation, to have a unitive experience, presupposes several categories or techniques of physiological and spiritual exercise transforming our ordinary consciousness into a qualitatively different realm of experience, in order to dispel terrestrial impulses and open new mental doors to the awareness of union.

*Yoni, the female organ as a matrix of generation. In tantric worship it acquires special significance as it represents the Ultimate Reality manifesting itself in its female principle, as Prakṛiti. Andhra Pradesh, c. 19th century. Wood.*

The Yoga-Sūtra of Patañjali, in its second aphorism, describes yoga as the 'inhibition of the modification of the mind'. Concentration implies 'one-pointedness' (ekāgratā) of the attention, fixing the attention on a single stimulus in order to achieve perfect autonomy over 'variously directed, discontinuous, diffused attention' (sarvarthatā). In the daily round of life our attention is constantly diverted by a variety of external stimuli. Subconscious forces disperse our consciousness and introduce a myriad of mental associations, words, images, sensations; thus our minds are continuously at the mercy of these inner forces. Meditation calls for a complete censorship of this mental flux by focusing one's awareness on a specific end or stimulus: 'As soon as the waves have stopped and the lake has become quiet, we see its bottom. So with

शालग्रामवर्णेफलम्

पीताधनकरीज्ञेया    रक्ताराज्यकरीस्मृता ॥

अतिरक्तारोगदाच    कृष्णकीर्तिप्रदायिनी॥

पाएडुरापापहानित्यं    रूक्षाचेद्रोगदायिनी ॥

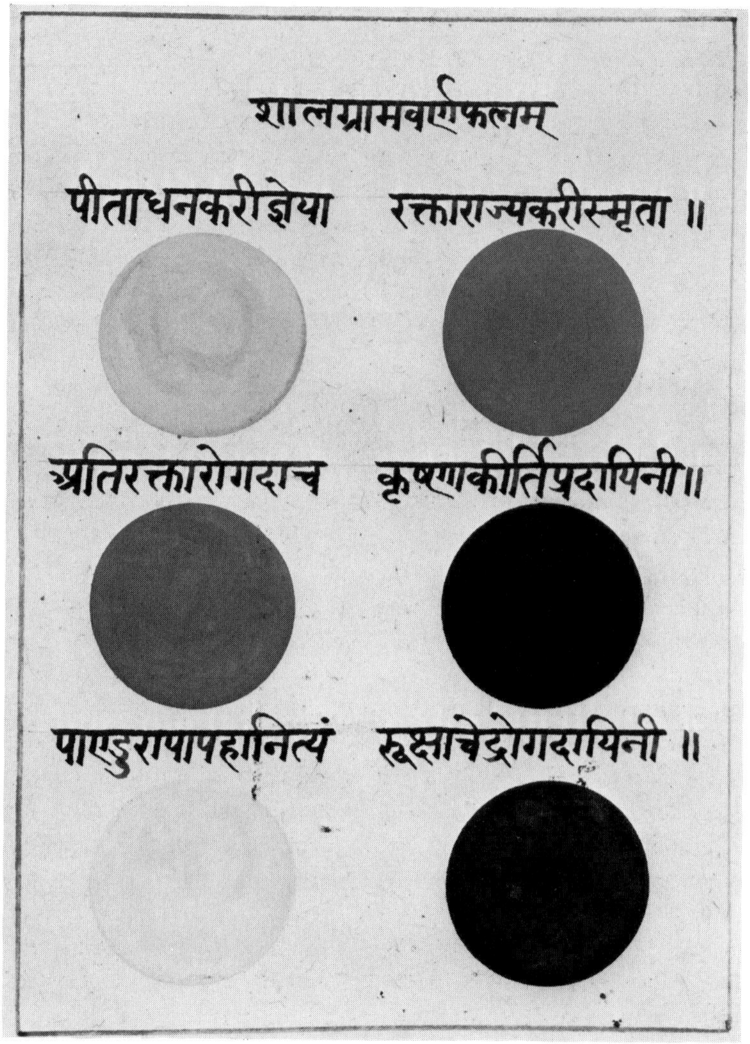

*A manuscript page of Śālagrāmas*
*for meditation, indicating the*
*auspicious results obtained from*
*their worship. Rajasthan, c. 18th*
*century. Ink and colour on paper.*

the mind: when it is calm, we see what our own nature is; we do
not mix ourselves with the modification of the mind; but remain
our own selves.'[35]

Meditation presupposes a subject, an object and an experiential
process. Though these three combine to form a unit, the emphasis
is on the process, which transforms and is the medium of
'awareness' and ultimate realization. Prāṇāyāma, dhāranā or
concentration, and meditation itself are phases of the same process.
Each successive phase is a subtle refinement of the former. If a
single act of attention is focusing one's mind on a particular object,
idea or feeling, then concentration is an intensification of the same
process by blocking off our awareness of every distraction from the

object of concentration. Meditation is a more intensified form, characterized by voluntary control of the mind leading to a condensed experience of a modality of being beyond our ordinary state of mind.

Traditional symbols are aids to recollection and serve as reminders of reality momentarily forgotten in the humdrum of worldly distractions. There are several which are used as supports to concentration, ranging from the frequently used concentrative, absorbing visual objects such as simple graphic signs, dots and concentric circles, to complex structural power-diagrams like the yantras and maṇḍalas. Others are sculptural forms such as the Śiva-liṅga and Śālagrāma, used as foci of concentration. Classical yoga also describes focusing concentration on the exterior surface of the body. A traditional method is to fix one's attention, with the eyes half-closed, on the tip of the nose ('nasal gaze') or towards the space between the eyebrows. Another simple method is to stare at a candle flame. An object-centred meditation is simply an 'eye-alogue'. The adept maintains a steady gaze on the object. With the control of concentration stray thoughts are eliminated and the external world is temporarily shut out. This exercise is more difficult than it first appears, and beginners find it very difficult to concentrate on an object for a prolonged period of time; they are distracted from the meditative object and invariably find their attention shifting hither and thither. Each time it happens the beginner must return his concentration to the meditative object and start afresh.

Another common aid to meditation is to concentrate one's attention on various sensory modalities such as the repetitive mantras, or internally generated sounds. The sounds may be natural, such as that of a waterfall, the roaring of the sea, the

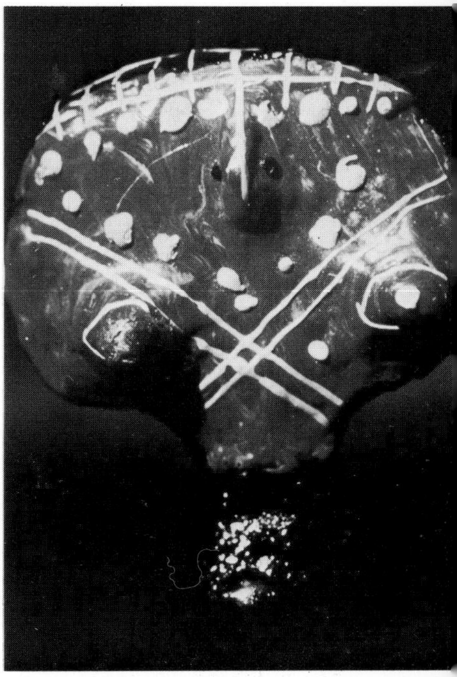

*Jagannāth, the Lord of the Universe. Midnapur, West Bengal, contemporary. Lacquer on sunbaked clay.*

*Necklace of Rudrākṣa beads for japa, repetition of mantras. South India, 19th century. Dried seeds.*

humming of bees, or the sound of a flute, or the adept may sit in a natural environment and concentrate on an imagined sound.

An inner meditative experience through visualization of a divine image is another method practised by the tantrikas. The technique of visualization normally involves withdrawing the energy flowing through the conscious function and directing it inwards. When this happens our inner vision projects an image on a mental screen, and we see and experience that form on the surface of the mind. Such visions are neither pathological fantasies nor dreams. In a dream one sees several images arising from the unconscious mind; visualization differs from a dream in that it is self-induced, even though it uses a picture-language similar to a dream's; it is nearer to consciousness. Visualization is performed in a meditative or solitary place, and the adept, with eyes closed, mentally constructs an image of the chosen deity. What is projected by deliberate effort on the inner screen of the mind is not a personal construct but an iconographic imprint, based on elaborate descriptions found in the traditional texts. The visualization is strictly pursued, following the canonical imagery, and each part of the deity's body and its symbols are highly dramatized to regulate the creative imagination of the adept. The adept is like a craftsman weaving together the threads of a canonical archetype, or a sculptor building a minutely-detailed mental image. The created mental image should not be disturbed by inner restlessness or thought since visualization is followed by identification. The adept concentrates very deeply on each aspect of the divinity, imagining that he is slowly being transformed into it. This exercise demands an active play of creative imagination.

*Śiva-liṅga in yoni-pedestal, the union of male and female organs symbolizing cosmic totality. Banaras, 19th century. Stone.*

The common thread uniting all meditative techniques is that meditation takes the adept to a centre of his own psychic forces by gathering up his variously directed energy into a nucleus. In this way the aids become 'bridges' along the path of sādhanā. There are two major effects of meditation: 'centering' and, the other which follows as a consequence of it, the experience of an altered state is necessarily arational and intuitive in experience and content.

The basic function of all techniques is to heighten the influx of intuitive insight, and that is why these techniques have recourse to mediums which involve each of our senses: sound through mantra; touch through mudrās, nyāsas, āsanas; smell and breath through prāṇāyāma; the mind through meditation, concentration, visualization. Each of these involves a basic sensitivity, and in combination they trigger an altered state so that the intuitive side of our consciousness finds its fullest play.

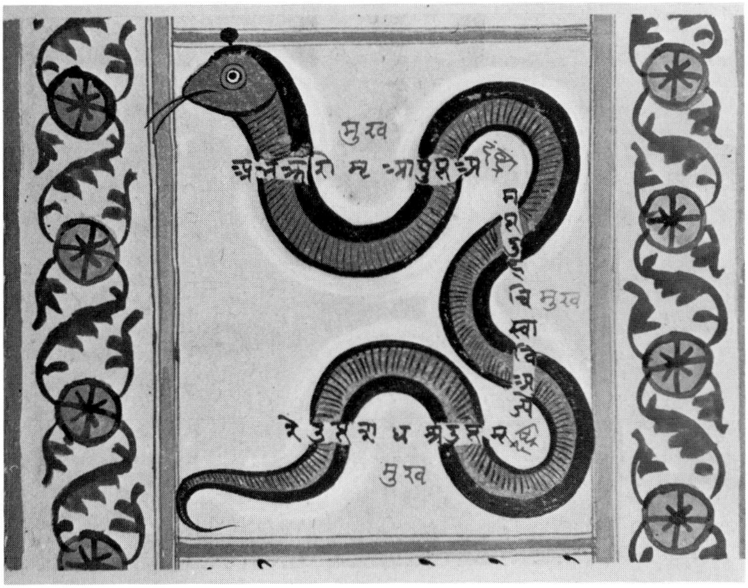

*Kuṇḍalinī as the emblem of microcosmic energy. Rajasthan, 19th century. Gouache on paper.*

*Yogi with chakras, Sahasrāra (the 'Lotus of a Thousand Petals') is the place of union between Kuṇḍalinī and Pure Consciousness. Rajasthan,* c. *18th century. Gouache on paper.*

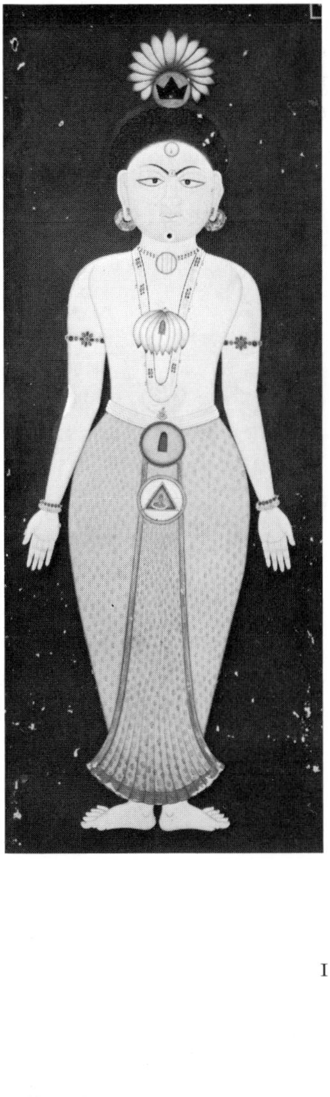

After such a survey of various techniques, we must return to the most fundamental of all questions: What is the evolutionary mechanism in the human body which generates the illimitable power to transform? What is the basis of the concept of the subtle energies operating in the human organism? The tantrikas describe it as the mysterious Kuṇḍalinī Śakti. In verse 3 of the *Satchakra-Nirupana,* the Kuṇḍalinī is described thus: 'She is beautiful like a chain of lightning and fine like a [lotus] fibre, and shines in the minds of the sages. She is extremely subtle, the awakener of pure knowledge, the embodiment of all bliss, whose true nature is pure consciousness.' At first glance it is not at all clear what the Kuṇḍalinī is. The verse describes the Kuṇḍalinī as an extremely subtle force which has the potency to transform. Can we then say that Kuṇḍalinī is the force that impels, a power that transforms, a feeling that unites? – No, it is something more.

The Kuṇḍalinī is the microcosmic form of universal energy or, more simply, the vast storehouse of static, potential psychic energy which exists in latent form in every being. It is the most powerful manifestation of creative force in the human body. The concept of Kuṇḍalinī is not peculiar to tantras but forms the basis of all yogic practices, and every genuine spiritual experience is considered to be an ascent of this power. The Kuṇḍalinī is described as lying 'coiled', 'inactive' or in 'trance sleep' at the base of the spine, technically called the Mūlādhāra Chakra or root centre, blocking the opening of the passage that leads to the cosmic consciousness in

*A manuscript page illustrating Śakti with Kuṇḍalinī. Rajasthan, c. 19th century. Gouache on paper.*

the brain centre. In most cases the Kuṇḍalinī may lie dormant all through one's life time, and an individual may be unaware of its existence. The closest parallel to this concept in modern terms is what contemporary behavioural scientists term the gap between our potential and actual self. According to their findings, the average individual uses only 10% of his capacities while the greater part of his potentialities, talents and abilities remain unrealized. The Kuṇḍalinī Śakti, however, should not be confused merely with an individual's creative capacities but should be conceived as a force which has the potency to awaken an undeniable psychic power inherent in all of us. No tangible description of the Kuṇḍalinī in symbolic or physiological terms will suffice, for it is a highly potential ultra-subtle vibration which eludes the 'surgeon's knife'. However elusive its nature, its efficacy can be judged only by experiencing it and the effect its arousal produces in the human body.

It is believed that man, within his corporeal frame, embraces all the subtle planes of the universe; beyond his physical existence there is a parallel 'etheric-double' which constitutes his subtle body. The subtle envelopes are related to the gross body at several psychic points. The numerous etheric channels are known as nāḍis (from the root *nād* meaning motion, vibration), and of them the most important ones are the lunar nāḍī, Iḍā, the solar nāḍi, Piṅgalā, and the central subtle channel, Sushumṇā. Though attempts have been made to identify these subtle nerves with various parts of the human anatomy, they are untraceable by direct physical means. It is mainly through the mechanism of this etheric structure that the vital current of Kuṇḍalinī is awakened.

The Mūlādhāra (mula-root) centre at the base of the spinal column between the anal orifice and the genital organs (sacral plexus) is the starting place of all the main nāḍis. The Sushumṇā, situated at the perineum, runs through the central channel of the spinal column and extends up to the crown of the head. On either side, and running parallel to it, are Iḍā on the left and Piṅgalā on the right. Though Iḍā and Piṅgalā separate from the Sushumṇā at the Mūlādhāra Chakra, they meet the Sushumṇā again in the region of Ajñā Chakra, situated between the eyebrows (cavernous plexus), and again they divide and separate into the left and right nostrils. Along the Sushumṇā channel there are the six major psychic centres also known as chakras, and one above the head and lying outside the body; together they make the seven major psychic vortices in the subtle body. These chakras are revealed to practising adepts only, through yoga.

Attempts are sometimes made to identify the chakras with several parts of the body. Rieker, however, correctly observes:

> If the system of chakras were identical with the central nervous system (CNS), then either all our academic knowledge would be wrong, or the yoga teachings would be empty fantasies. But neither is the case. Our knowledge about the CNS applies to the material aspect only, while chakra theory goes to the deepest sources of all dynamic processes in man, down to the deepest cosmic functions, to which we are undeniably bound.[36]

The chakras are figuratively referred to as lotuses, and each of them is related to a colour; each lotus's number of petals indicates the rate of vibrations of that particular chakra. Thus, only four frequencies are attributed to the root centre, where energy is at its lowest and resistance is highest, but as one ascends the scale, the frequencies increase considerably. The letters inscribed on the petals of the chakra lotuses should not be regarded as mere parts of the alphabet: they indicate sound vibrations and the varying degrees of energies working in the different centres. Similarly, the colours which the chakras reflect are related to their frequencies. Of the several interpretations offered for the symbolic use of lotuses the one which explains their function is that when the veils obstructing the chakras are lifted they open up more like flowers from within.

The seven chakras and their symbolic interrelation with sound, colour, form, significance and function have been described extensively in the tantras:

(1) *Mūlādhāra Chakra,* a major root centre of physical experience, is conceived of as having four red petals on which are inscribed in gold v, sh, ś, s within a yellow square representing the earth element with the bīja mantra Laṁ. An inverted triangle is placed in the centre of the square, enclosing the unawakened and mysterious Kuṇḍalinī, in trance-sleep and lying in three and a half coils around the Svyaṁbhu-liṅga. This represents the unmanifested or quiescent form of the Kuṇḍalinī. This chakra is associated with the cohesive power of gross matter and the element of inertia, the sense of smell, etc. The presiding deity of the chakra is Brahmā with the Śakti, Dākinī. The four letters represent the root variations and are related to the power of speech.

(2) *Svādishṭhāna (pleasant) Chakra,* the second centre in the ascending order of the Kuṇḍalinī, is situated at the base of the genital organ with six vermilion petals bearing the letters b, bh, m, y, r, and i. In the pericarp is represented the water element, stainless and luminously white, in the shape of a half-moon with the bīja mantra Vaṁ. On top of the bīja mantra sits the presiding deity Vishṇu flanked by the Śakti, Rākinī or Chākinī. This chakra governs the sense of taste.

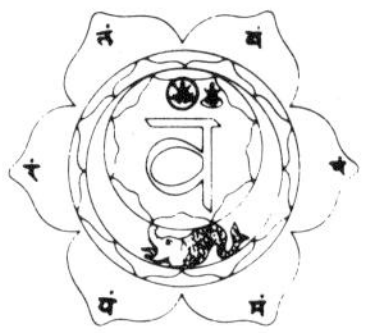

(3) *Maṇipūra (gem-site) Chakra,* near the navel (lumbar or epigastric plexus), is a blue lotus with ten petals inscribed with the letters ḍ, ḍh, ṇ, t, th, d, dh, n, p, ph. In the centre of the lotus,

a red triangle 'radiant like the rising sun' is related to the element of fire. Its bīja mantra is Raṁ. The presiding deity of this chakra is Rudra with the Śakti Lākinī. This chakra is related generally to the sense of sight.

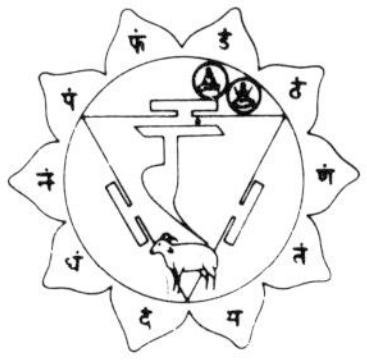

(4) *Anāhata (unstruck) Chakra,* in the region of the heart (cardiac plexus), has twelve letters – k, kh, g, gh, ṅ, ch, chh, j, jh, ñ, ṭ, ṭh – inscribed on golden petals. In the middle are two interpenetrating triangles of a smoky colour enclosing another golden triangle 'lustrous as ten million flashes of lightning', with a Bāna-liṅga inside the triangle. This chakra is associated with the element air, and above the two triangles is its presiding deity, the three-eyed Īśa with Kākinī Śakti (red in colour). Its bīja mantra is Yaṁ and it is principally associated with the sense of touch.

(5) *Visúddha (pure) Chakra* is located at the juncture of the spinal column and medula oblongata, behind the throat (laryngeal or pharyngeal plexus). It has sixteen petals of smoky purple inscribed with the letters of sixteen vowel sounds – a, ā, i, ī, u, ū, ri, ṝi, ḷi, ḹī, e, ai, o, ou, ṁ, ḥ – and within its white pericarp is a white circle enclosing a triangle that is inscribed with the bīja mantra Haṁ. The presiding deity is Sadāśiva in his Ardhanārīśvara (androgynous) aspect, and the chakra is associated with the element ether and controls the sense of hearing.

(6) *Ājñā (command) Chakra,* situated between the eyebrows, commands the various states of concentration realized through meditation. It is a two-petalled white lotus with the letters h and ksh. In its centre is an inverted white triangle with the white Itara-liṅga and the bīja mantra Oṃ. The tutelary Śakti is Hākinī, and it is associated with the various cognitive faculties of the mind.

(7) *Sahasrāra (thousand)* is the 'Lotus of the Thousand Petals' located about four finger-breadths above the crown of the head; it is also called Brahmarandhra and is the meeting-place of the Kuṇḍalinī Śakti with Pure Consciousness. Its petals are inscribed with all sound potentials, represented by all the letters of the Sanskrit alphabet. The tantrika Satyananda Giri explains that Kuṇḍalinī has to cross further, through eighteen mahāvidyās, i.e., eighteen energized subtle centres encircling the Sahasrāra region, finally to unite with Śiva, in an act known as maithuna-yoga.

The Sahasrāra is the centre of quintessential consciousness where the integration of all polarities is experienced. It is a centre which neutralizes all sounds and all colours, integrates all cognitive and conative functions and embraces the static and dynamic energies of the various centres into an all-pervasive unity. It is here that the Kuṇḍalinī terminates her journey after having traversed the six chakras: 'It is in this centre that the rupture of plane occurs, that the paradoxical act of transcendence in passing beyond saṁsāra, "emerging from time", is accomplished.' A man cannot stay in this state more than twenty-one days unless the Kuṇḍalinī reverses her course and comes down to the relative plane. But this experience retains its spontaneity and remains an unforgettable event in one's lifetime.

XIII *Enlightened Sādhaka. The opening of the Sahasrāra chakra above the head indicates that the yogi has attained the peak state of enlightenment. Maharashtra,* c. *19th century. Gouache on paper.*

XIV *Priest performing nyāsa with ritual ingredients during the Kālī-pūjā on Dīvālī, the darkest night of the year, when the 'festival of lights' takes place all over India.*

XVI

Jung states that in the process of what he terms individuation, the psyche becomes 'whole' when balance among the four 'functions', thinking, feeling, sensing and intuiting, is achieved. If we draw a parallel between Jung's ideas and the system of chakras we find that at each energy vortex a new element is encountered in ascending order, earth, water, fire, air, ether. The five vortices each manifest a new sense which is a limitation and possibility of the others. Thus, at the root centre, associated with the element earth, the attributed quality is cohesiveness and inertia, a level in which one may remain content without having any desire to change or expand into any other state. At the same time, just as the root of a tree implies the possibility of its growth, the earth centre also denotes an opportunity to expand awareness. Likewise the energy of the second chakra, associated with water, like its corresponding element, tends to flow downward in order to contract. The third chakra, which is associated with fire, like its flames implies an upward movement in order to consume. The fourth chakra is associated with air, and like its element is characterized by a tendency to revolve into different directions in order to relate itself with other possibilities. Finally, the fifth chakra, corresponding with the element of ether, is like a receptacle within which all elements operate.

The process of becoming is not unilinear, moving in one direction either up or down, but it is dialectical, with pulls and pushes at every level. The Kuṇḍalinī does not shoot up in a straight line, but at each stage of its unfolding it must undo the knots of different energies. With each successive untying a specific transformation occurs. The element-symbols associated with the vortices convey something about the positive and negative polarities functioning within the personality of an individual. When the Kuṇḍalinī ascends through the psychic centres it assimilates the different energies released from the centres, and the sādhaka experiences manifold interplay of visionary experiences and sensations of sound, light, colour, etc. At the etheric level of Ājñā Chakra, the centre between the eyebrows, the lower half of the dialectical functioning of the personality can be perceived and controlled. At this level, one sense predominates, the experience of awareness or the power to command, which can harmonize the energies.

In Jung's patients the process of individuation transcends the barriers of polarities interacting within their personality with the help of a therapist; similarly, the tantric initiate, through a long process of apprenticeship under the strict guidance of a guru, learns

XV *Kālī as visualized by a Sādhikā, Sudhā Mā, while in trance. Calcutta, contemporary, based on traditional form. Gouache on paper.*

XVI *The psychic centres and their related symbols, detail from an illuminated manuscript page. Nepal, c. 1761. Gouache on paper.*

to balance the dialectical process of the lower chakras with the aid of his will. Just as in Jung's subjects once a balance is attained psychic individuation results in a uniquely new awareness, so also with the adept, such awareness awakens when all functions are equilibrated.

## *Āsana or ritual of union: individual*

Tantra āsana is a mode of transcending the human condition; through it the gross sexual energy of man and woman can be transformed into superpotency by total integration of opposing polarities. Through planned meditative practices of sexo-yogic āsanas, Kuṇḍalinī, the psychic force lying dormant in the human body, is roused towards its upward move from Mūlādhāra Chakra to the brain centre, Sahasrāra, to unite with cosmic consciousness. The tantrikas believe that by manipulating this energy inherent in gross sex one can find creative powers to ascend to the spiritual plane, a plane of transcendental union for the realization of pure joy (ānanda). The tantrikas have experienced and tasted the power of sex in order to return in full awareness of the primal state of oneness.

Through the ages, the sex act has been generally associated with procreation or physical gratification. The tantrikas, however, were among the first to free sex from its limited orientation and recognize its spiritual values and capacities. The spiritualization of sex, its revitalization, its sublimation and its acceptance as a valid mode in the domain of ritual practices are to a certain extent due to the tantrikas' practical exploration. The sexual attitude of a practising tantrika is unconditional: sex is seen neither in the context of morality nor as an ascetically inhibiting act, nor as indulgent or permissive. The āsana ritual is free from emotion and sentimental impulses. It is sustained by the technical possibility of using sex as a medium of realization. Sex is neither immoral nor moral. It is amoral. The tantrika differs from sex-phobics in that he considers that the neglect of the psycho-physiological factors which touch the roots of our instincts as a certain cause of remaining in bondage. Liberation is a change of perspective, and realization can only dawn if the physical body can be transcended by using it in the quest for transformation. The body is a mere instrument, a yantra, and no code of social ethics can hold it prisoner. It is seen as divine in itself, a vital energy capable of acting with tremendous force on the mental state, which in turn reacts on the spiritual plane.

*Āsana in which a couple embrace as a 'creeper enfolds a tree', called 'latā-sādhanā'. Orissa, c. 18th century. Line and colour on paper.*

*Liṅga-yoni with pūjā (worship) offerings laid on it. Kangra, Himachal Pradesh, 18th century. Gouache on paper.*

Tantra is perfectly in agreement with the notion that sex or the blending of the polarities into one is the universal basis of all phenomena irrespective of dimension and magnitude. The universality of this concept on the physical plane from the subcellular to human level is demonstrated by the fact that

Micro-sex (small sex) is the biological foundation of macro-sex (big sex). About this there can be no argument whatever. All sexual phenomena in nature are designed to produce a result, a blending of the genetic codes of two members of the same species. The glow and sparkle of sex as we humans experience it, the cuddling, kissing, tumescence, copulating, orgasm, all serve one purpose only. They set the stage for a cellular drama that involves the sperm's odyssey through the tunnels and portals of the female genital tract, its quest for the waiting egg, its union with this egg.[37]

But what is said about the desire for union on the biological level applies to the whole cosmic system. The complete drama of the universe is repeated in this human body. The individual and universal, according to the tantra, are built on the same plane. The intensity of joy derived from sexual gratification, whether it is dissipated in a gross form or revitalized in a subtle form for a spiritual pursuit, differs only in degree. In its existential content, the ritual of union is functionally detachable from the conceptual. Here the male and female are both playing roles. They do not wish to 'explain', but to act in order to 'feel'. In all respects the ritual is confined to being an expressive encounter in visible and intelligible forms, in a relationship which yields satiety through a series of personifications, transformations, visualizations, identity and transference rituals. As the ritual gathers momentum the play of creative imagination and feeling are brought into focus by empathy; through this apprehension, both the male and the female partners are seen 'anew' by each other and they move together towards the fulfilment of unity. Thus in essence the ritual of union remains a 'felt-experience' – a product of the Dionysan nature rather then the Apollonian, or analytic in content.

The ritual is performed with a partner who is considered the reflection of Śakti, and unless the adept has the attitude of complete surrender to the object of his worship, in this case the female participant who plays the role of the divine energy, the practice of āsana cannot be successful. The 'devout woman' epitomizes the entire nature of femaleness, the essence of all the Ṣaktis in their various aspects. She becomes a perennial source of joy. From whatever stratum of society she comes she must bear certain auspicious signs in appearance and physical condition in order to be an ideal participant: she must be in good health, have lotus eyes, full breasts, soft skin, slender waist 'swelled into jewelled hips' (*Lalaita Vistāra*). Similarly, the male adept also has to meet specific physical requirements.

The methods of tantric āsana incorporate three main controls and mark out five subdivisions in the entire course of the discipline:

(1) *Control of mind or autonomy of thought:* The adept has to develop the ability to concentrate and consciously learn to exercise control over the mind. On the physical plane, āsana is

*Early stone carving of 'latā-sādhanā'. Khajuraho, Madhya Pradesh, c. 12th century.*

'ekāgratā' or concentration on a single point. Just as concentration on one object puts an end to the digressions of the mind, so āsana ends physical mobility by reducing a number of positions to a single archetype – it is the first concrete step taken for the purpose of abolishing the diversities of human intimacy.

(2) *Control of breath through mastering the technique of prāṇāyāma:* We have seen earlier how these techniques, apart from meditative exercises, play a basic part in forcing prāṇa to strike the latent Kuṇḍalinī. It is upon this that the tantras lay the highest emphasis.

(3) *Control of semen and ova in the human body:* Contrary to common belief the practice of āsana involves the retention of sexual energy, and herein lies the acid test of tantric sādhanā. The accumulated orgasmic energy increases inner pressure, transmuting the sex force into a potency so great that the psychic current is liberated. The transubstantiation of sexual potency confirms that the brief period of carnal joy, though it may become a visionary moment, remains shortlived, whereas the bliss derived from the spiritual union through the practice of āsana is an everlasting experience of ecstasy.

From the triple control over mind, breath and sexual ejaculation which constitutes the main techniques of āsana, the whole force of esoteric practice of preparation, purification, worship, meditation, unification is directed towards synthesis.

Prior to the commencement of the ritual, a choice of environment, and determination of the propitious time and hour, are made with the help of the guru. Tradition recognizes only one day each month to be the most auspicious: the eighth or fifteenth day of the dark fortnight; otherwise, a Tuesday on the eighth or fifteenth day of the full moon is prescribed.

Equally important is the place of worship. The tantrikas repeatedly stress the need to perform rituals in solitary places in an atmosphere free from noise and pollution. Our mental state of being is inextricably linked with the quality of the environment. We are at our best when our feelings and actions are synchronized into a perfect state of harmony. In congenial surroundings our efficiency is at its best and internal frictions are reduced. On the other hand, an uncongenial atmosphere leads to a fossilization of thoughts and feelings. The environment helps to co-ordinate the outer and the inner to make life more coherent and rewarding. It is therefore necessary that the place of worship should inspire our inner spiritual urges to flow naturally within us. Rieker explains the importance of a favourable atmosphere for meditative purposes: 'Man without environment, let us assume this possibility theoretically, could neither create nor change his inner self, for he would lack an outer measure of his inner relationships. And thus the inner self of Man is not, a priori, decisive, but only in his *momentary* relationship to his environment.'[38]

The acts of bathing (ablution), dressing, sitting for worship, offering of ritual ingredients, along with others like nyāsa and bhūta-śuddhi (purification of body and elements) are performed to tune the environment, body and mind.

## *Preparation*

After both partners have bathed, śakti (the female partner) is liberally and gently massaged with scented oils: jasmine for her hands, keora for her neck and cheeks, champa and hina for her breasts, spikenard for her hair, musk for her abdomen, sandal paste for her thighs, and khus for her feet. The primary aim of using

*Rādhā, the beloved of Lord Kṛishṇa, encircled by sixteen female energies. Rajasthan,* c. *18th century. Gouache with gold on paper.*

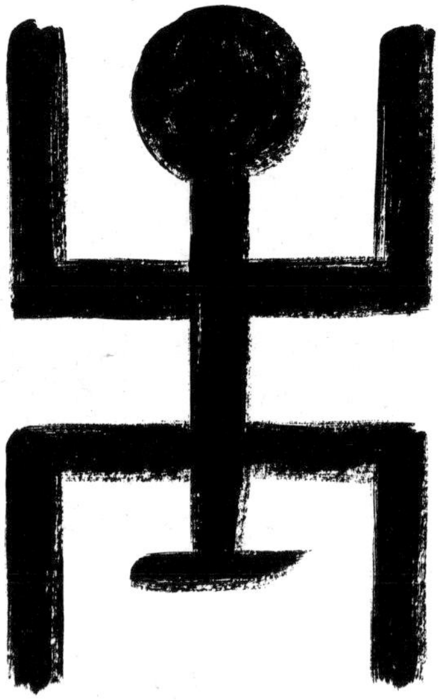

*Auspicious symbol representing a devī (female divinity) drawn with vermilion paste on a libation jar.*

certain scents is to stimulate the Mūlādhāra Chakra region which, being on the earth plane, is directly related to the sense of smell. A vermilion dot is drawn between śakti's eyebrows to mark the place of the opening of the third eye. Dressed in red raw wool or silk cloth sādhaka sits cross-legged while his śakti sits opposite him. The ritual ingredients are aesthetically arranged at the place where the rite is to begin. A tray holding flowers, including hibiscus, blades of green grass, grains of rice, tulsi leaves (a sacred plant), flower garlands, all thoroughly washed with water, vermilion and red sandalwood paste, is on the right side of the sādhaka along with an oil lamp, incense burner, and cooked foods. In front of the sādhaka are ritual water containers, and a libation jar (for a tantrika, 'a pot shows the universe'), with five green mango leaves across its top, symbolizing the five elements, and resting on a lump of kneaded clay, are kept, along with the Śri-pātra, or sacred wine cup. Each ritual article has a symbolic meaning and helps the preparatory training for both the ritual partners.

## *Purification*

After completing the initial discipline, sādhaka commences the purification ritual by reciting the āchamana (sipping) mantra: Oṃ ātmatattvaya svāhā ('The self in the worshipper is no other than the consciousness within him'), or Oṃ Śivatattvya svāhā, Oṃ Śaktitattvāyā svāhā, realizing that all his activities, both physical and mental, proceed from this consciousness, Śiva-Śakti, in order to have a full grasp of the successive stages through which he is to proceed during the communion. He draws a triangle on the ground with fingertips dipped in vermilion or sandal paste, representing Prakṛiti, and says the mantra:

*Om. āsane upavesanamantrasya*
*merupṛṣṭharṣi sutalam chandaḥ*
*kūrmo devatā āsanopaveśane viniyogaḥ*
*oṃ prithivī tvyi dhṛitā lokāḥ*
*devī tvaṃ viṣṇurā dhṛitā*
*tvaṃ ca dhāraya māṁ devī*
*pavitraṃ kurucāsanaṃ*

Sādhaka thus purifies the surrounding atmosphere and sanctifies the seat (āsana represents the earth) which is a mat, deerskin or raw wool. Touching his mouth with his right hand he purifies it with the mantra 'Oṃ tadviṣṇorparamaṃ padaṃ', his nose with the mantra 'sadā paśyanti sūrayaḥ', his eyes with the mantra 'dībība chakṣurātatam'. He then salutes his guru while reciting the following mantras:

touching his mouth:
  oṃ gurubhyo namaḥ

touching the middle of his forehead:
  oṃ paramagurubhyo namaḥ

touching the top of his head:
  oṃ parāparagurubhyo namaḥ

touching the right side of his body:
  oṃ Ganeṣāya namaḥ

With palms together touching the top of his head the sādhaka says:
  oṃ Hūṃ Hrīṃ Śiva-Śaktibhyāṃ svāhā

*Stamps for making auspicious signs on the body before ritual worship. South India, 19th century. Brass.*

## *Protection*

Now follows the ritual of protective measures. The power of the divinity is ritualized into each part of the body (aṅga-nyāsa) in order to form a protective circuit and activize the energy centres of sādhaka's body. In the following mantra different parts of the body are associated with various aspects of energy so that the entire physical field of the adept is protected and revitalized. Mantras uttered during the rite are so designed as to create appropriate vibrations within the psychic field. The adept utters each mantra three times, touching respective parts of his body with the thumb, ring and middle fingers:

*Hrīṃ, may Ādyā (Primordial Energy) protect my head.*
*Śrīṃ, may Kālī protect my face.*
*Krīṃ, may the Supreme Śakti protect my heart.*
*May she who is the supreme of the supreme protect my throat.*
*May Jagaddhātrī protect my two eyes.*
*May Śaṇkarī protect my two ears.*
*May Mahāmāyā protect my power of smell.*
*May Sarvamaṅgalā protect my power of taste.*
*May Kaumārī protect the power of my teeth.*
*May Kamalālayā protect my cheeks.*
*May Kṣmā protect my upper and lower lips.*
*May Mālinī protect my chin.*
*May Kuleśvarī protect my throat.*

*May Kṛpāmayī protect my neck.*
*May Vasudhā protect my two arms.*
*May Kaivalyadāyinī protect my two hands.*
*May Kapardīhī protect my shoulders.*
*May Trailokyatāriṇī protect my back.*
*May Aparṇā protect my two sides.*
*May Kamaṭheśvarī protect my hips.*
*May Viśālākṣī protect my navel.*
*May Prabhāvatī protect my organ.*
*May Kalyāṇī protect my thighs.*
*May Pārvatī protect my feet.*
*May Jayadurgā protect my vital breaths.*
*May Sarvasiddhidātā protect all parts of my body.*

As to those parts which are not mentioned and are unprotected, may the eternal Primeval Kālī protect all such.

At this stage nyāsa is introduced into the ritual. Nyāsa is a great help in creating a favourable mood in the adept aspiring for the divine nature to permeate his body. After the purification and protection of the gross body, follows the bhūta-śuddhi or purification of the elements of which the body is composed. It starts with the mantra:

*Oṃ bhūtasṛingāṭaśirah suṣumṇāpathena jīva-śivaṃ*
*paramaśivapade yojayāmi svāhā*
*oṃ yaṃ liṅgaśarīraṃ śoṣaya śoṣaya svāhā*
*oṃ raṃ saṅkocaśarīram daha daha svāhā*
*om paramaśivasuṣumṇāpathena mūlaśṛṅgāṭakaṃ*
*oṃ hrīṃ durgārakṣaṇyai svāhā.*

In the above mantra, known as paranyāsa, the sādhaka, the individual being, is identified with Parama-Śiva, the Universal Being. By this mantra the aspirant symbolically envisages that the impurities of his material body are burned away. He then becomes all-luminous and divine.

## *Transformation*

Having purified the element of his own body the sādhaka proceeds gradually to purify the body of his śakti with an appropriate ritual known as Vijayā-śodhana. Through the goddess, one gains the vision of reality. The woman who becomes the personified goddess opens a doorway to a deeper transpersonal experience.

Only when she is seen through divine eyes does the sādhaka apprehend the innate divine qualities of the physical woman.

Sādhaka now draws the Vijayā-maṇḍala around the libation jar which is placed on the ground. Ritual ingredients and five spoonfuls of wine (kāraṇa) are sprinkled over it. Through the finger gestures of the yoni mudrā and nyāsa the sādhaka symbolically transforms his partner into the radiance of Śakti's body with the following mantra which is the dhyāna or mūla (root) mantra of the goddess Saṃvit who is also called Bhairavī, an aspect of Śakti:

*Birth as an image of creation. South India, 18th century. Wood.*

I

*Aiṃ samvidā asya mantrasya*
*dakṣiṇāmūrti ṛṣisāndūlankritaṃchaṇdah sadāśiva devatā*
*saṃvit sānniuopane viniyogaḥ.*

II

*Oṃ siddhyadyaṃ saṃvitśrī śivabodhinīṃ karalasat*
*pāśāṅkuśāṃ bhairaviṃ*
*bhaktābhiṣṭavarapradam sukuśalāṃ*
*saṁsārabandhocchidāṃ*
*piyūsāmbudhimanthanodbhava rasaṃ sambitbilās-*
*āspadām vīrājārelta pādukāṃ*
*suvijayāṃ dhyāyet jagatmohinīṃ.*

In order to create an appropriate vibration around his śakti, the adept recites this mantra:

III

*Om saṃvide brahma-sambhūte brahmaputrī sadānaghe*
*bhairavānāñca tṛptyarthaṃ*
*pabitrobhava sarvadā*
*oṃ brahmāṇyaih namaḥ svāhā.*

For the protection of śakti, the adept claps three times and utters the bīja, Phaṭ, simultaneously thumping the ground three times with his left heel. Then follows the sublimation of senses by invocation to the ten Śaktis with the mantra:

*Sumitrā sunīti devī vijayā carcitā parā*
*amṛitā tulsī tuṅgā tejomayī sureśvarī*
*etāni daśanāmani kare kṛtvā paṭhedbudhah*
*duḥkha dāridryanāśyet paraṃ jñānam avāpṇuyāt.*

The sādhaka begs a blessing from śakti, identifying her with chidrūpa-mahāśakti (supreme śakti), with the following prayer:

*yāścakrakramabhūmikā vasatayoḥ nāḍiṣu yā samisthitā*
*yā kāyadrumaromakūpanilayā yāḥ samsthitā dhātuṣu*
*uchvāsormi marutlaringa nilyā niḥśvāsavāsāśca yāstā*
*devoh ripu bhkṣyabhakṣaṇa parā stṛipyantu kaulārcitā*
*yā divyakamapālika ksītigatā yā devatāstoyagā*
*yā nityaṃ prathitaḥ prabhaḥ śikhigatā yā mātariśvā sryāḥ*
*yā vyomāmṛita maṇḍatāmritamayā yāssarvagāḥ sarvadā*
*tā sarvāḥ kulamārga pālanaparāḥ śāntiṃ prayacchuntu me.*

This prayer is followed by a salutation to his own śakti with the mantra:

*Oṃ saṃviddevī garīyasīm guṇanidhim*
*vaiguṇyavidhāyinīṃ*
*mahāmohamadāndhakāra śamanīm tāpa-*
*trayonmīlinīṃ*
*vande viramukhāmbujā vilāsinīṃ*
*sambodhinīm dīpikāṃ*
*brahmamayī vivekavijayā*
*vidyā mūrtaye namaḥ.*

## *SYMBOLIC PRESENCE OF THE GURU*

At this stage, the sādhaka invokes the symbolic presence of the guru. He places two seats on the ground to represent the guru and his śakti, and mentally visualizes that the guru and his śakti have occupied the seats. Then begins the mental worship of the guru with various ritual ingredients. With thumb and ring-fingers of both hands he offers scent with the following mantra:

*I*
*Laṃ prithvyātmakam gandham saśaktika-*
*śrī gurave samarpayāmi namaḥ*

he offers red flowers with the mantra:

*II*
*Haṃ ākāśātmakam puṣpān saśaktika-*
*śrī gurave samarpayāmi namaḥ.*

In the same way he makes offering of incense, light and food with the mantra:

*III*
*Vaṃ vāyavyātmakaṃ dhūpāṃ saśaktika-*
*śrī gurave samarpayāmi namaḥ.*

*IV*

*Raṃ vanhyātmakam dīpam saśaktika-*
*śrī gurave samarpayāmi namaḥ.*

*V*

*Vaṃ amritātmakam naivedyam saśaktika-*
*śrī gurave samarpayāmi namaḥ.*

*VI*

*Aiṃ sam sarvātmakam tāmbulam saśaktika-*
*śrī gurave samarpayāmi namaḥ.*

Joining the middle and ring-fingers and thumb of his right hand, and placing it above his head on the Sahasrāra chakra, the adept makes a mental offering to the guru:

*Saśaktikaśrī guruṃ tarpayāmi svāhā*
*hrīṃ hrīṃ hrīṃ*
*saśaktikaśrī gurupādukām tarpayāmi svāhā*
*saśaktikaśrī paramaguruṃ parāparaguruṃ*
*parameṣṭhi guruṃ tarpayāmi svāhā*
*hrīṃ hrīṃ hrīṃ.*

(3 times) *Saśaktika divyaugha sidhayuga*
*mānavaugha gurupanktibhyāṃ*
*tarpayāmi svāhā*
*hauṃ hrīṃ hūṃ*

(3 times) *Saśaktika divyaugha sidhaugha mānavaugha*
*garupanktīnām śrīpādukaṃ*
*tarpayāmi svāhā.*

*The yoni at the feet of the Devī (goddess), one of the images in the Sixty-Four Yoginī Temple, representing ādyā-śakti, the primal energy. Bheraghat, Madhya Pradesh, c. 12th century. Stone.*

(12 times: the guru's Gāyatrī mantra)

*Oṃ aiṃ guru devāya vidmahe*
*caitanyarūpāya dhīmahi*
*tanno guru prachodayāt oṃ.*

He visualizes the guru as identified with his (the sādhaka's) ishṭa-devatā (chosen deity) by concentrating on the guru's ideal image (guru-dhyānam):

*Sudhāsphatikasaṅkāśam virājitam*
*gandhānulepanaṃ nijaguruṃkārunyenāvalokitaṃ*
*vāmoruśaktisaṃyuktam śuklāmbarabhuṣitam*
*saśaktim daksahastena dhṛtām cārukalevarām*
*vāme dhṛtotpalañśca suraktiṃ suśobhanam*
*ānanda rasollāsa lochandvya pankajamdhyayet.*

He repeats five times the bīja mantra Hauṃ, Hrīṃ at the imagined feet of the guru. At this point, it is believed, the power of the guru and his śakti are projected on to the adepts, and they themselves become guru and his śakti. The adepts visualize themselves as identified with the pervading reality, Śiva-Śakti, and, having gone through the ritual of the control of the senses by invocation and purifying rites, they submerge themselves into the immensity and appear to be space-clad or naked.

The sādhaka then places before him two bowls in the name of the guru and his śakti and pours wine into them:

*Om jaya jaya vijaya vijaya*
*parabrahma svarūpiṇī*
*sarvajanaṃ me vaśānaya*
*Hūṃ Phaṭ svāhā*

He gives one bowl of wine to his own śakti who drinks half and the rest is taken by the sādhaka.

Sādhaka imagines that he is sitting on the guru's right lap and his śakti on the imagined guru's left lap and they embrace each other and utter the following mantra 12 times:

*Laṃ – Mūlādhāra*
*Vaṃ – Svādishṭhāna*
*Raṃ – Maṇipūra*
*Yaṃ – Anāhata*
*Haṃ – Viśuddha*

Sādhaka and his śakti then enjoy the ritual of divine nectar. He sucks in a single breath at each of śakti's breasts to awaken in himself the sensation known as amṛta-pān ('taking of nectar'). This ends the ritual of the guru.

## *Śakti worship*

It is not physiological sight but psychologically seeing her as a mental screen onto which is projected a series of personifications, that changes the adept's ordinary perception of a woman into a special kind of perception – Śakti. The transference of divinity is not something which is detached from the real but is within the reach of experience. The man and the woman both are parts of a drama to which they conform in perfect lucidity. Their interplay is a complementary movement of thought and feeling; there is no place for abstraction here, but only constant reference to a tangible human condition. Hence the experience of the transubstantiation of a woman into a goddess is viewed as a very special revelation of reality which can be seen, felt, and apprehended in no other way than what it is.

*Devī. Kulu Valley, Himachal Pradesh, c. 18th century. Bronze.*

The man and woman encounter themselves in one another; in doing so more completely does one relate to one's inner self. This continuous activity of 'seeing' into one another through the various ritual acts climaxing in sexo-yogic āsana plunges the group into an anonymity in which personal ego-sense is dissolved for the acceptance of the common goal. By the process of ritual projection, the adepts are imbued with divinity until both the male and female, who represent the dialectical principles, achieve an existential awareness of unity similar to the symbol of the circle: 'So 'haṃ: I am He' or 'Sā 'haṃ: I am she', for 'There is no difference between Me and Thee.'

Sublimation techniques are based on regulating seminal ejaculation, which is achieved by combined thought and breath control, along with certain āsanas such as Padmāsana, Siddhāsana, Śavāsana, Yoniāsana, Jānujugmāsana, Chakrāsana, Puhapaka-āsana, Ratiāsana, Bhagāsana, and certain mudrās, prominent among which are Vajroli, Sahajoli, Yoni, Khecharī and Mahā-mudrā.

Sexual energy is also controlled through Hatha-yoga. The proper practice of these mudrās, bandhas or āsanas, prāṇāyama, etc., ensures retention of sexual energy in both partners. If, by chance, orgasm occurs, the fluids can be withdrawn into the body by Vajrolimudrā. Through bandhas and āsanas, expansion and contraction of the pelvic region are also possible, the most effective being the Uddiyana-bandha, Mūla-bandha and Mahāvedha. True maithuna is the consummation of a difficult apprenticeship.

The next stage of the ritual consists of its higher level, Śakti worship. The adept visualizes the essence of his śakti as an abstract

*Kālī Yantra. Rajasthan, 18th century. Gouache on paper.*

yantra of the Devī – a bindu in the triangle with its apex upwards at Sahasrāra, the top of the head. He shares food and other ritual objects with his śakti and draws an inverted triangle with a bindu inside it, within a circle on the ground at śakti's right side; he worships the yantra, the abstract symbol of Śakti, with an offering of red flowers, preferably jabā (hibiscus), and the mantra:

*Oṃ māṇḍukyāya namaḥ*
*oṃ kālāgnirudrāya namaḥ*
*oṃ anantāya namaḥ*
*oṃ varāhāya namaḥ*
*oṃ prithvyai namaḥ*
*oṃ nālāya namaḥ*
*oṃ kesarāya namaḥ*
*oṃ padmāya namaḥ*
*oṃ karṇikāya namaḥ*
*oṃ maṇḍalāya namaḥ*
*oṃ dharmāya namaḥ*
*oṃ vairāgyāya namaḥ*
*oṃ aiśvaryāya namaḥ*
*oṃ jñanāya namaḥ*

*oṃ anaiśvaryāya namaḥ*
*oṃ avairāgyāya namaḥ*
*oṃ adharmāya namaḥ*
*oṃ ajñānāya namaḥ*
*oṃ jñānātmane namaḥ*
*oṃ kriyātmane namaḥ*
*oṃ paramātmane namaḥ.*[39]

After the recitation of the mantra, the sādhaka places a libation bowl on the yantra and sprinkles wine with the red flower. He then worships his śakti with the mantra:

*Oṃ aiṃ kandarpāya namaḥ*
*oṃ hriṃ kāmarājāya namaḥ*
*oṃ klīṃ manmathāya namaḥ*
*oṃ blūṃ makardhvajāya namaḥ*
*oṃ strīm monobhavāya namaḥ.*

and says the following mantra on four sides of his śakti:

*Oṃ baṭukāya namaḥ*
*oṃ bhairavāya namaḥ*
*oṃ durgāyai namaḥ*
*oṃ kṣetrapālāya namaḥ*

He then uses vermilion paste to draw an upward-pointed triangle with a bindu in its centre on the forehead of his Śakti and begins to worship her from the Ajñā chakra region downwards with the following mantra, in which he personifies her as the three aspects of Devī as Durgā, Lakṣmī and Sarasvatī:

*Oṃ hsauh sadāśiva mahāpreto padmāsanāya namaḥ*
*oṃ aiṃ klīṃ strīṃ blūṃ ādhāraśaktiśrī padukāṃ pūjayāmi namaḥ*
*oṃ Durgāyai namaḥ*
*oṃ Lakṣmyai namaḥ*
*oṃ Sarasvatyai namaḥ.*

Finally he worships Ganeśa, bestower of attainment.

## *Body worship*

This stage of the ritual implies a sensuous and aesthetic experience which takes into account the ever-present interphysical relationship between man and woman. However transitory its nature, the physical communion is a limitation of the absolutely real. The sādhaka worships his śakti's hair and face as representing

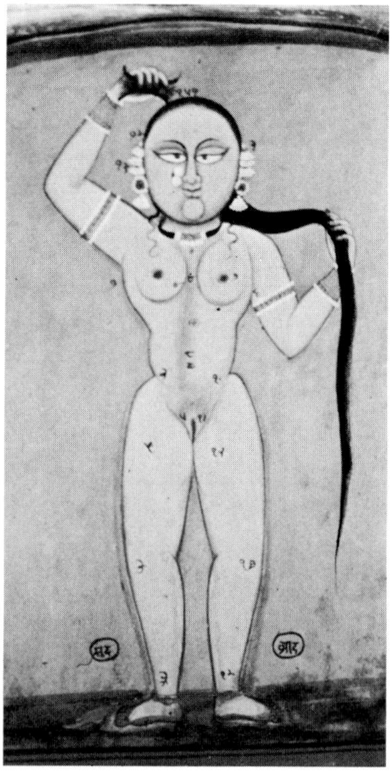

*A female figure marked to indicate the Amṛitakalā, which are energized on auspicious days of the white and dark halves of the month. Rajasthan, c. 18th century. Gouache on paper.*

the essence of the sun and the moon, and then begins the elaborate ritual of Kāma-kalā, touching all the parts of her body, from her right toe to her head, while reciting the mantra:

*Oṃ aṃ śraddhayai namaḥ*

*oṃ āṃ kīrtyai namaḥ*

*oṃ iṃ rataye namaḥ*

*oṃ īṃ bhūtayae namaḥ*

*oṃ uṃ kāntaye namaḥ*

*oṃ ūṃ monobhāvaya namaḥ*

*oṃ ṛṃ monoharaye namaḥ*

*oṃ ṝṃ monoharinyai namaḥ*

*oṃ lṃ madanaye namaḥ*

*oṃ lṃ utpādinyai namaḥ*

*oṃ eṃ mohinyai namaḥ*

*oṃ aiṃ dīpinyai namaḥ*

*oṃ oṃ sodhanyai namaḥ*

*oṃ auṇ vasaṅkaraye namaḥ*

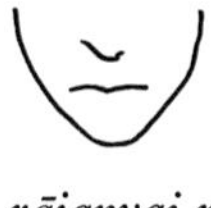

*oṃ aṃ rājanyai namaḥ*

*oṃ aḥ priyadarśanaye namaḥ.*

Then, from the top of her head to her left toe, the sādhaka touches his śakti's body, accompanying his gestures with this mantra:

*Oṃ aṃ puśaye namaḥ*
*oṃ āṃ basaye namaḥ*
*oṃ iṃ samanaye namaḥ*
*oṃ īṃ rataye namaḥ*
*oṃ uṃ pritaye namaḥ*
*oṃ ūṃ dhritaye namaḥ*
*oṃ ṛṃ sudhaye namaḥ*
*oṃ ṝṃ somaye namaḥ*
*oṃ ḷṃ marichaye namaḥ*
*oṃ ḹṃ aṃśumālinai namaḥ*
*oṃ aiṃ angiraye namaḥ*
*oṃ aiṃ vasinyai namaḥ*
*oṃ auṃ chāyaye namaḥ*
*oṃ auṃ sampurnamaṇḍalaye namaḥ*
*oṃ aṃ tuṣṭaye namaḥ*
*oṃ aḥ amṛtaye namaḥ*

## *Yoni worship*

The sādhaka then proceeds to worship his śakti's yoni with the following mantra, offering water, flower and kāraṇa (wine):

*Oṃ aiṃ candrāya namaḥ* (water)
*oṃ aiṃ sauryāya namaḥ* (flower)
*oṃ aiṃ agnaye namaḥ* (wine)

He then places as an offering red sandal paste and flowers on her yoni with this mantra:

*Hrīṃ strīṃ hūṃ namaḥ*
*oṃ bhagamālinyai namaḥ*
*oṃ aiṃ hrīṃ srīṃ aīṃ yaṃ blūṃ*
*klinne sarvāni bhagāni vaśamanaya me*
*oṃ strīṃ hrīṃ klīṃ blūṃ bhagamālinyai namaḥ*
*aiṃ hrīṃ srīṃ saśaktika namaḥ*

This mantra is recited in the name of Bhagamālinī, the third goddess of the three very closely associated deities of Devī Tripurāsundarī. They are the first three predominant goddesses of the fifteen nitya-kalā. In the trikoṇa-yantra (triangular yantra) of Sahasrāra, Devī Tripurāsundarī is surrounded by the goddess Kāmeśvarī, Vajreśvarī and Bhagamālinī. Since the name Bhagamālinī is erotically suggestive because of the pun on the word

*Ādyā-Śakti, the Ultimate Ground, genetrix of All Things. Alampur Museum, Andhra Pradesh,* c. *11th century. Stone.*

bhaga, which means both female organ and divine power, she is often referred to in the ritual.

Sādhaka then begins worshipping his own ishṭa-devatā, or chosen deity (here, the goddess Kālī), with the following mantra:

*Oṃ krīṃ pādyaṃ samarpayāmi namaḥ* (feet)
*oṃ krīṃ arghyam samarpayāmi namaḥ* (offering the water)
*oṃ krīṃ ācamaniyam samarpayāmi namaḥ* (sipping)
*oṃ krīṃ snānīyam samarpayāmi namaḥ* (bath)
*oṃ krīṃ gandhaṃ samarpayāmi namaḥ* (perfume)
*oṃ krīṃ puspam bilvañca samarpayāmi namaḥ* (flowers and bilva leaves)
*oṃ krīṃ naivedyaṃ samarpayāmi namaḥ* (food)
*oṃ krīṃ pānayaṃ samarpayāmi namaḥ* (water)
*oṃ krīṃ tāmbulaṃ samarpayāmi namaḥ* (betel leaves)
*oṃ krīṃ dakṣhiṇāṃ samarpayāmi namaḥ* (sacrificial fee)

## *Śakti as goddess*

Touching the feet of his śakti, now a goddess, the sādhaka recites the hymns to the Devī as if she has now become the goddess Kālī:

*Oṃ yā devī sarvabhūtesu śaktirūpena saṁsthitā*
*namastasyai namastasyai namastasyai namo namaḥ*

and he recites:

*That power who is defined as Consciousness in all beings,*
*reverence to Her, reverence to Her, reverence to Her,*
*reverence, reverence.*

*Kālī. Kalighat, Calcutta, c. 19th century. Gouache on paper.*

*That Power who is known as Reason in all beings,*
*reverence to Her, reverence to Her, reverence to Her,*
*reverence, reverence.*

*That Power who exists in all beings in the form of Sleep,*
*reverence to Her, reverence to Her, reverence to Her,*
*reverence, reverence.*

*That Power who exists in all beings as Hunger,*
*reverence to Her, reverence to Her, reverence to Her,*
*reverence, reverence.*

*That Power who exists in all beings as Shadow,*
*reverence to Her, reverence to Her, reverence to Her,*
*reverence, reverence.*

*That Power who exists in all beings as Energy,*
*reverence to Her, reverence to Her, reverence to Her,*
*reverence, reverence.*

*That Power who exists in all beings in the form of Thirst,*
*reverence to Her, reverence to Her, reverence to Her,*
*reverence, reverence.*

*That Power who exists in all beings as Forgiveness,*
*reverence to Her, reverence to Her, reverence to Her,*
*reverence, reverence.*

*That Power who exists in all beings in the form of Species,*
*reverence to Her, reverence to Her, reverence to Her,*
*reverence, reverence.*

*That Power who exists in all beings as Bashfulness,*
*reverence to Her, reverence to Her, reverence to Her,*
*reverence, reverence.*

*That Power who exists in all beings as Peace,*
*reverence to Her, reverence to Her, reverence to Her,*
*reverence, reverence.*

*That Power who exists in all beings in the form of Faith,*
*reverence to Her, reverence to Her, reverence to Her,*
*reverence, reverence*

*That Power who exists in all beings as Loveliness,*
*reverence to Her, reverence to Her, reverence to Her,*
*reverence, reverence.*

*That Power who exists in all beings as Fortune,*
*reverence to Her, reverence to Her, reverence to Her,*
*reverence, reverence.*

*That Power who exists in all beings as Vocation,*
*reverence to Her, reverence to Her, reverence to Her,*
*reverence, reverence.*

*That Power who exists in all beings in the form of Memory,*
*reverence to Her, reverence to Her, reverence to Her,*
*reverence, reverence.*

*That Power who exists in all beings as Compassion,*
*reverence to Her, reverence to Her, reverence to Her,*
*reverence, reverence.*

*That Power who exists in all beings as Fulfilment,*
*reverence to Her, reverence to Her, reverence to Her,*
*reverence, reverence.*

*That Power who exists in all beings as Mother,*
*reverence to Her, reverence to Her, reverence to Her,*
*reverence, reverence.*

*That Power who exists in all beings in the form of Illusion,*
*reverence to Her, reverence to Her, reverence to Her,*
*reverence, reverence. (Chaṇḍī, v:16–80)*

After this, the sādhaka's internal worship of śakti starts with his visualizing a floating circle of rays of light as though reflected from snow, with red light mixed in it, and there appears Śakti sitting in Padmāsana with Śiva. In the final act of surrender sādhaka mentally extinguishes those aspects of himself such as ego-sense, pride, greed, illusion, and lust, which are hindrances to his goal by offering different kinds of flowers, each symbolically representing these aspects.

## *Liṅga worship*

After this the liṅga is worshipped by reciting the following mantra ten times:

*Oṃ auṃ īśānāya namaḥ*
*oṃ auṃ aghorāya namaḥ*
*oṃ auṃ vāmadevāya namaḥ*
*oṃ auṃ sadyojātāya namaḥ*
*oṃ auṃ tatpuruṣāya namaḥ*
*oṃ nivṛttyai namaḥ*
*oṃ pratisṭhayāi namaḥ*
*oṃ vidyāyai namaḥ*
*oṃ śāntātītāyai namaḥ*
*oṃ ayuteśvarāya namaḥ*
*oṃ kubjāyai namaḥ*
*oṃ kāmakalāyai namaḥ*

*oṃ samayāyai namaḥ*
*oṃ cakreśvaryai namaḥ*
*oṃ kālikāyai namaḥ*
*oṃ dikkālavāsīnyai namaḥ*
*oṃ mahācakresvrayai namaḥ*
*oṃ tārāyai namaḥ.*

*Jānujugma-āsana. Orissa,* c. *19th century. Ivory.*

## *Fulfilment and union*

The adept then contemplates mental sexual intercourse. Dissolving in the fire of Śakti's yoni all the actions of the sense organs, regulating the vital breath so as to make it enter the Sushumnā, he recites the mantra Hrīṃ 108 more times, touching the breast of the Śakti with his right hand, and then Hrīṃ 108 times while touching her yoni.

Śakti places her hands over the sādhaka's head and recites thrice:

*Uttisthata:* Get up.
*Jāgrata:* Wake up.
*Virobhava:* Be strong.
*Nityamukta svabhāvānubhava:*
Realization of the everlasting and free original self.

Now I am giving you the command to immerse yourself within me. I am your guru, and enjoy yourself now with the full bliss within me. I am your Śakti and you are mine. According to the command of my Kaula Avdhūt, I as viśva-yoni [universal-yoni] am asking you to implant your cosmic liṅga in my field. My Sat-guru is here to protect you from your negative desires.

Think that at this moment you are not my husband; you are Śiva in the form of my Sat-guru and I am nothing but Śakti.

May my divine self bless you and lead you to the eternal joy of bliss.

*Viparit-ratī, sexual union with Śakti on top of the sādhaka. Orissa, 18th century. Ivory.*

Sādhaka is by this time no longer an adept but has been transformed as Bhairava, and as Śiva he worships his Śakti with nine symbolic flowers: (1) holding, (2) embracing, (3) kissing, (4) touching, (5) visualizing, (6) seeing, (7) sucking, (8) penetrating, (9) meditating, while uttering the mantra, 'Sivo 'ham: I am Śiva', 'Śivo 'ham: I am Śiva', 'Śivo 'ham: I am Śiva'.

If Śakti desires she may enact the opposite role, known as Viparit-ratī, that is the role of the sādhaka. In that case the union is effected by Śakti on top of the sādhaka, who lies like a corpse, or Śavāsana, and does not move at all. Śakti is now the male and the guru, herself acting in the great drama and transfusing the potentially charged energy of the ritual. After a prolonged stay in either position, both the adepts end the ritual with the mantra AIṂ KLĪṂ HRĪṂ SRĪṂ and finally recite HAUṂ HRĪṂ as long as possible.

In the initial stages of sādhanā, if the aspirants cannot prolong the union, they may change the āsana positions, for instance from Padmāsana to Jānjugmāsana and to Śavāsana for relaxation. The period of retention of energy may also be gradually increased. Sometimes herbal preparations are taken orally to increase its duration, such as bhāng seeds (*cannabis indica*) with the seeds of the tulsi plant; the Indian basil (*ocymum sanctum*) chewed with betel leaves also produces the desired result.

During sexual union, the minds of the adepts are withdrawn from their physical environment as they identify themselves completely with one another. After prolonged practice, the sexual energy can be retained and sublimated until the psychic current is liberated. This experience of bi-unity is termed *samarasa* in tantric texts and is a state parallel to samādhi.

*Sexo-yogic pose, from an illuminated manuscript page. Orissa, c. 18th century. Gouache on paper.*

## *Collective āsana or ritual of union*

The ritual of union is also performed collectively. The rite is designated as Pañcha-makāra, or five M's, and is practised by both the Vāmāchāris, or left-hand tantrikas, and Dakshiṇācharis, or right-hand tantrikas. When performed in a circle, it is known as Chakra-pūjā. In every instance it is a planned, intensive, emotional group-experience, and in no case may either a single couple or too many participate. Generally eight males and eight females form a chakra or circle.

A careful screening of the participants is undertaken by the guru over a specific period of time, usually a year, before actual initiation into a group takes place. A participant's competence, apart from his physical condition, is tested, with special regard to his mental disposition. *Kulārnava Tantra* lays down eight negative criteria – hatred, doubt, fear, shame, backbiting, conformity, arrogance and status consciousness – and so long as these tendencies are prevalent a participant is not fit to practise this esoteric ritual.

The aim of the chakra-pūjā is to expand consciousness by the five categories which are the objects of human desires, hence the use of these tattavas, the five M's: madya (wine), māṁsa (meat), matsya (fish), mudrā (fried cereals), maithuna (sexual union). Conventionally regarded as barriers they are accepted in this ritual by the left-hand tantrikas as steps on the ladder of perfection. The tantrikas point out that the main principle of this ritual is not to

*Bhairavī-chakra illustrating the five M's, ingredients of the tantric Pañcha-makāra rite. Rajasthan, c. 19th century. Gouache on paper.*

shrink from the senses but to conquer them through experience: 'Perfection can be attained easily by satisfying all desires' (*Guhya-Samaj Tantra*), a statement which is echoed so vividly in Aldous Huxley's letter to Timothy Leary:

> Tantra teaches a yoga of sex, a yoga of eating (even eating forbidden foods and drinking forbidden drinks). The sacramentalizing of common life, so that every event may become a means whereby enlightenment can be realized, is achieved, essentially, through constant awareness. This is the ultimate yoga – being aware, conscious even of the unconscious – on every level from the physiological to the spiritual.[40]

The five ritual ingredients beginning with M, apart from their literal meanings, are reminders of yogic processes. If they are hypostatized into mental configurations, the ritual becomes a right-hand tantric practice, or Dakshināchāra. Thus madya (wine) becomes the symbol of 'intoxicating knowledge'; māṁsa (meat) implies the control of speech (from the word ma, meaning tongue); matsya (fish) represents the two vital currents moving in the Īḍā and Piṅgalā subtle channels on each side of the central subtle channel Sushumnā; mudrā (parched cereal) symbolizes the yogic state of concentration; maithuna (sexual union) symbolizes meditation upon the primal act of creation. Those right-hand practitioners who follow rājasik sādhanā use material substitutes for the five M's. Wine is substituted for by coconut juice, meat by ginger, radish or pāniphala (the fruit of a water plant), mudrā by rice, wheat or grain, and maithuna by two types of flowers, karavī resembling the liṅga and aparājitā representing the yoni. It is believed that some of these rites were introduced by the Indian tantrika master Vasishṭha, who brought to India various antinomian practices known as chināchāra from Mahāchina ('Greater China'), which is identified with China or Tibet.

The place where the Pañchamakāra rite is to be performed must have a pleasant aroma, with incense burning, and a serene atmosphere. The ideal time for the rite is midnight. The actual performance should take place fifty-four minutes past three o'clock in the morning and continue for one hour and thirty-six minutes, a time considered auspicious for final sexual union. No less important is the arrangement of light to enhance the ritual. Castor oil lamps, which produce a violet light, are considered an ideal stimulant.

The Pañchamakāra rite begins with the initiation of the participants by the guru or the Chakreśvara, the leader of the chakra, who remains the directing centre of the group throughout the rite. The adepts pay reverence to the guru and to the circle with folded hands; each adept sits with his śakti on his left, while the

*Adharachumbana Āsana. Basohli, Jammu and Kashmir, c. 18th century. Gouache on paper.*

*Rati-āsana. Khajuraho, Madhya Pradesh, c. 12th century. Stone.*

guru sits in the centre of the chakra. Thereafter the whole ritual unfolds like the individual āsana, with the same mantras, nyāsas, prāṇāyāma, purification, identification, concentration, etc. The rite progresses by transforming the ordinary woman into Śakti, while the sādhaka, viewing her as an incarnation of the goddess Devī, recites: 'Oṃ srīṃ bale bale tripurāsundarī yonirūpe mama sarvasiddhing dehi yonimukting kuru kuru svāhā.'

In Pañchamakāra, after the consecration of the wine kept in the Śri-pātra, the cooked meat, fish and cereals are generally placed on a silver tray, and the wine cup is held between the thumb and third finger of the left hand by guru's śakti, who sips the wine and passes the cup to the adepts until all the participants drink the wine in turn, holding the cup in the same fashion. The meat is taken with the first cup of wine, the fish with the second, cereals with the third; in this way, once the first four M's are consumed, the fifth, maithuna, takes place.

In all phases of the ritual of union the emphasis is laid on knowledge and unity through personal encounter, which in turn is responsible for changing the individuals through face-to-face contact of feeling, indulging, acting, being aware in a complex relationship of body, mind, senses, man and woman become a unity. Sex tears away the differences of the ego. But like all human activity, sexuality is also of equivocal significance. It can lead an adept to the shore of inner realization or doom his humanity. To the extent the partners participate in the harmonious complementary whole with an intense awareness of their spiritual affinities, their actions serve to lead them to the deepest possible experience. On the other hand, if the adepts of the group are alienated from one another and indulge in self-defeating ego-games they will merely perpetuate a situation contrary to liberation. For this reason tantras such as the *Kulārnava* emphasize that those who indulge in this ritual mainly for the sexual acts, or for hedonistic purposes with no reference to spiritual ends, are only defeating themselves. This ritual has become suspect through gross misinterpretation of the original texts; the fault, however, is not in the tantras, but in us.

## *Confrontation*

The notion that the spiritual life is a soft, flowing, uninterrupted stream is given the lie by facts. Periods of storm and stress and of panic-stricken tension are created in rituals in order to reduce conflict and lead the adept to an impasse point so that he can

*Saptamuṇḍi-āsana. Mandi, Himachal Pradesh, 18th century. Gouache on paper.*

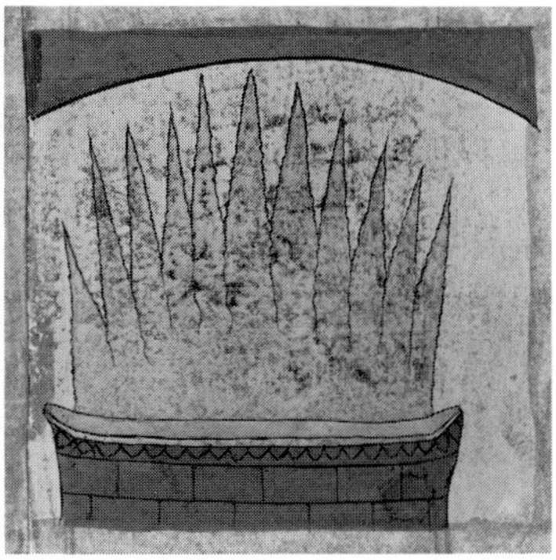

*The Principle of Fire. Rajasthan, 18th century. Gouache on paper.*

outgrow the merry-go-round of self-defeating ego-games and accept the contradictions and polarities of his own personality structure. Buddha's life is a reminder of such instances, when in his search for enlightenment he had to encounter fear-inspiring threats from Māra and his host of evil demons. The advanced tantrikas practise a type of āsana known as Śavāsana at cremation grounds. Such a place stresses the truth of transience and the aspirant's heart itself becomes a cremation ground – pride and selfishness, status and role, name and fame are all burnt to ashes. Meditation on certain types of corpses at midnight are considered best for overcoming fears and temptations that confront the adepts. It takes courage not to shrink from such emotionally disintegrating panoramas, which are not directly part of our conscious attention in our normal day-to-day life.

Recognition of the fierce aspects of life carries shock-effects of varying degrees, depending upon the strength of the adept's conviction, before tranquility can be established. However, it is not at all necessary that all sādhakas should go to such terror-inspiring sites; the same result may be achieved by introspection. Perhaps because of their strong associations with the mysterious, terrifying situations and atmospheres charged with powers that can frighten the aspirant, such as midnight and cremation grounds, were considered suitable for an explosion of psychic potential. Another meditative occult practice is carried out with the aid of five, or nine, human skulls and is called Pañcha-muṇḍi, or Nava-muṇḍi, āsana. The adept sits in Padmāsana (the lotus position) on human skulls, a discipline necessary to help him confront and purge from consciousness his own terror.

These confrontations are a source of renewal, and a doorway to a new productive impulse which comes to the adept's aid with a constructive view of the situation. They help to obliterate distinctions between the objects of attraction and revulsion and stress that all extremes, the individual's conscious and unconscious self with its contradictions, the ostensibly positive and negative aspects of existence, form an inseparable unity.

The views advanced by modern psychologists such as Jung, who recognized the importance of a shock experience in order to face the 'shadow self' or the 'dark' side of the personality structure for a total integration of the psyche, are in no way different in essence from what the tantric adept aspires to achieve from these awe-inspiring rituals. In *The Symbolic Quest* Edward C. Whitmont explains the Jungian concept of the significance of confronting the 'shadow':

> The confrontation of one's own evil can be a mortifying death-like experience; but like death it points beyond the personal meaning of existence. . . . It [the shadow] represents the first stage toward meeting the Self. There is, in fact, no access to the unconscious and to our own reality *but* through the shadow. Only when we realize that part of ourselves which we have not hitherto seen or preferred not to see can we proceed to question and find the sources from which it feeds and the basis on which it rests. Hence no progress or growth in analysis is possible until the shadow is adequately confronted – and confronting means more than merely knowing about it. It is not until we have truly been shocked into seeing ourselves as we really are, instead of as we wish or hopefully assume we are, that we can take the first step toward individual reality.[41]

In the abstruse symbolism of tantras, the ten aspects or energies of the Primal Śakti, or the ten objects of transcendental knowledge, daśa-mahā-vidyās, signifying the various degrees and stages of existence, have a similar transformative function. The ten Mahāvidyās are (1) Kālī, the power of time; (2) Tārā, the potential of re-creation; (3) Śoḍaśī, the embodiment of the sixteen modifications of desire; (4) Bhuvaneśvarī, substantial forces of the material world; (5) Bhairavī, who multiplies herself in an infinity

*Mahāvidyās, the Śakti-transformations representing transcendental knowledge. Ten aspects of Śakti – Kalī, Tārā, Soḍashī, Bhuvaneśvarī, Bhairavī, Chinnamastā, Dhūmavatī, Bagālā, Mātangī and Kamālā – embody all levels of knowledge. Jaipur, late 19th century. Gouache on paper.*

of beings and forms; (6) Chinnamastā, distributing the life energy into the universe; (7) Dhumābatī, associated with unsatisfied desires; (8) Bagalā, destroyer of negative forces; (9) Mātaṅgī, the power of domination; (10) Kamalā, the state of reconstituted unity. Philip Rawson summarizes these transformations thus: 'These Śakti-transformations may be worshipped separately, in series, or even in combined images symbolic of transitional stages. Each one of them represents a limitation of the total persona of Kālī herself, but is an inevitable part of that whole. Without the drastic experience of disintegration, no search for integration means anything.'[42]

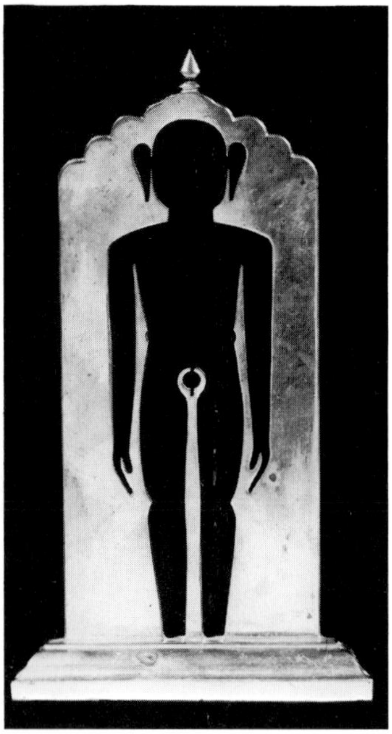

*Jaina icon of the Jina as released spirit. Rajasthan, c. 19th century. Brass.*

## *Stages of psychic growth*

The pilgrimage of the ego from its incipient potential state to self-actualization – an unwinding of the inner energies to expand, to be, to become – is a slow gradual process which begins at the very advent of spiritual life. The ultimate goal of the human ego treading the tantric path is liberation or enlightenment through the experience of ecstasy: to become a total being through the awareness of one's psychic potencies. Psychic ascent can be viewed in terms of sharply defined phases which can be subdivided into various categories: first, preparation and incubation; second, self-actualization and realization.

The psyche, as a condensed nucleus of energy with the possibility to expand, first begins to be aware of its unbounded potentiality and concurrently accepts the belief system, in this case tantra, in which it is going to be actualized. Then begins the quest for a spiritual preceptor who can direct and point out the signposts on the path. When the sādhanā begins and under the guidance of the guru various techniques are adopted, the neophyte, by following a continuous, uninterrupted physical and mental discipline, allows these disciplines to infiltrate into his life and actions. He absorbs the technique in a process analogous to incubation, until their daily performance and observance becomes as natural to him as breathing.

The special states of consciousness conducive to psychic ascent consist mainly in narrowing down the field of concentration by becoming more centralized, and gathering into a nucleus one's own energies through the use of various concentrative and absorptive methods in relation to one's temperament and potencies. Prescribed techniques may include the recitation of mantra, use of yantra, mudrā, nyāsa, prāṇāyāma, daily pūjā, meditation, etc. By daily practice, the sādhaka enhances his possibilities of entering into unusual states of mind, albeit such awareness in the preliminary stages is only one aspect of the whole manifestation. Once a balance is struck between external aids and the sādhaka's inner rhythm, the next step of sādhanā which follows simultaneously as a consequence of outer worship is the inner control of the mind by a total 'disintegration of the ego'. This stage consists of facing and confronting the shadow self, the unconscious forces, and the perception of the creative, destructive continuum of the polarity principles manifesting as one. At this stage, either one advances towards total liberation or returns to material conditions. Many who cannot bear the forcefulness or arduous task of the discipline may even abandon the search. The next stage is one of reintegration, a harbinger of a new creative birth – a state before psychic actualization slowly begins to dawn.

The second stage, which is anticipatory to the final stage, may be called self-actualization. It is a stage when the aspirant begins to apprehend that awareness is not inseparable from other aspects of experience: he is a part of the totality of which he is a centre. This is a state of equanimity of *samayana,* the state of emptiness, of mental tranquility, serenity, imperturbability, self-restraint, accompanied by a cessation of cognitive, cognative and volitional function. At this level, the sādhaka is 'centred' or 'balanced', always at ease. Nothing in life is too great or final to move him, since he is no longer at the mercy of opposing sense-reactions.

Self-actualization may also be manifested in the attainment of supernatural powers, or siddhis, such as duplicating one's body at will, walking on water, etc. The lives of some of the famous tantric Nātha saints give glowing descriptions of their superhuman occult powers. In all cases the attainment of siddhi is considered to be a lesser grade of enlightenment. Ramakrishna always used to warn his disciples not to become siddhāi and deprecated and implicitly decried it: 'If asceticism can teach you after twenty years only to walk on water better pay the boatman and save your time.'

The physiological symptoms of self-actualization may be perceptible in the adepts of Kuṇḍalinī-yoga. The ascent of the Kuṇḍalinī as it pierces through the chakras is manifested by certain physical and psychical planes of awareness. In the preliminary stages the body trembles and the yogi can feel the explosion of psychic heat passing like a current through the Sushumnā. Ramakrishna describes his own experience of the leaps and bounds of this phenomenon as 'hopping', 'pushing up', 'moving', 'zig-zag'. As the Kuṇḍalinī ascends further other signs of awakening begin to appear. The yogis describe how, at first, a number of auditory experiences of inner sounds are had, in which the sounds heard interiorly resemble some of the sounds of the external environment such as the sound of a waterfall, the humming of bees, the sound of a bell, a flute, the tinkling of ornaments, etc. In such experiences, the head may become giddy and the mouth fill with saliva, but the aspiring yogi must go further till he can hear the innermost, unstruck subtle sound or *nād* identified with inner silence. Along with these there may be many sensory reactions of a visual nature. The yogi may, in his closed-eye-perception, visualize a variety of forms such as dots of light, flames, geometrical shapes till all of these in the final state of illumination

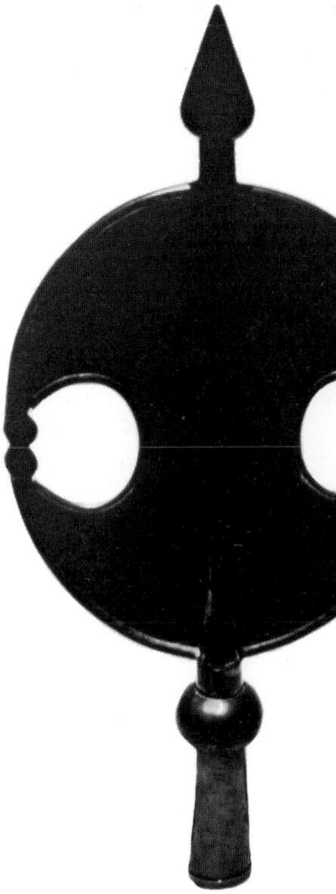

*Vaishṇava symbol of Lord Chaitanya. Bengal, c. 18th century. Brass.*

dissolve into an inner radiance of intensely bright pure light in which the yogi has the sense of being immersed into a blaze of dazzling flame.

An altered state of consciousness differs from our ordinary perception of reality. First, the illumined yogi has a holistic perception of reality which he directly apprehends through the inherent harmony in unity of all things, together with various sensory reactions. Second, his ascent from one level of consciousness to another alters a normal dimension of linear time-experience as a constant flow of events sequentially organized as past, present and future into an experience which transcends time and in which all events simultaneously exist in the 'infinite present'.

*Śiva-Śakti, illustrating Śiva and Śakti as the embodiment of universal energy, Kuṇḍalinī, in the centre of his body. Himachal Pradesh, c. 18th century. Gouache on paper.*

The last stage of psychic ascent culminates in illumination or unity-mergence. The psyche, having traversed a long and winding road, now enters a new domain. The aspirant becomes totally integrated within himself, having cast aside all illusions and delusions. There is no ambiguity in his life. He is merged with the object of his worship, slowly dissolving all the grosser elements of his personality into a subtle constancy for final abandonment. This stage is characterized by an experiential realization of what the classical Hindu tradition (including tantra) calls Sat (Being), Chit (Consciousness), Ānanda (Bliss), the triad of substances of Śiva-Śakti in union. If we take a mundane view of these concepts, these three may appear as separate substances. But in an 'altered' or 'metamorphosed' state of consciousness, such as that lived by one who has realized, they form a tri-unity, each submerging into one single unified experience. In our ordinary experience we dissociate the object of pleasure from the person who experiences it. Thus a painting is different from the painter, a poem is distinct from the poet, music is separated from the musician; but in altered states these distinctions are abolished – the painter becomes the painting, the poet the poem, the musician the music, the sādhaka the very essence of the bliss of union characterized by Sat-Chit-Ānanda.

One who has attained these transformations has no more desires. All external aids become symbols of phases and forces. They are no more than 'links' in different parts of the whole, and all the means that we require to reach the ultimate goal, however high, lie within us: 'What need have I of an outer woman? I have an inner woman within myself.' When roused, she (Kuṇḍalinī, the 'inner woman') shines like 'millions of lightning flashes' in the centre of the sādhaka's body. He then thinks that he himself is shining like everything that is reflected. He looks upon the entire objective world that is reflected as surging within him. He then neither chants mantras, nor performs mudrās or prāṇāyāma, nor worships gods and goddesses. For he looks upon all that is in himself.

Pattinattar, the Tamil tantrika siddhāi poet, expresses the joy of realization thus:

*The eightfold yoga*
*The six regions of the body*
*The five states*
*They all have left and gone*
*Totally erased*
*And in the open*
*Void*
*I am left*
*Amazed*
*There is but a red rounded Moon*
*A fountain of white milk*
*For delight*
*The unobtainable Bliss*
*Has engulfed me*
*A precipice*
*Of light.*[43]

The origin and goal meet in a single focal point: UNION.
The knower and the known become ONE.

# Notes

1 Woodroffe, *Principles of Tantra*, II, p. 39
2 Barnett, *The Universe and Dr Einstein*, p. 90
3 Schindler, *Goethe's Theory of Colour*, p. 205
4 Naranjo and Ornstein, *On the Psychology of Meditation*, II
5 D. Bhattacharya, *Love Songs of Chaṇḍidas*, p. 18
6 Ibid., p. 153
7 Solomon, *LSD*, p. 69
8 Eliade, *Yoga, Immortality and Freedom*, p. 250
9 Mookerjee, *Tantra Art*
10 Rawson: review of *Tantra Art* in *Oriental Art* XIII, 4, 1967
11 Coomaraswamy, *The Transformation of Nature in Art*, p. 67
12 Lucio Fontana's statement, 1965
13 Zimmer, *Myths and Symbols in Indian Art and Civilization*, pp. 141–2
14 Jenny, *UNESCO Courier*, December, 1969, pp. 16, 18
15 *Abstract Art Since 1945*, p. 289
16 Tucci, *The Theory and Practice of the Mandala*, p. 51
17 Ibid., p. 50
18 Zimmer, Ibid., p. 90
19 Rawson, *The Art of Tantra*, p. 139
20 Boner, *Principles of Composition in Hindu Sculpture*, p. 25
21 Quoted by Koestler in *The Roots of Coincidence*, p. 63
22 Seal, *The Positive Science of the Ancient Hindus*, pp. 40–1
23 Prabhavananda, *The Spiritual Heritage of India*, pp. 213–14
24 Ibid.
25 Rola, *Alchemy*, pp. 20–1
26 Ray, *History of Chemistry in Ancient and Medieval India*, p. 132
27 Walker, *Hindu World*, I, p. 286
28 Parker, *The Compleat Astrologer*, p. 50
29 Krishna, *The Biological Basis of Religion and Genius*, pp. 42–3
30 Quoted by Reyna in *The Philosophy of Matter in the Atomic Era*, p. 96
31 Rieker, *The Yoga of Light*, p. 157
32 Gupta, *Lakṣmī Tantra*, p. 189
33 Quoted by Fabun, *Dimensions of Change*, pp. 199–200
34 Gupta, op. cit., p. 206
35 Vivekananda, *The Yogas and Other Works*, p. 627
36 Rieker, op. cit., p. 36
37 De Ropp, *Sex Energy*, p. 4
38 Rieker, *The Secret of Meditation*, p. 52
39 Documentation of a number of mantras by Kalyan S. Coll has been of great help
40 Letter of Aldous Huxley to Timothy Leary, 11 February 1962
41 Whitmont, *The Symbolic Quest*, pp. 164–5
42 Rawson, op. cit., pp. 133–4
43 Kamil V. Zvelebil, *The Poets of the Powers*, pp. 101–2

# Glossary

ADHIKĀRA, a disciple's competency to practise spiritual discipline.

ĀDYĀ ŚAKTI, the Primal Energy.

ĀGAMAS, sacred tantric scriptures.

AJAPA MANTRA, the involuntary repetition of a sacred formula.

ĀJÑĀ CHAKRA, centre between eyebrows in the subtle body.

ĀKĀŚA, generally, ether, a kind of matter subtler than air.

ANĀHATA CHAKRA, the heart centre in the subtle body.

ANĀHATA SABDA, unstruck sound.

ĀNANDA, essential principle of joy, bliss, spiritual ecstasy.

AṆIMĀ, power to become small as an atom through yoga.

AÑJALI, the mudrā in which the two hands extended upwards are held palm to palm.

AP, the material element of water.

APĀNA, one of the energies that goes downwards, controlling the vital air in the abdominal region.

ARDHANĀRĪŚVARA, the androgynous form of Śiva.

ĀSANA, steady posture, yogic pose, a condition of balance and poise.

ĀSRAMA, a hermitage or dwelling place dedicated to spiritual pursuits.

AUM, the three sounds which compose the root mantra, Oṃ (q.v.).

AVADHŪTA, a rebel renunciate.

AVATĀRA, a divine Incarnation.

ĀYURVEDA, ancient Indian medical system based on the Vedas.

BANDHA, muscular flexion, yogic practice in which certain organs of the body are 'locked' in a position.

BHAGĀSANA, 'vulva pose', a secret sexo-yogic posture in which the male member is 'locked', in prolonged erection inside the yoni of a female partner, while certain internal esoteric acts are performed.

BHAIRAVA, destructive aspect of Śiva.

BHĀVA, emotion: aesthetic state or feeling which enlivens the senses, the vehicle of rasa (q.v.).

BHOGA, enjoyment.

BHŪTA, any of the five elemental conditions of matter.

BHŪTĀDI, rudimentary matter devoid of any physical substance.

BĪJA MANTRA, a seed sound formula corresponding to a particular psychic potentiality. Tantra texts state that the universe has evolved out of the fifty original bīja mantras which correspond to the fifty letters of the Sanskrit alphabet.

BINDU, dot: a sacred symbol of the universe in its unmanifested form, in tantra also equated with semen.

BRAHMĀ, the first god of the Hindu trinity, the creator.

BRAHMAN, the Absolute Reality, transcendental or pure consciousness, not to be confused with Brahmā.

BRAHMARANDHRA, crown of the head.

BUDDHI, the principle of intelligence; that intelligence-stuff which reveals knowledge of the cosmic unity.

CHAITANYA, pure consciousness.

CHAKRĀSANA, a sexo-yogic circle pose.

CHAKRAS, literally 'wheel' or 'circle'; technically, the psychic centres of energy situated along Sushumṇā in the subtle human body, also known as padmas (lotuses).

CHAKREŚVARA, leader of the chakra-pūjā, the communal ritual of union.

CHINNAMASTĀ, one of the Mahāvidyās, Devī in her destructive and creative aspect, signifying apparent dissolution and return to the First Cause.

CIT, the Absolute, the pure consciousness attributed to the knowledge of the one reality.

CIT-ŚAKTI, consciousness as power, the supreme energy.

CITTA, basic mental awareness.

CHITTĀKĀSA, mental or physical inner space.

DĀKINĪ, the presiding Śakti of the mulādhāra chakra.

DAKSHIṆA-MĀRGA, 'right-hand' path of the tantra.

DAMARU, an hour-glass shaped drum used by the Śaivites.

DEVATĀ, a form of divinity, generally male.

DEVĪ, a form of female divinity, goddess, śakti.

DHĀRAṆĀ, concentration.

DHYĀNA, meditation, sustained inner concentration beginning with concrete and ending with abstract awareness.

DĪKSHĀ, initiation by a guru.

DĪPA, a sacred oil lamp.

DURGĀ, closely related to Kālī, and generally identified with her.

EKĀGRATĀ, one-pointed.

GĀYATRĪ MANTRA, a sacred formula, one of the most important of all mantras.

GHAṆṬĀ, bell.

GHAṬA, a pot or sacred vessel.

GORAKHNĀTH, a great tantrika siddhāi (*c.* AD 1120) of the Nāthas, founder of the order of the Kānphātā Yogis.

GUṆA, attribute, quality; the three guṇas are the substantive qualities of Nature – sattva, rajas and tamas – of which the world is composed.

GURU, spiritual preceptor.

HĀKINĪ, the śakti who presides over the ājñā chakra.

HAṀSA, literally a swan, used to indicate spiritual unfolding.

HAṬHA-YOGA, a yoga system incorporating bodily disciplines leading to psychic development.

IḌĀ, the left subtle nāḍi, or psychic channel, coiling round the Sushumṇā and ending at the left nostril.

INDRIYAS, the ten faculties of sensation and perception in the human body: five 'knowing' agents, jñānendriyas – hearing, touching, seeing, tasting and smelling; five 'action' agents, karmendriyas – walking, handling, speaking, procreation and evacuation.

ISṬA-DEVATĀ, an individual's chosen deity.

JAGADGURU, the world teacher.

JĀGRAT, waking consciousness.

JAMBU-DVĪPA, the earth seen as the gigantic jambu (rose-apple) tree of Mount Meru casting its protective shadow over the island which is the earth.

JAPA, constant repetition, either silently or audibly, of a mantra.

JĪVAN-MUKTA, liberated in this life; spiritually free but still manifest in human form.

JĪVĀTMAN, the individual self.

JÑĀNA, self-knowledge, knowledge of the absolute through meditation.

JYOTI, spiritual light, Kuṇḍalinī

KAIVALYA, realization of one's self as being identical with Reality.

KĀKIṆĪ, the śakti of the anāhata chakra.

KĀLA, time: the power that conditions or limits the existence of unchangeable elements in matter.

KĀLĀGNI, the lowest plane (bhuvana) of existence.

KĀLĪ, the Divine Śakti, representing the creative and destructive aspects of nature.

KALPA, aeon; a 'day' of Brahmā the creator.

KĀMA, enjoyment, especially in love; desire as cosmic power.

KĀRAṆA, cause, source; wine, in tantric chakra-pūjā, ritual of union.

KARMA, action; the law of universal cause and effect.

KAULA, 'left-hand' sect of tantrism.

KHECHARĪ-MUDRĀ, a yogic pose in which the tongue is thrust up to close the nasal orifice.

KLĪṂ, a bīja mantra often used in tantric rituals.

KOŚA, sheath; an individual human being is conceived of having five sheaths or kośas.

KṚISHṆA, incarnation of Vishnu; the Divine Lover.

KṢITI, the earth element.

KULĀRNAVA TANTRA, an important tantra of AD 1150.

KUMBHAKA, retention of breath during the practice of prānāyama.

KUṆḌALINĪ, dormant psychic power lying coiled up like a serpent at the base of the spine.

LAGHIMĀ, power to attain weightlessness through yogic practice.

LĀKINĪ, the śakti of the maṇipūra chakra.

LAKSHAṆA, auspicious sign; feature of self-expression; attribute.

LATĀ-SĀDHANĀ, tantric discipline requiring a female partner, latā, literally 'a creeper'; tantric term for a woman embracing a man as the creeper enfolds a tree.

LAYA, merging, cessation, total dissolution.

LAYA-YOGA, the awakening of KUṆḌALINĪ.

LILĀ, the divine play.

LIṄGA, phallus; generative force in its creative aspect; according to Skanda Purāṇa, the liṇga is the name for space, in which the whole universe is in the process of formation and dissolution.

LIṄGA-ŚARĪRA, totality of the subtle or psychic body.

LOKA, world, plane of existence.

LOTUS, symbol of purity, unfolding.

MADHU, honey, sacred wine.

MAHĀKĀLA, an aspect of Śiva, personification of the disintegrative forces of the cosmos.

MAHĀMUDRĀ, sexo-yogic āsana known as 'great posture' in which the practitioner sits with the left heel pressed against the perineum (yoni-place) with the right leg stretched outward, and holding the right foot with both hands. The nine orifices of the body are contracted and the chin is pressed closely into the chest (jalandhara) for the control of the breath.

MAHĀVIDYĀ, transcendental knowledge of the Nature.

MAITHUNA, sexual union.

MĀLĀ, rosary.

MAṀSA, meat, one of the five M's in the tantric ritual of union.

MANAS, mind, the mental faculties of coordination, reasoning, assimilation.

MAṆḌALAS, a mystic diagram of squares and circles, symbolic of cosmic forces, used as support for concentration.

MAṆIPŪRA CHAKRA, navel centre in the subtle body.

MANTRA, sacred formula based on the principle that sound has a spiritual significance and power; incantation.

MĀRGA, path.

MĀYĀ, creative power, the limiting principle, illusion of the real nature of the world-appearance.

MERU, the mythical mountain supporting the world, merudaṇḍa; symbolically, the spine.

MITHUNA, paired.

MOKSHA, liberation.

MUDRĀ, seal, finger gesture; yogic control of certain organs as an aid to concentration which produces psychic responses.

MUKTI, liberation from the wheel of life and bondage of existence.

MŪLĀDHĀRA CHAKRA, the root chakra at the base of the spinal column in the subtle body.

MŪLA-PRAKṚITI, primordial root Energy.

NĀDA, motion; vibrational energy manifesting as sound; primeval and inner sound.

NĀDA-BINDU, primal vibration; the seed sound out which the universe emanates.

NĀḌI, psychic or astral nerve channel in the physical body.

NAMAḤ, salutation.

NĀMA-RŪPA, name and form.

NĀRĀYAṆA, an aspect of Vishṇu.

NIRVĀṆA, final emancipation.

NIYAMA, control, yogic discipline of the mind and body.

NYĀSA, projection of divine entities into various parts of the body.

OJAS, vital energy.

OṂ, seed mantra compounded of three sounds, aum, embracing all the secrets of the cosmos which are, as it were, gathered to a point within it.

PADMA, lotus; symbolic name of the chakras.

PAÑCHABHŪTAS, five gross elements; earth, water, fire, air, ether or space.

PAÑCHARĀTRA, the Vaishṇava philosophy.

PARA, last stage of consciousness.
PARAM, the supreme.
PARAMĀṆU, a gross atom.
PARĀTPARĀ, supreme of the supreme.
PARĀ VĀK, the unmanifest vibratory movement of cosmic ideation.
PASHYANTI, literally, 'seeing'; sound emerging towards the visible.
PAŚU, one who is bound, the individual soul.
PATAÑJALI, author of the systematized treatise on Yoga-Sutra (*c.* 100 BC–AD 300).
PRAJÑĀ, wisdom, First Principle.
PRAKṚITI, counterpart of Purusha; creative energy the source of objectivity referred to as the primeval female or Nature.
PRALAYA, the end or dissolution of a cycle of aeons.
PRĀṆA, life-force, the vital energy of the cosmos.
PRAṆAVA, the primal sound.
PRĀṆĀYAMA, yogic breath-control.
PREMA, love, wherein there is no longer a distinction between the lover and the beloved.
PṚITHVI, earth principle.
PŪJĀ, ritual worship.
PURĀṆAS, 'old'; 'ancient' Hindu scriptures expounding in legendary form the powers and deeds of gods and goddesses.
PURUSHA, Pure Consciousness, counterpart of Nature or Prakṛiti.
PURUSHA-PRAKṚITI, Consciousness in its relation to Nature, male-female, static-kinetic.

RAJAS, the principle of motion, a constituent of Prakṛiti.
RAJAS, female seed, menstrual flow.
RĀJASIKA, active quality of the mind.
RĀKINĪ, the śakti dominating the svādhishthāna chakra, at the base of the genitals.
RASA, essence of a thing, aesthetic delight, the substance of aesthetic experience, pleasure in the pure source of feeling.
RECHAKA, exhalation.
RETAS, physical substance.
RIṢHI, an inspired seer or sage.
RUDRA, originally a Vedic deity of many aspects; later mythology associates Rudra with Śiva.
RUDRAGRANTHI, one of the knots that Kuṇḍalinī has to pierce in its ascent.

ŚABDA, sound, cosmic sound.
ŚABDABRAHMAN, the Brahman as the primal sound energy.
ŚABDA-TANMĀTRA, infra-atomic sound potential.
SAD-GURU, a teacher of spiritual wisdom.
SĀDHAKA, seeker; one who is disciplined.
SĀDHANĀ, spiritual discipline.
SĀDHU, holy man.
SAHAJA, spontaneous, inborn, innate; a minor sect influenced by tantrism.
SAHAJOLI, one of the mudrās by which to reverse the downward tendency of seminal energy.
SAHASRĀRA CHAKRA, the psychic centre above the head, symbolized by the thousand-petalled lotus above the head where the Kuṇḍalinī Śakti unites with Śiva.
ŚAIVA, votary of Śiva.
ŚĀKINĪ, the śakti presiding over the viśuddha chakra located in the subtle body.
ŚAKTI, kinetic aspect of the Ultimate Principle; the power that permeates all creation; also the divine consort of Śiva.
SAMĀDHI, the deep meditation, trance, superconscious state in which identification is realized; the final goal of yoga.
SĀṀKHYA, one of the major systems of Indian philosophy founded by the sage Kapila (*c.* 500 BC), which influenced tantrism.
SAMYĀVASTHĀ, state of equilibrium, undifferentiated condition.
SAṄKALPA, personal determination, resolution or will to achieve the desired goal.
SAṄDHĀBHĀSĀ, esoteric terminology of tantrism.
SANNYĀSA, the final stage in the pilgrimage of life which cuts the thread of all bondage.
SANSKĀRA, an imprinted impression or memory-trace, fruit of karmic action.
ŚĀNTI, spiritual peace.
ŚARĪRA, the material body, substance.
ŚĀSTRAS, sacred books of divine authority, scriptures.
SAT, Being, Pure Existence.
SAT-CHIT-ĀNANDA, Being Consciousness, Bliss, as a unity; the peak stage of realization.
SATTVA, the highest of the guṇas, principle of equilibrium, truth, purity.
ŚAVĀSANA, the 'corpse'-like yogic posture for complete relaxation.
SIDDHĀSANA, one of the most important yogic postures.
SIDDHI, acquisition of paranormal powers, fruits of yogic practices but not their ultimate aim.
ŚIVA, the third god of the Hindu Trinity, the Destroyer; in tantrism, Pure Consciousness manifesting in creative union with Śakti or Prakṛiti.
SOMA, a certain type of vine from

which wine was made; an intoxicating drink known in Vedic times.

SPHOTAVĀDA, concept of sound.

SṚISHṬI, creation.

STHŪLA, gross.

SUDHĀ, nectar.

ŚUKRA, male seed.

SŪKSHMA, subtle.

ŚŪNYA, void.

SUSHUMṆĀ, the subtle channel in the centre of the spinal column through which the Kuṇḍalinī rises.

SVĀHĀ, the terminal word of some mantras.

SVĀDISHṬHĀNA CHAKRA, the chakra at the base of the genital organ in the subtle body.

TAMAS, power of inertia; the lowest of the three guṇas.

TANMĀTRAS, infra-atomic energy potentials.

TANTRA, one of a series of scriptures that emphasize practical ways of self-enlightenment, especially relating to the power of Śakti.

TĀNTRIKA, one who follows the discipline of tantra.

TAPA, self-discipline.

TARPAṆA, libation of water allowed to fall from the palm of the hand.

TATTVA, 'thatness'.

TATTVAJÑĀNA, knowledge of Nature, of all powers and principles.

TEJAS, fire, heat, energy.

TRĀṬAKA, to look at the space between the eyebrows, or to gaze without any blinking, concentrating the vision on a single point or object.

TRIKONA, a triangle.

UDĀNA, the upward movement of vital life-force in prāṇayāma.

UPANISHADS, spiritual doctrines of ancient Indian philosophies composed in their present form between (*c.* 1000 BC and 800 BC). The fundamental concept of the Upanishads is the identity of the individual soul with the Universal Soul, and is essentially an inquiry into the nature of the ultimate Reality.

UPĀSANĀ, worship.

VAIKHARĪ, the fourth stage of the gross physical sound or vibration manifesting as word.

VAIŚESHIKA, one of the six systems of Indian philosophy; its founder, the author of *Vaiśeshika-sutra,* was Kaṇāda (*c.* 250 BC–AD 100).

VAJROLI-MUDRĀ, one of the mudrās by which sexual energy is controlled and reabsorbed into the body. The adept is expected to draw in the female seed through the member into his body during the union, in a process called *sahajoli.* Care is to be taken during the act that emission of the semen does not occur. If his semen is released into the female body, both the male and female fluids are subsequently drawn back into his body through *amaroli.*

VĀMA-MĀRGA, 'left-hand' path of the tantras.

VĀYU, vital air.

VEDAS, the original source-books of India, revealed knowledge of the Aryans, consisted of 100,000 verses and are in four divisions, the Rig-Veda (*c.* 2000–1500 BC), the earliest literature of the world; the Yajur-Veda; the Sāma-Veda; the Atharva-Veda.

VIBHŪTI, examples or expression of supernatural powers.

VĪRA, an initiate in tantric rites is called vīra or hero, as distinguished from the paśu, the uninitiated, one in bondage.

VISHṆU, the second god of the Hindu Trinity, the Preserver.

VIŚUDDHA CHAKRA, the throat centre in the subtle body.

VIŚVARŪPA, the universal form of the absolute.

VYĀNA, one of the five vital airs (vāyu) distributed in the body.

YANTRA, a form symbol, aid to contemplation, geometrical representation of a deity.

YOGA, union; a system of philosophy; the path on which the individual self is united with the Universal Self; teaching about that path of realization.

YOGI, one who seeks to attain essential identity with the Reality.

YOGIN, a student of yoga; feminine, *yogini.*

YONI, the primal root of the source of objectiviation; a triangle pointing downwards symbolizes the yoni, the female sex organ, symbol of cosmic mysteries.

YONI-MUDRĀ, sexo-yogic āsana known as 'vulva-posture'. In this the adept is required to sit in siddhāsana and contract the perenium (yoni-place) between testes and anus.

YONISTHĀNA, 'yoni-place', or perineum, corresponding to the position of the female vulva.

YUGA, aeon, the four yugas are Satya or Kṛita-yuga, Tretā-yuga, Dvāpara-yuga, and Kālī-yuga, the present age of mankind.

ZERO, void; the dot.

# Bibliography


Abhinavagupta, *Tantrasara*, ed. with notes by M. R. Sastri, Bombay, 1918

*Abstract Art since 1945*, various contributors, foreword by Jean Leymarie, London, 1971

Agehananda, Swami Bharati, *The Tantric Tradition*, London, 1965 and Ontario, 1966

Akhilananda, Swami, *Hindu Psychology, its meaning for the West*, London and New York, 1948

Aurobindo, Sri, *On Yoga: The Synthesis of Yoga*, Pondicherry, 1965

—— *On Tantra*, compiled by M. P. Pandit, Pondicherry, 1967

Avalon, Arthur (*see* Woodroffe, Sir John)

Bach, George R., and Goldberg, H. *Creative Aggression*, New York, 1974 and London, 1976

Bagchi, Probodh Chandra, *Studies in the Tantras*, Part I, Calcutta, 1939

Banerjea, J. N., *Pauranic and Tantric Religion*, Calcutta, 1966

Barnett, Lincoln, *The Universe and Dr Einstein*, London and New York, 1948

Bhattacharya, B., *The Indian Buddhist Iconography*, Calcutta, 1958

Bhattacharya, Deben, ed. *The Mirror of the Sky: songs of the Bāuls from Bengal*, London, 1969

—— *Chaṇḍidāsa – Love Songs of Chaṇḍidās*, London, 1967

Bhattacharya, Sukhamay, *Tantra-Parichay*, Santiniketan, B.S., 1359 (Bengali)

Blofeld, John, *The Way of Power – A practical guide to the Tantric mysticism of Tibet*, London, 1970

Boner, Alice, *Principles of Composition in Hindu Sculpture*, Leiden, 1962

Bose, D. N. and Haldar, Hiralal, *Tantras: Their Philosophy and Occult Secrets*, Calcutta, 1956

Bose, Sir J. C., *Avyakta*, Calcutta, B.S. 1358 (Bengali)

Brown, W. Norman, ed. *The Saundarya-Lahari*, Cambridge, Mass., 1958

Chakravarty, Chintaharan, *Tantras: Studies on their Religion and Literature*, Calcutta, 1963

Chatterji, Jagadish Chandra, *Kashmir Shaivaism*, Srinagar, 1962

Coomaraswamy, Ananada K., *Christian and Oriental Philosophy of Art*, New York, 1956

—— *The Transformation of Nature in Art*, Cambridge, Mass., 1934, New York, 1956

Daniélou, Alain, *Yoga, the method of re-integration*, London, 1951 and New York, 1955

—— *Hindu Polytheism*, London, 1964

Dasgupta, Shashibhusan, *An Introduction to Tantric Buddhism*, Calcutta, 1950

—— *Obscure Religious Cults as background of Bengali Literature*, Calcutta, 1946, 1962 (rev. ed.)

Dasgupta, Surendra Nath, *History of Indian Philosophy*, 5 vols., London, 1932–55

Datta, Bibhutibhusan, *History of Hindu Mathematics*, Bombay, 1962

De Ropp, Robert S., *Sex Energy*, London, 1970
Einstein, Albert, *Essays in Science*, New York, 1934
Eliade, Mircea, *Yoga, Immortality and Freedom*, London and New York, 1958
Evans-Wentz, W. Y., ed., *Tibetan Yoga and Secret Doctrines*, London, 1958 (2nd. ed.)
Garrison, Omar V., *Tantra: The Yoga of Sex*, New York, 1964
Goswami, Hemchandra, ed., *Kāmaratna Tantra*, Shillong, 1928
Govinda, Lama Anagarika, *Foundations of Tibetan Mysticism*, London, 1959 and New York, 1960
Guenther, Herbert V., *Yugānadha, The Tantric View of Life*, Banaras, 1952
Gupta, Sanjukta, tr., *Lakṣmī Tantra*, Leiden, 1972
Jacobs, Hans, *Western Psycho-Therapy and Hindu Sādhanā*, London and New York, 1961
Jaini, J. L., *Jaina Universe*, Lucknow, 1948
Jeans, Sir James, *Physics and Philosophy*, Michigan, 1958
Jung, C. G., *Archetypes and the Collective Unconscious*, Vol. IX, Part I, London and New York, 1959
—— *Man and His Symbols*, London and New York, 1964
—— *Maṇḍala Symbolism* (tr. by R. F. C. Hull), Princeton, 1972
Kane, P. V., *History of Dharmaśāstra (ancient and medieval religions and civil law)*, Vol. V, Part II, Poona, 1962
Kaviraj, Gopi Nath, *Tantra O Agam Shāstrer Digdarshan*, Calcutta, 1963 (Bengali)
—— *Tantric Bāṇgmoy me Śākta Dṛishti*, Patna, 1963 (Hindi)
Kaye, G. R., *Astronomy (Memoirs of the Archaeological Survey of India)*, No. 18, Calcutta, 1924
Kinsley, David R., *The Sword and the Flute: Kālī and Kṛṣṇa*, California, 1975
Koestler, Arthur, *The Roots of Coincidence*, London, and New York, 1972
Krishna, Gopi, *The Biological Basis of Religion and Genius*, London, 1971 and New York, 1972
—— *The Secret of Yoga*, London and New York, 1972
Leadbeater, C. W., *The Chakras*, Madras, 1966 and London, 1972
Mallik, Kalyani, *Nāthasampradāyer itihāsa, darśana o sādhanā pranāli* (History, philosophy and esoteric doctrine of Nāth Yogis), Calcutta, 1950 (Bengali)
—— *Siddha-Siddhānta-paddhati and other works of Nāth Yogis*, Poona, 1954.
Metzner, Ralph, *Maps of Consciousness: I Ching, Tantra, Tarot, Alchemy, Astrology, Actualism*, New York, 1971
Mookerjee, Ajit, *Tantra Art*, Paris, New York etc., 1967
—— *Tantra Asana*, Basel, New York etc., 1971
—— *Yoga Art*, London, 1975
Naranjo, Claudio and Ornstein, Robert E., *On the Psychology of Meditation*, New York, 1971 and London, 1972
Narayanananda, Swami, *The Kuṇḍalinī Shakti*, Rishikesh, 1950
Nikhilananda, Swami, *Ramakrishna: Prophet of New India*, New York, 1948 and London, 1951
—— *Vivekananda, The Yoga and Other Works* (compiled), New York, 1953
Orstein, Robert E., *The Psychology of Consciousness*, London, 1975

Panday, K. C., *Abhinavagupta*, Varanasi, 1963
Parker, Derek and Julia, *The Compleat Astrologer*, London and New York, 1971
Patanjali, *Yoga-Sutra*, (tr. from Sanskrit by Bengali Baba), Poona, 1949
Pott, P. H., *Yoga and Yantra*, The Hague, 1966
Prabhavananda, Swami, *The Spiritual Heritage of India*, London, 1962 and New York, 1963
Radhakrishnan, S., ed., *History of Philosophy: Eastern and Western*, New York, 1957 and London, 1967
Ramakrishna Mission Institute of Culture, *Cultural Heritage of India*, Vol. III, Calcutta, 1958
Rawson, Philip, *The Art of Tantra*, London and New York, 1973
Ray, P., ed., *History of Chemistry in Ancient and Medieval India*, Calcutta, 1956
Rendel, Peter, *Introduction to Chakras*, Northamptonshire, 1974
Reyna, Ruth, *The Philosophy of Matter in the Atomic Era*, Bombay, 1962
Rieker, Hans-Ulrich, *The Yoga of Light, Hatha Yoga Pradipika*, London and New York, 1972
—— *The Secret of Meditation*, London, 1974
Rola, S. K. de, *Alchemy*, London, 1973
Saraswati, Swami Janakananda, *Yoga, Tantra och Meditation*, Stockholm, 1975
Saraswati, Swami Pratyagatmananda, *Japasūtram*, Madras, 1971
Sastri, S. Subrahmanya and Ayyangar, T. R., tr., *Saundarya-Lahari*, Madras, 1972
Saunders, E. Dale, *Mudrā*, New York, 1960
Schindler, Maria, *Goethe's Theory of Colour*, Sussex, 1964
Schrader, F. Otto, *Introduction to Pañcarātras and Ahirbudhnya Saṁhitā*, Madras, 1916
Seal, Sir Brajendranath, *The Positive Science of the Ancient Hindus*, Delhi, 1958
Shankaranarayanam, S., *Glory of the Divine Mother (Devīmāhātmyam)*, Pondicherry, 1968
Sharma, Sri Ram, *Tantra-Mahāvijñāna*, Vols. I–II, Bareilly, 1970 (Hindi)
Singhal, D. P., *India and World Civilization*, Vols. I–II, Calcutta and London, 1972
Snellgrove, D. L., *The Hevajra Tantra*, London, 1939
Solomon, David, ed., *LSD: The Consciousness-Expanding Drug*, Berkley, 1964
Spiller, Jurg, ed., *Paul Klee: the thinking eye*, London and New York, 1961
Suryanarayanamurthy, C., *Sri Lalita Sahasranāmam*, Madras, 1962
Tucci, Giuseppe, *The Theory and Practice of the Maṇḍala; with special references to the modern psychology of the subconscious*, (tr. by Alan Houghton Broderick), London, 1961
Walker, Benjamin, *Hindu World*, Vols. I–II, London and New York, 1968
White, John de, *Frontiers of Consciousness*, New York, 1974
Whitmont, Edward C., *The Symbolic Quest: basic concepts of analytical psychology*, New York, 1969
Woodroffe, Sir John (Avalon, Arthur pseudonym), *The Garland of Letters; Varnamālā, studies in the mantra-śastra*, Madras, 1952

—— *Kāma-Kalā-Vilāsa,* Madras, 1953
—— *Principles of Tantra,* Vols. I–II, Madras, 1953
—— *Serpent Power,* Madras, 1953
—— *Tantrarāja Tantra,* Madras, 1954
—— *Kulārṇava Tantra,* Madras, 1965
—— *Hymns to the Goddess,* Madras, 1965
—— *Mahānirvāna Tantra* (Tantra of the Great Liberation), New York, 1972
Zimmer, Heinrich, *Myths and Symbols in Indian Art and Civilization* (ed. by Joseph Cambell), Washington, 1946
Zvelebil, Kamil V., *The Poets of the Powers,* London, 1973

# *Periodicals*

Chandra, Pramod, *The Kaula Kapalika Cult at Khajuraho,* in *Lalit Kala,* Nos. 1–2, April 1955–March 1956
Dasgupta, Shashibhusan, *The Role of Mantra in Indian Religion,* in *Bulletin of the Ramakrishna Mission Institute of Culture,* Vol. VII, No. 3, March, 1956
Hariharanand, Swami Sarasvati, *The Inner Significance of Linga worship,* in *Journal of the Indian Society of Oriental Art,* Vol. IX, 1941
Jenny, Hans, 'The Sculpture of Vibration', *UNESCO Courier,* December, 1969
Mookerjee, Ajit, *Tantric Art,* in *Times of India Annual,* 1965
—— *Tantra Art in Search of Life Divine,* in *Indian Aesthetics and Art Activity,* 1966
—— *Tantra Art,* in *Graphis,* 1966
—— *Tantra Art,* in *Lalit Kala,* 1971
Mukharji, P. B., *The Metaphysics of Form,* in *Bulletin of the Ramakrishna Mission Institute of Culture,* Vol. VIII, No. 8, 1956
—— *The Metaphysics of Sound,* ibid, Vol. VII, No. 9, 1956
—— *The Metaphysics of Light,* ibid., Vol. XII, No. 11, 1961
Mukherji, K. C., *Sex in Tantras,* in *The Journal of Abnormal and Social Psychology,* 1926
Sircar, D. C., *The Śakta Pithas,* in *The Journal of the Royal Asiatic Society of Bengal,* Vol. XIV, No. 1, 1948

# Index